I Believe in Church Growth

By the same author:

BORN INTO BATTLE
BODY BUILDING EXERCISES FOR THE LOCAL
  CHURCH

I Believe
in
Church Growth

Eddie Gibbs

HODDER AND STOUGHTON
LONDON SYDNEY AUCKLAND TORONTO

British Library Cataloguing in Publication Data

Gibbs, Eddie
   I believe in church growth.—(Hodder
   Christian paperback)
   1. Church growth
   I. Title
   270   V652.25

  ISBN 0 340 37277 X

Hodder and Stoughton Editorial Office: 47 Bedford Square, London WC1B 3DP.

To my wife Renee

Col. 2:19
Under Christ's control the whole body is nourished and held together by its joints and ligaments, and it grows as God wants it to grow.
(GNB)

Notes on Referencing system

As an aid to easy reference I have avoided page footnotes and end of chapter lists by following each quotation with the name of the author, the date of the publication and the page number. The titles of the books mentioned can be found at the end of the book in the Bibliography, listed alphabetically according to the author.

Contents

EDITOR'S PREFACE 11
AUTHOR'S PREFACE 13

1 GOD'S PEOPLE AND THE NATIONS 15
Church Growth Awareness 15
God's Concern for his Entire Creation 22
Abraham: a Blessing to the Nations 23
A Covenant to Embrace all Nations 25
A Glorified People Attracting the Nations 32
The Servant of the Lord: a Light to the Nations .. 36
Summary 40

2 CHURCH AND KINGDOM 43
The 'Gospel' in the Gospels 43
The Gospel of the Kingdom 46
The Old Testament Expectation of the
  Kingdom 48
The New Testament Realisation of the
  Kingdom 51
The Signs of the Kingdom 56
Entering the Kingdom 60
Growth of the Kingdom 65
Summary 68

3 GOSPEL AND CULTURE 71
Defining Culture 74

Christ in Relation to Culture   74
Culture and Biblical Revelation   80
Culture and Contemporary Communication   85
The Communication Process   88
Culture and Church Structure   93
The Impact of the Gospel on Cultures   98
Summary   102

4 MEASUREMENT AND MEANING   104
Answering Objections to Data-gathering   106
The Value of Data-gathering   111
Data-gathering at Local Church Level   114
Quality of Commitment   128
Use of Facilities   130
Community Profile   130
Future Projections   131
Summary   132

5 MEDIUM AND MESSAGE   134
Make Prayer Meetings the Power House   135
Establish a Positive Attitude   137
Build an Adequate Base   138
Agree on your Evangelistic Goal   140
Identify the Evangelists   142
Train the Christian Community to
    Communicate   145
Identify Receptive Groups and Individuals   147
Emphasise a Biblical Theology of
    Conversion   151
Develop a Long-term Strategy for Resistant
    Areas   156
Recognise the Evangelistic Potential of
    Groups   158
Achieve Visibility   158
Implement New Members Procedures   160
Summary   162

6 GROUPS AND GROWTH 163
Groups in the New Testament 164
The Strategic Importance of Groups 169
The Purpose of Groups 172
Dealing with Problems Likely to Arise in
Groups 177
Leadership for Groups 182
Summary 190

7 STRUCTURES AND STRATEGY 192
Defining Groups 193
Secondary Groups 194
Tertiary Groups 203
Incorporating Newcomers into Membership 209
Evangelism at All Three Levels 212
Summary 219

8 EQUIPPING AND MOBILISING 221
Why People are Reluctant to Get Involved 223
The Resources which the Lord Supplies 226
Gifts for Service 230
A Composite List of Gifts Mentioned in the
Bible 239
Gifted for Leadership 245
A Leadership Team to Facilitate Membership
Ministry 251
Summary 254

9 LEADERSHIP AND RELATIONSHIPS 256
The Need for Leadership 257
Styles of Leadership 259
Avenues of Change 262
Leadership Models 264
Skill Levels 274
Leadership Qualities 279
Summary 284

10 EXPECTATIONS AND PLANNING   285
    Planning that is Pleasing to God   286
    Establishing General Objectives   291
    Working for Consensus   293
    Achieving Specific Goals   297
    Formulating Workable Plans   301
    Drawing up an Organisational Framework   302
    Allocating Adequate Resources   303
    Stimulating Enthusiastic Participation   305
    Ensuring Good Internal Communications   306
    Coping with Change   309
    Resolving to Act   310
    Evaluating and Reformulating   311
    Conclusion   312

    BIBLIOGRAPHY   313

Editor's Preface

When has any book like *I Believe in Church Growth* been put out by an Englishman? It is not only an imaginative and illuminating new book, but almost a new *genre*. For a long time the churches in the West have been accustomed to think in terms of survival, not of growth. Battered by the disastrous results of the scientific controversies at the end of the last century, depressed by two world wars and the emerging secularism, all the denominations of mainline Christianity have been in retreat for years. Growth? Unthinkable!

Yet in the rest of the world it is not so. There are far more Christians in the world than there have ever been. Church growth is taking place (sometimes, as in South America and Africa, at a startling pace) in most parts of the world. The deadest areas are those traditionally associated with Christian culture, namely Western Europe: here the faith is in decline in most countries. But take Korea, Russia or China, Colombia or Uganda, or many parts of the United States, and a totally different picture emerges. The Church grows in size, vitality and sacrifice. Numbers are not the most important thing: qualities of character, service to others, confidence in the gospel, appropriate styles of leadership – these are some of the notable features. And in this book Eddie Gibbs, whose own background is far from the middle-class Anglicanism commonly found among English writers on religion, and whose experience is widely based in Europe, and, much more important, in Latin America, gives a fascinating diagnosis of the Church's disease in the West and offers some prescriptions. If every clergyman were merely to read the chapter on 'Leadership and Relationships' this book would have been eminently worth while.

When Eddie wrote the first edition of this book, I was delighted to welcome it. It was quite different from other books in the *I Believe* series, and I felt it could well be among the most influential of them. This has proved to be the case, and the book has been much in demand among church leaders. In this new and revised edition Eddie has slimmed the volume down for the general reader, and has updated it in certain areas. As a result I think this confident book will reach a much wider circle of those who are tired of stagnation in the church, and are ready to share in the growth which is bursting out in many parts of the world church. There is nowhere where this revolution in Christian attitudes and priorities might not take place – if we are prepared to pay the price.

Michael Green

Author's Preface

I am delighted that the publishers have made possible an abridged, popular edition of *I Believe in Church Growth*. The sections which have been deleted are those likely to be of less interest to the general reader. While undertaking the editorial work I also took the opportunity to update some of the data and to make corrections to the original text.

Many church leaders have expressed appreciation for the practical guidelines in the first edition. I pray that this abridged version will bring encouragement to a much wider Christian public.

An increasing number of church leaders are declaring that they believe in Church Growth not just as a theoretical possibility they are prepared to entertain, or even as a theological constraint which they are ready to acknowledge, but as a personal commitment which has been proven in their experience.

Eddie Gibbs
Pasadena, California
November, 1984

CHAPTER ONE

God's People and the Nations

CHURCH GROWTH AWARENESS

This century has witnessed numerical church growth on an unprecedented scale according to a number of recent reports. In 1970 Bishop Stephen Neill challenged the widely held view that the Christian percentage of the world population has already begun to decrease and will continue to grow less till the end of the century, asserting to the contrary that the percentage of Christians has been slowly increasing since the beginning of the century (Neill 1970:78, 79).

Detailed country by country surveys conducted by the Missions Advanced Research and Communications Centre as part of the Lausanne Committee for World Evangelisation programme have more than substantiated Bishop Neill's claim. Dr Ralph Winter reported that 'while non-Christians in Africa and Asia have more than doubled since 1900 and will more than triple by the year 2000, the number of Christians in Africa and Asia was in 1974 thirteen times what it was in 1900 and by 2000 it will be thirty-four times as large' (Evangelical Mission Quarterly Jan 1974:12). According to calculations made by C. Peter Wagner, Professor of Church Growth at Fuller Theological Seminary, Pasadena, every day sees 78,000 new Christians and 1,600 new churches open each week around the world. In Africa alone 6,052,800 new Christians were added to the Church in the year 1978 (Information Service Lausanne Committee for World Evangelisation June 1979).

One of the most dramatic examples of Asian church growth is to be found in South Korea. Dr Joon Gon Kim reports that twenty-five to thirty per cent of his country's population of 37 million are known Protestants. He also declares that sixty per cent of the soldiers are now professing Christians. On the final night of the four-day World Evangelisation Crusade held in Seoul, August 12–15, 1980, a crowd of 2.7 million gathered in the Yoido Plaza, a converted aerodrome! The Christians of South Korea are currently planning to send 10,000 of their number as missionaries to other parts of Asia! (ISL May 1980).

The Church in Indonesia has an annual growth rate of ten per cent, with an estimated two million people having been added to the Church in the last decade, mostly in the islands of Sumatra, Java and Kalimantan. Other growth spots include Nagaland in North India (now sixty-six per cent Christian), Burma, Sarawak, the Philippines, Singapore, and mainline China with its estimated Christian population of 50 million according to Jonathan Chae of the Chinese Research Centre in Hong Kong.

In Latin America, where the population is nominally Catholic, but with church attendance below ten per cent, the Protestant churches have made enormous gains this century. In 1900 there are estimated to have been about 50,000 Protestants, the majority of whom were migrants from Northern Europe. In the early 70s the Protestant community numbered around twenty million (Wagner 1973:25), and today they are estimated to have passed the fifty million mark. Alongside this Protestant growth there is widespread evidence of Catholic renewal with a variety of emphases.

Dr Donald Anderson McGavran, one-time missionary in India and now Dean Emeritus of the School of World Mission, Fuller Seminary, Pasadena, USA, was among the first to urge the missionary agencies to believe that there was a receptive climate to the gospel in many areas of the world. Twenty years ago in his book *How Churches Grow* he wrote about 'a change of climate like the end of an ice age'. He maintained in the face of his unconvinced critics, that 'the chill wind of suspicion of the Christian faith has abated. The glaciers of an anti-Christian nationalism have retreated. The sun of faith has risen higher in the heavens. Explain it in whatever metaphor you will, churches can multiply.' (McGavran 1959:2).

He was aware of the preoccupation of western missionary agencies with social issues, providing life support systems for ailing national churches which they had brought into being, promoting ecumenism and exporting patterns of church organisation suited to slow growth. The fact that the great majority of the world's missionary personnel came from Europe and the United States, where either rapid church growth was largely unknown or numerical decline was accepted as the irreversible norm, meant that missionaries were either content with meagre results or perpetuated a maintenance attitude. He considered that their presuppositions blinded them to the growth potential around them, and caused them to hold back from supplying essential resources needed to reap a spiritual harvest.

This overriding concern has continued to burn through his speaking and writing over the years. Six years after writing *How Churches Grow* his appeal appeared in the influential *International Review of Missions* periodical. There he challenged the 'seed-sowing' concept of missions, that 'the objective and measurable growth of churches must neither be expected nor counted as a measure of effectiveness'. He argued for a narrow definition of mission, emphasising the goal of church planting, in place of one which 'attempts to take in everything that the Church and the Christian faith ought to do'. For McGavran 'the whole gospel for all mankind means little, unless it is preceded by stupendous church-planting. There can be little hope of sustained signs of the Kingdom in the world without the influence of a

sufficient number of sons and daughters of the Kingdom. . . .
What the fantastically mounting population of this world
needs is fantastically multiplying churches. . . .' (IRM Oct
1965:451–461).

It was not until three years later that McGavran's out-
spoken article was challenged in the July number of *International Review of Missions*, which was dedicated entirely to the
subject. Most of the articles were hostile to his position, but
McGavran in his reply remained unrepentant. He declared
that he was surprised at the depth and thrust of the anti-
church growth sentiment in several of them, and hoped that
when they saw their combined and enthusiastic opposition
to the growth of Christ's Church, they themselves would be
surprised and possibly dismayed. He ended his article with
the observation that the preparatory documents for the
'Renewal in Mission' section of the Fourth Assembly of the
World Council of Churches said precisely nothing about
presenting the gospel to the two billion who now owe Jesus
no allegiance (IRM July 1968:335–343). Fifteen years later
that two billion is now nearer three billion.

At the heart of McGavran's position is the profound
conviction that God wants lost people found. He believes
that the Bible teaches that it makes an eternal difference
whether a man believes in Jesus Christ as God and Saviour
and becomes his disciple and a responsible member of his
Church (IRM June 1968:337).

This concern reappears in his most comprehensive
volume on church growth entitled *Understanding Church
Growth*, which was published in 1970. There he concedes
that 'Mission defined as "God's programme for man" is
obviously many-sided. Each aspect of it can be called mission. Has God assigned any priority among these myriad
good activities? . . . We believe He has. His will in these
matters can be learned from His revelation and is manda-
tory for Christians' (McGavran 1970:31). 'The Finding God
wants humankind brought into a redemptive relationship

to Jesus Christ, where, baptised in His Name, they become part of His Household' (1970:32).

Dr McGavran, now in his mid-eighties, has become the sprightly patriarch as well as the sparring prophet of the church growth movement. Advancing years have in no way drained his enthusiasm. He still travels the world to add to his encyclopaedic knowledge and to test the church growth principles he has propounded.

Dr McGavran's combative style reflects the polarisation which existed in the mission debate in the 50s through to the early 70s. Then evangelicals were attacking what they considered to be the syncretism and universalism of the liberals, while the liberals accused the evangelicals of preaching a truncated gospel of personal salvation to the exclusion of social justice as an essential element of the Good News.

At the present time these important issues are far from being resolved. Yet a significant shift has taken place. The polarisation has given way to cross-pollination as the former combatants learn to listen to one another and as radical voices emerge within the various camps. Playing a significant role in this experience are those non-western churches which are both witnessing rapid church growth and at the same time proclaiming a gospel message which speaks with striking relevance to their situation.

Many radical Christians would remain unimpressed by the statistics with which we began this chapter. They are more concerned with the content and quality of the commitment rather than the numbers involved. This is a legitimate concern. Enrolment as church members cannot uncritically be equated with a genuine, life-transforming turning to Christ. It is a legitimate question to ask. What are they turning from and what are they turning to? On the other hand quality must not be set against quantity, for God has sent his Church into the world to make disciples. He longs for more Christians as well as better Christians. Numbers are not simply numbers; they stand for people, and each digit represents an individual of intrinsic worth and dignity, for people are made in the image of God.

In the early days of the formulation of church growth thinking there was an over-emphasis on the numerical growth of the empirical church. This stress represented an over-reaction to the non-growth presuppositions of many influential voices at the time. In the past decade there has been a growing concern among those identified with the church growth movement to come to terms with the quality of individual commitment and nominality within the existing church. These opening two chapters attempt to provide a theological contribution in that area.

Another criticism of the church growth emphasis must also be taken seriously into account. Sometimes church growth has been represented as the totality of mission. This may arise out of an extremely negative attitude to the world by some evangelicals, which results in mission being regarded as a rescue operation, saving individuals from a doomed cosmos sliding into chaos. Alternatively, it is argued that for society to be transformed the overwhelming priority must be given to evangelism until there are sufficient Christians to be able to influence their situation. This position is argued by Dr McGavran in his *International Review of Missions* article in 1965. However, it must be conceded that such results do not follow automatically. Church growth can result in decanting people from the world to seek an alternative sub-culture in isolation, rather than equipping the saints to act as yeast, salt and light in the world.

When church growth is regarded as the sum totality of mission it results in a preoccupation with the empirical church to the exclusion of the world. In contrast to this ecclesiastical narrowing of mission the Scriptures represent mission as being from God and directed to the whole world and every area of life. The contribution of the church growth emphasis is to draw attention to the centrality of the

Church in God's cosmic plan, while its critics emphasise that God's concern is for the whole of his creation (Eph. 1:20–23; Col. 1:19–20). This being so, the Church must avoid an attitude of self-preoccupation, whether that be manifested by self-preservation or expansionism. The focus of our attention is not therefore the Church, but Christ and his world.

Orlando E. Costas, a Latin American Baptist theologian, has offered one of the most perceptive criticisms of church growth emphases from among the evangelical ranks. He writes:

> When church growth theorists affirm that the aim of evangelism is the multiplication of churches, they are advocating a theology that makes the Church the end of God's mission. Granted that the gospel is community-oriented, the question is whether the community is the objective or a result (a necessary and imperative one) of the communication of the gospel. Or to put it in other terms, whether the community is an ultimate or a penultimate goal of God's mission.
>
> Isn't the gospel the good news of the kingdom? Who is the centre of the kingdom – Christ or the Church? Who is the object of the kingdom – the community or the King? What is the aim of the kingdom – the exercise of Christ's righteous, peaceful, and loving reign in heaven and on earth in a restored and transformed universe, or the gathering of a community to Him? (Costas 1974:135).

These pertinent questions underline the fact that for the Church's witness to be authentic it must point beyond itself. Conscious of its weakness and source of life, the Church points to Christ who is Redeemer and Lord, and aware of its incompleteness it points forward to the Kingdom which, although already present in a provisional and fragmentary form, will one day come in completeness, power and manifest glory.

In order to appreciate the biblical expectations of growth, we turn now to a detailed examination of the witness of the people of God among the peoples of the world and in the following chapter consider the role of the Church as a sign and servant of the Kingdom which God is bringing into being.

GOD'S CONCERN FOR HIS ENTIRE CREATION
(Gen. 1–11)

The Dutch missionary theologian, J. H. Bavinck, writes that, 'At first sight the Old Testament appears to offer little basis for the idea of missions. This part of the Bible speaks of bloody wars and the annihilation of various heathen peoples; it appears to have very little room for mercy, nor does it seem ready to grant the blessings of the gospel to the heathen' (Bavinck 1961:11). Yet on closer reading we discover a more promising scenario.

The scene is set for mission in the Old Testament doctrine of creation. The Bible is unique among ancient records in making this the starting-point for the history of a nation. The entire world, including all its inhabitants, is regarded as belonging to God, for he created it in the beginning and continually sustains it (Gen. 1–2; Pss 24; 33:13; 47:2). His watchful eye is upon the world so that nothing escapes his notice. He exercises a universal jurisdiction, which means that not only Israel, but all the nations, are accountable to him. 'God is not localised in His interests and activities; He is the God of the nations. No one escapes his provisions, though nations may grossly misuse such. None evades His moral government. He is present in a certain sense everywhere, even though He has chosen to limit his unique disclosures to and through a particular people. Thus universality and particularism are not mutually exclusive' (Peters 1972:108).

ABRAHAM: A BLESSING TO THE NATIONS

Scripture explains the origin of the people of God not in terms of natural causes, but as a consequence of divine initiative. God calls an individual, Abram, out of Ur of the Chaldees. From the outset the people of God are the people of the word. They are those who hear and obey the command of God and place their confidence in his promises. The faith of Abram gave him a new identity signalled by the new name of Abraham, which God bestowed on him. This faith and that of the Patriarchs in general is not expressed as a response to specific laws, but in following where God directs. It is being prepared to step out without knowing beforehand the destination; to leave a life of settled security for one of pilgrimage, not really belonging any-where, and constantly encountering new situations (Heb. 11:8–10).

The most emphatic indication of God's intention for the nations of the world is to be found in his promise to the aged and childless couple Abram and Sarai. He reassured them with these words: 'I will give you many descendants, and they will become a great nation. I will bless you and make your name famous, so that you will be a blessing.

> I will bless those who bless you,
> But I will curse those who curse you.
> And through you I will bless all the nations.'
> (Gen. 12:2–3)

Such a far-flung, if unspecified, promise emphasises from the outset that God is not calling a people to himself to the exclusion of the nations but for the sake of all nations – that they might share in the blessing. The substance of this blessing does not become clear until the New Testament (Acts 3:25; Rom. 4:12; Gal. 3:8–16). His role is described in the new name which God gave him, 'Abraham', which sounds like the Hebrew for 'ancestor of many nations' (Gen. 17:5).

Abraham stands as a spiritual prototype. He hears the call of God to leave Babylonia and venture out in faith not knowing where that might lead him (Gen. 12:1; Heb. 11:8). His attitude of trust and confidence in God serves as a model of the kind of response that God seeks from man in every age. It is this which puts him in a right relationship to God. Man is justified by his faith not by his works (Rom. 4:9), yet that faith must be shown to be genuine by our practical response (Jas. 2:21, 23). In exercising faith Abraham was prepared to commit everything.

The Old Testament establishes Abraham as a reference point to remind Israel that her very existence has its historical roots in the call of God. His covenant with Abraham gave birth to the nation (Ex. 2:24; Lev. 26:42; 2 Kings 13:23; Ps. 105:9).

Through succeeding centuries Abraham presents a constant challenge to the people of God. He confronts their complacency and serves as a reminder of the saving initiative of God. Our Lord challenged those who presumed to say, 'We have Abraham as our father,' by telling them that God was able to make descendants for Abraham even from the stones scattered around them. (Matt. 3:9). Later in response to the faith displayed by the centurion Jesus challenged the Jewish bystanders, 'I tell you, I have never found anyone in Israel with faith like this. I assure you that many will come from the east and the west and sit down with Abraham, Isaac, and Jacob at the feast in the Kingdom of Heaven. But those who should be in the Kingdom will be thrown out into the darkness. . . .' (Matt. 8:10–12).

St Paul also speaks to the racially mixed churches in Rome and Galatia reminding them that they share a common ancestor in Abraham, who is the spiritual father of all who believe (Rom. 4:11). 'You should realise then, that the

real descendants of Abraham are the people who have faith'
(Gal. 3:7).

So the promise made many years before to Abraham
finds its fulfilment not simply in the emergence of the nation
of Israel, but in the Church of Jesus Christ. His life of faith
in God shows how mankind can enter the Kingdom and be
incorporated into the Church of Jesus Christ. It also underlines the fact that life and growth can occur in seemingly
impossible circumstances, for Abram and Sarai were well
past the years of normal parenthood when they were given
offspring. They were not simply encouraged to think in terms
of an intimate family circle to comfort them in old age, but
to see far into the future to a phenomenal expansion.

God helped Abram comprehend something of the im-
mensity of his purposes by pointing him first to the stars in
the sky, and then to the sand on the seashore, assuring him,
'You will have as many descendants as that.' (Gen. 15:5;
22:17; 32:12; 2 Sam. 17:11; 1 Kings 4:20). When we here in
urban Britain look up, we more often see clouds and look
down to see concrete! But behind the clouds are the myriads
of stars, and under the concrete (and indeed within the
concrete!) are the countless grains of sand of God's un-
breakable promise regarding the expansion of his Church.

A COVENANT TO EMBRACE ALL NATIONS

The term 'covenant' means an agreement or solemn pact.
Here we are concerned with the covenants (for more than
one are mentioned in Scripture) that God makes with
humankind. Such agreements are not the result of negotia-
tion between equal partners, but are the expressions of
God's gracious initiatives. They are neither merited nor
manufactured by man. They are given by God.

The covenant with Adam and Eve

Some scholars, particularly within the Reformed tradition,
see the first covenant obligation in the Adam and Eve story,

where these persons, made 'in the image and likeness of God', are first blessed by him and then commanded to 'have many children, so that your descendants will live all over the earth and bring it under control'. God tells them, 'I am putting you in charge of the fish, the birds, and all the wild animals. I have provided all kinds of grain and all kinds of fruit for you to eat' (Gen. 1:28, 29). This is the classic covenant form: the granting of a blessing 'which bestows not only a gift but a function' (Kidner 1967:52), leading to the acceptance of responsibilities and the assurance of provision. This command to propagate and to take charge is given to man as God's vassal. It is, therefore, not simply a cultural mandate, but a covenant mandate (Conn 1976:2, 3), to extend the conditions which prevailed in Eden throughout God's entire creation.

The covenant with Noah

The first occurrence of the term 'covenant' is to be found in Genesis 6:18, where God makes Noah and his family the sole exceptions to his purpose of destroying mankind through the Flood. He is spared because he is found to be a righteous man, that is, a man who stood in right relationship to God in response to his covenant obligations (von Rad 1961:116). God warns him of his intentions and instructs him to construct a boat according to his specifications in which he and his family and representative livestock will be able to survive. 'Everything on the earth will die, but I will make a *covenant* with you. Go into the boat with your wife. . . .' Here the covenant concept is essentially linked with God's saving intention. Noah 'goes into the ark not as a mere survivor, but as the bearer of God's promise for a new age' (Kidner 1967:89).

The full extent of the covenant blessings, beyond the initial act of preservation, is not spelt out until the flood waters have subsided and the occupants are free to roam on dry land again (Gen. 9:9–17). This covenant is *universal*, embracing 'all living beings', which includes animals as well as humans. It is *permanent*, applying not only to Noah and his generation, but to his descendants. Therefore it is termed an 'everlasting covenant'. Furthermore, it is *ratified by a sign* for all to see – the rainbow in the skies – which will serve as a reminder not only to man but also to God, of his promise never again to destroy all living beings by flood waters. The glory of the rainbow against the gloom of the clouds shines as a token of God's grace (Kidner 1967:102).

The Adamic and the Noachic covenants, which are both universal in their scope, provide the broad basis against which God's narrower, elective covenants should be seen. Through them God's gracious will is assured to all humankind.

The covenant with Moses

This covenant is superimposed on the Abrahamic pact to prepare the people of God to meet an entirely new situation. From being a people, or kinship group, they are now to become a nation alongside other nations. Israel is about to become 'a political entity and begins to take a place in the history books' (Goldingay 1975:6). The radical change of status from slavery to nationhood was only made possible by divine initiative, securing the release of Israel from the oppression of the Egyptians through a series of miraculous interventions.

As a small emergent nation, occupying militarily indefensible territory between the powerful pincer arms of Egypt and Babylon, she could not hope to survive without the protection of Yahweh her God. She was not only vulnerable to attack from outside her borders, but to moral and spiritual subversion from within generated by the Canaanite enclaves which survived the conquest. In anticipation of the complex legislation required by Israel's promotion to nationhood, the covenant with Moses 'itemises her commitment'

(Goldingay 1975:7) with detailed ethical, social and cultic requirements.

While the Mosaic covenant set Israel apart from the nations, it by no means excluded them from its benefits. There are specific provisions laid down for non-Israelites to become members of God's people. The qualification for membership is not birth, but willingness to commit oneself. From the time of the Exodus from Egypt foreigners formed part of the company (Exod. 12:38; Num. 11:4). The subsequent narrative continues to provide instances of an openness to others. This is seen in the case of the Midianite priest (Exod. 18:11, 12), Caleb the Edomite (Num. 13, 14), Rahab the harlot (Josh. 2:1–11, 6:25), the Gibeonites (Josh. 9:9, 10) and the surrender and willing allegiance of the inhabitants of Shechem (Josh. 24).

Let us now pause to summarise the main features of the covenant relationship in the Old Testament.

In the first place the covenant represents *an intensely personal relationship*. The God of Israel was one who calls by name. 'It is in the realm of the personal, which is the highest we know . . . only a person can send' (Davidson 1969:23). This was the experience of Moses at the burning bush (Exod. 3:4–10). God called him by name, 'Moses. Moses!' He identified himself as the God of his ancestors, Abraham, Isaac and Jacob.

Secondly, the covenant represents *a redemptive relationship*. Redemption signifies deliverance from bondage and propitiation for sin by the payment of a price. God's people in Egypt were preserved from the destroying angel by the offering of a passover lamb and the smearing of its blood on their door posts and lintels. This Passover sacrifice remained at the heart of the elaborate sacrificial system which was subsequently initiated, serving as an annual reminder of God's mercy. In the Jewish sacrificial system the price paid to secure forgiveness of sins was the shed blood of the innocent victim represented by the animal or bird offered in sacrifice. This price is not paid by the man offering the animal, but by God who gave the life which was to be sacrificed. In Hebrew thinking the life of the animal was considered to be in the blood, and God was the giver of life. Redemption, therefore, speaks of what God does for man to secure his release from the punishment, bondage and guilt of sin.

Thirdly, the covenant describes *a responsible relationship* initiated by God, establishing a mutual pact, in which man is held accountable before God for his actions. It is a call to an ongoing relationship as adopted children who are required to live a distinctive life-style to show to the world what God intends for his people, and requires of them. His people are called to be holy because he is holy (Lev. 19:2; cf. I Pet. 1:15; Heb. 12:14). The covenant relationship demands an unreserved allegiance to God and obedience to his commands. It emphasises that covenant privileges carry covenant obligations.

Fourthly, the covenant makes possible *an extendable relationship*. J. H. Bavinck, the Dutch missiologist, makes clear it is precisely this covenant relationship that opens up the possibilities for mission. 'If Jehovah is the God of Israel because He has made a covenant with Israel, it is conceivable that other nations will also some day be included in that covenant. For Israel has no individual and peculiar claim upon God; its privileged position is due solely to God's electing grace. Israel is not better than other nations, it simply bears greater honour and greater responsibility. And its distinction consists precisely in the fact that it may and shall be the means by which other nations shall one day receive the salvation of Israel's God' (Bavinck 1961:14). This glorious prospect is eventually realised through the operation of the new covenant which we now move on to consider.

The new covenant
As God's people repeatedly fail to live up to the demands of the covenant relationship and sense the inadequacy of the

sacrificial system to cover their failings, for there was no offering which could secure forgiveness for wilful disobedience, so they come to realise that God's demands can only be met in his strength. So, God speaks to his wayward people through the prophet Jeremiah, promising a new covenant. There will be a continuity with the old in terms of his promises and requirements, yet there is also a fundamental difference. The Lord declares, 'It will not be like the old covenant that I made with their ancestors when I took them by the hand and led them out of Egypt. Although I was like a husband to them, they did not keep that covenant. The new covenant that I will make with the people of Israel will be this: I will put my law within them and write it on their hearts. I will be their God, and they will be my people. None of them will have to teach his fellow-countryman to know the Lord, because all will know me, from the least to the greatest. I will forgive their sins and I will no longer remember their wrongs. I, the Lord, have spoken' (Jer. 31:31–34).

The essential distinction lies in the fact that the new covenant will not be one of external requirements and restraints, but of an inward motivation and constraint, for the law will be written on their hearts.

The covenant idea testifies to God's consistent desire to establish an intimate relationship with his people. In the Old Testament the main thrust relates to his special commitment to Israel, and their persistent unresponsiveness constantly frustrates his wider purposes. All that we can detect are occasional hints and prods which only become explicit in the New Testament.

The Epistle to the Hebrews twice refers to the prophecy of the New Covenant in Jeremiah, chapter 31. The author sees its fulfilment in the coming of Christ, who inaugurates the New Covenant by becoming both the Great High Priest and the all-sufficient sacrifice for sins (Heb. 8:7–13; 10:15ff; 4:14ff; 7:23ff; 9:25ff). This is not simply the fanciful exegesis of a Judeo-Christian apologist, for Christ himself, in offering the cup to his disciples during the Last Supper, declared, 'Drink this all of you, . . . this is my blood which seals God's covenant, my blood poured out for many for the forgiveness of sins' (Matt. 26:27, 28; see also Mark 14:24; Luke 22:20; 1 Cor. 11:25). The Lukan and Pauline versions explicitly state that the cup represents God's '*new covenant*', and some versions of the other Gospel accounts include the adjective '*new*'.

The coming of the Holy Spirit on the disciples individually and corporately provides that new relationship anticipated by the prophets. In the Upper Room the Lord reassured his followers he would not leave them orphaned, but would send another Comforter, who would dwell among them and teach them (John 14:17). He abides with them both to witness *to* them to the Lord's living presence and to witness *through* them to reveal the nature and power of God to the world (Acts 1:8). In addition to operating through his followers that same Spirit is at work in the world to 'convince (convict) the world concerning sin and righteousness and judgement' (John 16:8).

Thus the New Covenant holds out the prospect of mission which is startlingly realised through the witness of the disciples and the thousands throughout the Mediterranean world who responded to their testimony. There is a further faint echo of Jeremiah's prophecy in Paul's words to the Corinthian believers whose radically changed lives read like an open letter from Christ himself (2 Cor. 3:1–3).

This covenant relationship also serves as a constant reminder to the Church that she herself is subject to him. She has no monopoly on God, and she has no magical power with which to manipulate him. Her task is to bear faithful witness to a covenant relationship which she has neither earned nor deserved. Her witness is at best partial and approximate. In drawing people to herself she points beyond herself to a covenant-keeping God who grieves over, struggles with and yet delights in his people. A growing Church must be continually experiencing correction, reformation and renewal.

A GLORIFIED PEOPLE ATTRACTING THE NATIONS

The Old Testament emphasis is not on Israel moving out in mission, but on the nations spontaneously converging on Jerusalem. They are attracted by the evidence of the God of Israel uniquely and gloriously present in the midst of his people. So they come to pay homage to a foreign deity, not compelled by conquest but convinced by the covenant God has established with Israel and extends to the world.

Pilgrims en route for Zion will encourage others to join their ranks: 'Those from one city will say to those from another, "We are going to worship the Lord Almighty and pray for His blessing. Come with us"' (Zech. 8:21). The response will be widespread including 'many peoples and powerful nations'. Wherever Jews are to be found they will become the centre of attention surrounded by those seeking to share their destiny because the news has been spread abroad that God is with them (Zech. 8:23; see also Hab. 2:14; Zech. 8:22, 23; Mal. 1:11).

'Arise, Jerusalem, and shine like the sun; the glory of the Lord is shining on you! Other nations will be covered by darkness, but on you the light of the Lord will shine; the brightness of His presence will be with you. Nations will be drawn to your light, and kings to the dawning of your new day' (Isa. 60:1–3).

Israel is called by God to be a witnessing people. The form of her witness is not so much a missionary force as a magnetic presence. Her quality of life was intended to demonstrate to the surrounding nations that God was in her midst. As a consequence they would be attracted to Jerusalem where the throne of God was located to enjoy his presence and offer him sacrifice and service. '. . . As far as is known, Judaism was never a missionary force in the sense that organised efforts were made by the Jews as a whole to win others. We have no evidence that Jews were sent to Palestine with the express purpose of winning converts to Judaism, or that Jews of Palestine felt any personal responsibility for this work. It was left to the individuals who made contact with non-Jews in the lands to which they were scattered to make converts or not as they felt inclined' (Rowley 1950:92).

The clearest challenge to Israel to be open to the possibility of other nations responding to God's law appear in the stories of Ruth, Jonah and Daniel. The first of these shows how a foreign Moabite woman becomes a member of one of the most respected families in Israel, thereby becoming the great-grandmother of King David. The book of Jonah describes the begrudging responses of a prophet of Israel to the Lord's command to warn Nineveh, capital of Assyria, of God's impending judgement. He cannot come to terms with God's intention to have mercy on the implacable enemy of Israel. The prophet's intolerance is in stark contrast to God's patience. Jonah chose to sulk outside the city, longing for God's judgement to fall, rather than proclaim the message of God's love to the repentant Ninevites (Jonah 4:2). He is more concerned about a castor oil plant which perished, thus denying him shade, than with the fate of the 120,000 people in the city who were so confused they didn't know their right hand from their left. The isolated and resentful Jonah is held up to Israel as a mirror image of their exclusiveness.

The third story describes how Daniel and his friends were transported to Babylon during the time of the exile. It tells how they face the challenge to their way of life presented by their conquerors. Yet God enables them to remain faithful. Furthermore, he gives them insights beyond those possessed by the greatest minds of that renowned civilisation. The message is clear. Provided

Israel remains faithful to the Lord, she has nothing to fear and much to give. She holds the key to unlock the meaning of history.

It is evident from our Lord's condemnation of the leaders of the law and Pharisees who sailed the seas and crossed whole countries to win one convert (Matt. 23:15) that some zealous individuals did feel inclined to propagate their religion. But those were exceptions. In the main, Gentiles were left to take the initiative if they felt attracted to Judaism. Those Gentiles who attached themselves to the Synagogues of the Jews were technically known as 'god-fearers'. It was this group which was frequently ready to respond to Paul's preaching as he visited synagogues throughout Asia and Macedonia to proclaim and argue the gospel during his missionary journeys.

Before Israel could become a light to the nations she had to experience a genuine conversion herself. Jeremiah describes her as unfaithful Israel needing to turn back to God. When she demonstrated a genuine repentance then she would know the mercy of God and his law would be written in their hearts. 'When that time comes, Jerusalem will be called "The Throne of the Lord", and all nations will gather there to worship me.' (Jer. 3:17; 31:31–34). As the details of this expectation unfold it becomes clear that this spontaneous coming will not be within the normal course of history, but will be a direct result of the coming of the Messiah and the outpouring of the Holy Spirit (Joel 2:28).

In the New Testament we find that this stress on the centripetal movement of magnetism is not entirely displaced by the centrifugal movement of mission. The New Testament church is described in a number of places as an *attracting* fellowship. The Lord prayed for his disciples just prior to his arrest and crucifixion, 'May they be one, so that the world will believe that you sent me. I gave them the same glory you gave me, so that they may be one, just as you and I are one: I in them and you in me, so that they may be completely one, in order that the world may know that you sent me and that you love them as you love me' (John 17:21–23). The unity of which the Lord speaks is not a regimented uniformity but a supernatural harmony, orchestrated by God through his Spirit at work within them. The word 'glory' refers to the manifest presence of God among his people.

Christ assured his followers that his death on the cross would itself have enormous drawing-power. It brought about the overthrow of the 'ruler of this world' so that Satan would not be able to restrain those whom the Spirit moved to respond to the gospel. 'When I am lifted up from the earth, I will draw everyone to me' (John 12:32).

The church in Jerusalem so manifested the presence of God through miracles and wonders that everyone was filled with awe, and their depth of commitment and degree of practical concern made such an impression that they enjoyed the good will of all the people. They could not simply be ignored. 'And every day the Lord added to their group those who were being saved' (see Acts 2:43–47). This response did not simply occur as a result of their evangelistic zeal, but through the fact that they were such an effective advertisement to the value of knowing God.

Writing in old age John reflects on the nature of the invitation which the Church issued. 'What we have seen and heard we announce to you also, so that you will join with us in the fellowship that we have with the Father and with His son Jesus Christ. We write this in order that our joy may be complete' (1 John 1:3, 4). The Church has no hesitancy in inviting others to join them because what they enjoyed was worth sharing. To deny others would be to deprive them of blessing.

There can be no spiritually significant church growth without church renewal. Our Lord warned that not all

growth is valuable or even desirable. Weeds which have
every appearance of being wheat will grow up alongside the
genuine wheat, but would bear no fruit and would ultimately
be separated for burning (Matt. 13:24–30; 36–43). A fig
tree with foliage but no fruit was cursed by Christ (Luke
13:6–9). True growth is not so much the result of activism
and popularity, as an evidence of a unique quality of personal and corporate life, which comes into being because
God is with his people.

THE SERVANT OF THE LORD:
A LIGHT TO THE NATIONS

The servant appears in Isaiah, chapters 41–55, where he is
mentioned eighteen times. Scholars have argued at length
over his identity. In the earlier references it seems to be the
nation as a whole who is referred to. This is quite explicit
in Is. 41:8.

> But you, Israel my servant,
>   you are the people I have chosen,
>   the descendants of Abraham, my friend.

The context underlines the fact that servanthood was a
privilege, they were chosen by God for the role and could
count on his protection. He had been at work behind the
scenes to create the conditions for Israel to return to Israel
from exile. Cyrus, the Persian emperor, had, without realising it, been God's instrument to help God's servant Israel
(45:4) by overthrowing their Babylonian captors (41:2, 25).
If Cyrus could not be expected to realise the significance of
current events, Israel had no excuse. She had failed to learn
the lessons of the exile, which had come upon her on
account of her disobedience, neither did she apparently see
the hand of God to secure their return, which prompted
God to exclaim,

Is anyone more blind than my servant,
more deaf than the messenger I send?
Israel, you have seen so much,
but what has it meant to you?
You have ears to hear with,
but what have you really heard?

(42:19, 20)

God does not abandon his servant Israel. He calls upon
her to bear witness to him as the one true God, who in
contrast to man-made idols, lives and speaks. He predicts
what is to happen and provides insight into the significance
of events (43:10; 44:6–8). Their obstinacy in refusing to
listen to God's voice meant that they were both defeated
militarily and depleted in numbers.

If only you had listened to my commands!
Then blessings would have flowed for you
like a stream that never goes dry!
Victory would have come to you
like the waves that roll on the shore.
Your descendants would be as numerous as grains of sand,
and I would have made sure they were never destroyed.

(48:18–19)

But God gives her another chance.

Go out from Babylon, go free!
Shout the news gladly; make it known everywhere:
The Lord has saved his servant Israel!

(48:20)

He restores her to her land (48:2) and calls upon her to bear
her witness to him as the one true God.

Within the concept of the servant as the personification
of the nation begins to emerge an individual servant
who embodies Israel's mission, and surpasses her in the

fulfilment of that mission (Rowley 1950:119). The first glimpse occurs in chapter 42:1–4, where the servant of the Lord is described as filled with the Spirit and with the assurance that he will succeed in his mission to bring justice to every nation. His approach to achieve this end will be a gentle one. He will speak in a quiet and restrained manner, he supports the bruised and broken plant, and blows into flame the dying spark.

The servant has a two-fold task, which is described in chapter 49:1–6. His first assignment is to bring back his scattered people to enjoy their true spiritual heritage (v.5). His second assignment is of a much wider nature presenting an even greater challenge.

> I have a greater task for you, my servant.
> Not only will you restore to greatness
> the people of Israel who have survived,
> but I will also make you a light to the nations –
> so that all the world may be saved.
>
> (49:6)

The light of revelation and regeneration brought by God's servant will not be confined to Israel but will become the light for the entire world. However, this will not be accomplished without suffering. He will be rejected by men, despised and brutally ill-treated so that people will not bear to look at him. Yet his very suffering will attract world-wide attention.

> But now many nations will marvel at him,
> and kings will be speechless with amazement.
> They will see and understand
> something they had never known.
> The people reply,
> Who would have believed what we now report?
> Who could have seen the Lord's hand in this?
>
> (52:15–53:1)

When its significance is explained to them they will be overwhelmed, it will seem utterly incredible. In the first place *he was an innocent victim*. His God-inflicted suffering was undeserved. The pain he bore was the punishment which those who tortured and killed him should have borne.

But he endured the suffering that should have been ours,
the pain that we should have borne.
All the while we thought that his suffering
was punishment sent by God.
All of us were like sheep that were lost,
each of us going his own way.
But the Lord made the punishment fall on him,
the punishment all of us deserved.

(53:4, 6)

In the second place *the punishment inflicted upon him was for their healing*.

We are healed by the punishment he suffered,
made whole by the blows he received.

(v. 5b)

In the third place he was a *voluntary victim*. He made no attempt to resist, v. 7, 8, and prayed for sinners that they might be forgiven. In the fourth place he will *survive the suffering of death*. He will see his descendants (v. 10). After a life of suffering he will again have joy (v. 11).

In the fifth place he will know that it has *all been worth while*. He will see his offspring and be given a place of honour.

These prophecies find their remarkable fulfilment in the self-giving ministry of Christ. He forged the essential link between the concepts of Messiahship and Suffering Servant which had not occurred to his contemporaries. The growth of the people of God was not to come about through military conquest but along the costly pathway of crucifixion which would lead to resurrection. The Lord viewed his own cross not in terms of extinction, but germination. He declared, 'a grain of wheat remains no more than a single grain unless it is dropped into the ground and dies. If it does die, then it produces many grains' (John 12:24). This was not only true for him in his unique act of redemption, but it was an abiding principle by which his followers were called to live (John 12:25; Luke 9:23). There can be no sustained growth until we have learned to die daily. We cannot preach the cross effectively unless we are carrying it.

Whereas in the prophet Isaiah the concept of the Servant starts with the nation and then narrows to an individual, in the New Testament the unique servant enlists and empowers his followers in his servanthood. 'As the Father has sent me even so send I you.' And when Paul in the introductory paragraph of so many of his letters to the churches describes himself as a servant of Jesus Christ, he is not describing a servile position, but one of highest honour. Those who have leadership positions in the Church of Jesus Christ do not lord it over the followers, but act as towel-bearing servants (John 13:1–17).

SUMMARY
In this chapter we have briefly reviewed the relationship of the people of God to the nations of the world. This presents us with a consistent picture, namely that it is God's declared purpose that his people will grow in numbers not simply through biological growth (i.e. by children of Christian parents becoming church members), but as they exert a powerful spiritual influence upon the world.

God's call and promise to an *individual* (Abraham) results in a *family*. The family diversifies into a group of tribes – a *people* sharing a common kinship. The people become institutionalised as a *nation* ruled by a king. As a consequence of Israel's persistent disobedience God permits the kingdom to be overthrown, and the nation driven into exile is reduced to a *remnant*. But in the providence of God that remnant is not intended as a survival from the past but as a stump from which future growth can develop. The remnant therefore becomes a *religious community* – the servant of the Lord – membership of which is not confined to any ethnic, geographical or political groupings, but is open to all who are committed to the word of God (in Old Testament terms, 'the torah', his law). 'Here is the birth of the confessing church.' (Goldingay 1975:2, 19).

We learn that church growth is on God's agenda, not simply through a few isolated 'missionary texts' but through the long strands of teaching which extend back from the New Testament through the previous centuries of divine revelation recorded in the Old Testament. If such growth appears on God's agenda then it should also appear on ours!

At the same time, we must heed the warnings of Old Testament scholars not to read back into the period the concerns of the New Testament for the mission of the people of God to all nations. There is little or no evidence of their awareness of such a calling. Israel's consciousness of her election led to an exclusiveness which blinded her to her spiritual responsibilities to the nations. In place of a concern for mission we find the constant drive for preservation and prosperity. Here are warning notes for the Church to heed today, otherwise our concern for church growth will be wrongly motivated.

One further element must be underscored lest it escape our attention. The divine intention for, and possibility of, mission emerges most clearly in the worship of the people of God and as they hear the challenge of the prophetic word. Mission has its starting-point not in ideas and plans, but in praise offered to God and in learning to listen intently to him. It is the praying rather than the talkative church which is most likely to be effectively engaged in mission. We will return more than once to this vital, yet frequently neglected, point.

CHAPTER TWO

Church and Kingdom

THE 'GOSPEL' IN THE GOSPELS

Each of the Gospels, representing different versions of our Lord's life, were written with a clear evangelistic purpose. They were produced to introduce enquirers to the authentic and essential facts of the gospel and used as a basis of instruction for those who were preparing for baptism.

Michael Green draws attention to the fact that the Gospels represent an entirely new literary form, which was neither history, nor biography, but a highly selective weaving together of fragments using preaching and teaching 'arranged in order to show what sort of person Jesus was, to give the evidence on which the disciples had followed him and had adjudged him the Messiah and Son of God, and by the strongest possible implication, challenge the readers to make the same act of faith in Christ as they themselves had done.' (Green 1970:229, 230).

In a more recent book he suggests that the gospel was also made available as widespread and cheaply as possible by a novel process. The gospel was bound in a compact book form rather than produced as a bulky scroll, with paper made from cheap papyrus rather than the very expensive vellum (i.e. treated skins) (Green 1979:125). These also made for easier reference with page turning being easier than unwinding a scroll to find your place. The early Christians may therefore be credited with the invention of the forerunner of the popular paperback!

There has been a great deal of argument as to what a new enquirer needs to know before or immediately upon making a decision to follow Christ for that decision to be meaningful. As we have seen, the Gospels were written to meet that need, so by examining carefully their contents we will gain an overall impression of the range of information which the early Christians deemed to be necessary for an adequate on-going commitment to be made. In the great majority of cases this teaching would be communicated orally, for Gospels were in short supply and many converts were illiterate. As a general rule those who could read had to make their own copy. Having to write it out was a good way to absorb the contents.

By switching from concentration on a few 'proof texts' in evangelism to a more balanced and comprehensive approach adopted by one of the four Gospels we might see better short and long-term results in our evangelism. They give a clear picture of the identity of Christ, show the radical all-or-nothing nature of commitment to him, describe the life of discipleship as a corporate not individualistic activity, spell out the cost involved, and show how our present experience relates to the Kingdom of God, which is both present and yet still to come.

The first three Gospels each place a heavy emphasis on the 'Kingdom'. Matthew, to suit Jewish susceptibility, prefers to speak of the 'Kingdom of Heaven' rather than the 'Kingdom of God', because Jews were reluctant to utter the divine name. He refers to the Kingdom fifty-two times, while Mark uses it nineteen times, Luke forty-four times and John only four.

The lack of Kingdom emphasis in John is probably explained by the fact that he is writing more in retrospect and possibly to play down false expectations in the contemporary Jewish understanding of the Kingdom. The 'Kingdom of God' is only mentioned twice (3:3, 5) because it 'calls to mind that apocalyptic Judaism which John seems for the most part to avoid. Perhaps this general avoidance suggests his criticism of that Judaism which was content to await the miraculous vindication of Israel in the Kingdom of God and to ignore the necessity for inward conversion and rebirth' (Barrett 1960:173). If John, apart from the important reference in Chapter 3, which we shall consider later, avoids the term Kingdom of God, he does on the other hand lay more stress than the other three Gospels on Jesus as King of Israel (Barrett 1960:346). The Gospels therefore lay a heavy emphasis on the gospel of the Kingdom and the Kingship of Jesus.

The writings of Donald McGavran do not make clear the relationship he sees between the Church and the Kingdom. At several points he seems to use the terms interchangeably. Church planting becomes synonymous with Kingdom building. Mission is not simply self-proliferation, for the Church is not the Kingdom. As Rene Padilla cautions, 'To speak of the kingdom of God is to speak of the purpose of God, of which the empirical church is little more than a pale reflection' (Padilla 1975:43). The failure of church growth thinking, at least in its early formulations, to differentiate between Church and Kingdom has led to a great deal of misunderstanding and criticism. It has resulted in Christian mission being caricatured as denominational aggrandisement, or a plan for survival for western-based churches and their related mission agencies. Church growth thinking has been slow to come to terms with the problem of nominality within existing churches, and has consequently given the impression that mission is simply making more and more people to become like ourselves. It has not sufficiently emphasised that the Church itself is in the process of becoming and through its disobedience can present a distorted or even completely erroneous picture of the Christian life. In recent years this aspect has been corrected to a large extent through the response of Third World Christian thinkers and the radical discipleship movement which is emerging among younger Christians in the more affluent nations.

THE GOSPEL OF THE KINGDOM

From the outset the Gospels establish the relationship between the coming of the Kingdom and the appearance of the Christ. John the Baptist, as the last in the long line of Old Testament Prophets, called upon the nation to repent to prepare for the Kingdom whose coming was imminent (Matt. 3:2). When his public voice was silenced through imprisonment, Jesus established the continuity of his ministry with that of John. Like him, he calls the nation to turn away from their sins because the Kingdom of heaven is near (Matt. 4:23; 9:35), but with a significant new emphasis. Whereas for John the Kingdom came as a threat to a people who were unprepared, for Jesus it represented good news to those who felt unworthy or excluded.

'The transition from "the days of John the Baptist" (Matt. 11:12) to Jesus' independent career was signalled by the priority of "the reign of God" over "the wrath about to come". . . . The call to baptism bore immediately on the restoration of Israel and the concomitant salvation of the nations. The key to the difference is the motif "free gift", with which Jesus charged the expression "the reign of God". This is why his proclamation came eventually to be known as "gospel" or "news of salvation"' (Meyer 1979:130).

As the Gospel narrative unfolds we are quickly made aware that the good news signifies more than rescue from divine wrath. It is the establishing of God's Kingly rule, which entails both God's provision for his people and requirements from them.

The inauguration of the Kingdom is an act of God and not the result of human achievement. However, its coming is not automatic; it requires a response from man. For this reason the message of the Kingdom has to be both proclaimed as fact and promise. Christ himself came *preaching* the Good News of the Kingdom, describing its nature and calling for a response. His silent presence was not sufficient of itself. The Kingdom needed explaining and people needed exhorting. If presence was inadequate by itself as a strategy to extend the Kingdom in the ministry of Christ, it is even more deficient when left to his stumbling followers.

This need for proclamation is expressed with sensitivity in section three of the World Council of Churches Conference on World Mission and Evangelism Report (Melbourne May 12–24, 1980) *The Church Witnesses to the Kingdom*, in the following paragraph:

> The proclamation of the Word of God is one such witness, distinct and indispensable. The story of God in Christ is the heart of all evangelism, and this story has to be told, for the life of the present Church never fully reveals the love and holiness and power of God in Christ. The telling of the story is an inescapable mandate for the whole Church; word accompanies deed as the kingdom throws its light ahead of its arrival and men and women seek to live in that light (1:3).

In fact Christ explicitly commanded his disciples to proclaim the Kingdom. He sent out the Twelve to the towns and villages of Israel with this charge, 'Go and preach, "The Kingdom of heaven is near!"' (Matt. 10:7). Subsequently, with the sending out of the Seventy, they were to announce, 'The Kingdom of God has come near you' (Luke 10:9).

Seeing the extent of the need and the readiness of the response, Jesus calls upon his followers to pray to the owner of the harvest that he will send out workers to gather in his harvest (Matt. 9:37; Luke 9.2). Elton Trueblood comments, 'when Christ said the labourers were few, He and those to

whom He spoke were surrounded by large numbers of
priests and semi-professional religious men. The priests in
Jerusalem were so numerous that they had to take turns in
performing Temple ceremonies. The dearth was of persons
who could give the only kind of witness that counts with
those looking for help, the kind that is couched in the first
person singular' (Trueblood 1961:51). The Kingdom must
be announced by 'insiders' and not simply treated as a
subject for speculation.

Within hours of his death, Jesus sets forth a world-
embracing scenario. 'And this Good News about the
Kingdom will be preached through all the world for a
witness to all mankind; and then the end will come'
(Matt. 24:14). This leaves no doubt as to the universal and
abiding significance of the Kingdom concept. Gospel
preaching will be seriously deficient if this dimension is
omitted. The Kingdom gives content and purpose to the act
of commitment. It represents a radical and all-embracing
transfer of allegiance. It is therefore essential for the
Christian witness to understand to what 'the Kingdom'
refers in Scripture.

THE OLD TESTAMENT EXPECTATION
OF THE KINGDOM

Although the Old Testament nowhere expressly mentions
the Kingdom of God, the world is represented as existing
under his cosmic rule (Ps. 24:1; 93:1; 95:3). His sovereignty
is not confined to the created order but includes political
powers. As the King of the Nations (Jer. 10:7; Ps. 47:3;
99:2), he exerts his sovereign power by guiding their for-
tunes and acting in judgement. Certain individuals and
peoples become instruments of his justice and anger. Thus,
in a number of ways through the Psalms and Prophets the
Old Testament continually reminds us that God is King
(Snyder 1977:14). While for the prophets the envisioned
universal rule of God is an eschatological event, for the

Psalmist the enthronement of Yahweh is 'a present reality experienced in the cultic ceremony' (Klappert 1976: Vol. II, 372–389).

For the prophets the new age of the Kingdom represented an era of peace, prosperity and justice for Israel brought about by radical economic and social changes (Mic. 4:1–5; Zech. 9:10; Is. 2:4; 9:7; 42:3 and 65:21ff). It would also transform the created order, resulting in geological changes bringing about a favourable climate and fertility of the soil, so that Israel surpassed her early reputation of being a land of 'milk and honey' (Is. 11:6–9; 32:14–20; 38:1f; Zech. 14:3f; Amos 9:13). Conflict in nature would be resolved, with the lion lying down with the lamb. Humanity would also be renewed, both physically with the disappearance of sickness, and the diminution of the power of death; and spiritually with men being given a 'new heart' through the Spirit coming upon all flesh and spreading a universal knowledge of God (Jer. 23:5f; 31:31; Ezek. 36:24–28; Zech. 8:20–23; Joel 2:28). As we noted in the previous chapter, the nation of Israel occupied a central place in the realisation of this hope, serving as the gathering-point of the nations (Is. 24:23; Zech. 14:9; Obad. 21). She would not achieve this position of prominence through conquest but through example and inspiration.

Thus, when John the Baptist and then Jesus spoke of the 'Kingdom of God' or the 'Kingdom of Heaven' they were not introducing a novel concept which needed explaining. On the contrary, the idea of the Kingdom had a long history in the life of Israel, and the coming of Christ coincided with a feverish wave of expectancy within the nation. They longed for deliverance from Roman oppression, and were encouraged to think that they would not have much longer to wait as the prophetic voice was heard once more in the land after centuries of silence. As the crowds listened to Christ's unconventional preaching and observed his miracles they acknowledged him as sent from God. After Jesus feeds the Five Thousand the crowd respond by declaring, 'Surely this is the Prophet who was to come into the world!' As they advance on him Jesus realises that they are about to seize him to make him King (John 6:15).

Similarly, when he enters Jerusalem crowded with pilgrims and with a politically charged atmosphere, they prepared a royal route and cry out, 'Praise God! God bless him who comes in the name of the Lord! God bless the coming kingdom of King David, our father! Praise God!' (Mark 11:10). Matthew in his version makes clear that this was no mistaken identification. The event was staged to fulfil Zechariah's prophecy of the Messianic King riding into Jerusalem (Matt. 21:5). However, the crowd missed the symbolism of his riding on a donkey in humility rather than a horse as military conqueror.

Chief among the political activists were the zealots, who were the Jewish first-century freedom fighters. Their motivation was not simply political or patriotic, but religious. By their guerrilla activities they hoped to generate a revolt against Rome, thereby hastening the coming of the Kingdom. In the New Testament we read of the insurrection under Judas and Theudas (Acts 5:36, 37), and a further revolt under an unidentified Egyptian (Acts 21:38). The eventual destruction of Jerusalem was brought about by the Romans to crush the rebellion of Bar Kokhba who was styled by the Akiba, the most famous rabbi of the time, as the Messiah (Ladd 1974:62).

Israel's expectation of the Kingdom was not confined to the political activists and zealots. It was also shared by the pious saints, referred to as 'the quiet in the land'. Other groups such as the Essene sect had withdrawn completely from society to await the eschatological consummation of the Kingdom. They expected the angels to come down and join battle with them – 'the sons of light' – against their enemies – 'the sons of darkness' – and to give them victory over all other peoples (Ladd 1974:62).

Within the New Testament we find reference to pious individuals who were awaiting the redemption of Israel through the mission of a Messiah who would be King David's greater son. Such longings find expression in the Song of Mary (Luke 1:46–55), the prophecy of Zechariah (Luke 1:68–79), among Andrew, Simon Peter, Philip and Nathaniel as disciples of John the Baptist, who were encouraged by their self-effacing master to transfer their allegiance to Christ (John 1:29–50), by spiritually discerning Pharisees such as Nicodemus (John 3:1–8), and in the case of Joseph of Arimathea, a member of the Jerusalem Council, who 'was waiting for the coming of the Kingdom of God' (Luke 23:50, 51).

So Christ ministered in Israel to those who had preconceived notions about the coming Kingdom. His many references to the Kingdom recorded in the Gospels must be seen against this historical background and contemporary context.

After being so intimately with Christ and hearing his parables of the Kingdom and private commentary interpreting those stories, his disciples still expected the Kingdom to come in the material and nationalistic terms of the Old Testament (Acts 1:6). To what extent were they in line with Jesus' teaching?

THE NEW TESTAMENT REALISATION OF THE KINGDOM

Our Lord emphasises the continuity with the past when he inaugurates his public ministry with the announcement, 'The right time has come, and the Kingdom of God is near! Turn away from your sins and believe the Good News' (Mark 1:15). 'The two Testaments are organically linked to each other. The relationship between them is neither one of upward development nor of contrast; it is one of beginning and completion, of hope and fulfilment. And the bond that binds them together is the dynamic concept of the rule of God. There is indeed a "new thing" in the New Testament . . . it has introduced a tremendously significant change of tense. In referring to the Kingdom the Old Testament spoke in such terms as "Behold, the days are coming". But in the New Testament we encounter a change: the tense is a resounding present indicative – the Kingdom is *here*!' (Bright 1953:196, 197).

For Jesus, the Kingdom of God represented an approaching new order of things. This new order was no distant hope but already operative . . . God's final saving act was already operative in Israel: now is the new creation, time of the new wine and the new cloak (Mark 2:21f)! The fields are 'white' (John 4:35), the harvest 'great' (Matt. 9:37)! Now is the wedding, the espousal of Israel! 'Can the wedding guests mourn?' (Mark 2:19). The young man dead through sin 'is alive again' (Luke 15:24, 32), 'so it is right to be glad' (Meyer 1979:131). The reign of God has already come upon you (Matt. 12:28).

But in what sense can the Kingdom be understood to have arrived in the person and ministry of Jesus? Part of the mystery is unravelled by our appreciating the differences in the concept of 'time' within the Bible and our modern western understanding. For us time is a quantity concept. For the Hebrews, on the other hand, it was a quality measure. They thought in terms of a right or wrong time, rather than long or short duration. Ecclesiastes 3:1–8 well illustrates their way of thinking, 'There is a time for everything, a time for every occupation under heaven: a time for giving birth, dying, planting, killing, healing, knocking down, building, etc.' 'For the Hebrew, to know the time was not a matter of knowing the date, it was a matter of knowing what kind of time it might be. Was it a time for tears or a time for laughter, a time for war or a time for peace? To misjudge the time in which one lived might prove to be disastrous' (Nolan 1976:74).

The task of the prophet was therefore supremely to

interpret 'the times'. So when our Lord spoke about the Kingdom of Heaven being at hand, he was referring to its being qualitatively present. His public ministry inaugurates this new 'quality time', and his ascension to the throne of power and sending of the Spirit upon his disciples represents its coming in power. The Kingdom of God as a new dimension of living opens up to those who turn away from their sins, evidencing a radical break with the past. For them it begins to be present as an 'insiders' experience. At the same time, for those who have not arrived at, or hold back from such a step of faith, the Kingdom is not yet.

Our Lord came to inaugurate the Kingdom. As he began his ministry it was present in his person. He represented the dawn of a new age which would never be engulfed by darkness. His amazing words and miraculous deeds were signs of the coming Kingdom. As his disciples were identified with him in his ministry and experienced the healing powers of the new age operating through them, so they became partakers of the Kingdom. Wherever they went they represented a frontier of the Kingdom (Luke 10:1). To the Pharisees, who were blind to the evidence before their eyes, and were postponing their hopes to the future, our Lord responded, 'No one will say, "Look, here it is!" or, "There it is!" because the Kingdom of God is within you' (Luke 17:21). The Greek word *entos* translated here as 'within' should more accurately be rendered 'among' you or 'in your midst' (Nolan 1976:46). The point Jesus was making was that it was all around them and they hadn't noticed!

In the Acts and Epistles Christians are regarded as experiencing the Kingdom as a present reality. It is evidenced in the lives of believers who serve Christ in 'Righteousness, peace, and joy which the Holy Spirit gives' (Rom. 14:17). Paul describes the Christians in Colossae as having been rescued from the power of darkness and 'brought' (past tense) into the Kingdom of his dear Son by virtue of the saving work of Christ (Col. 1:13). The church in Thessalonica is urged to live the kind of life that pleases God, who calls them ('now,' not 'one day') 'to share in his own Kingdom and glory' (1 Thess. 2:12). While John the Divine describes himself to the seven churches in Asia as 'your partner in patiently enduring the suffering that comes to those who belong to his Kingdom' (Rev. 1:9).

Alongside this emphasis of the Kingdom as a present reality to be experienced and enjoyed, there is an equally strong strand of teaching which speaks of the Kingdom as in the future and, therefore, to be anticipated and longed for. This second strand, like the first, runs through the entire New Testament. It is associated with the final curtain descending on present world history, when Jesus will descend from heaven in power to destroy his enemies and restore the entire creation. This coming of the Kingdom will be a time of separation (Matt. 25:34; Luke 13:28) and judgement (Matt. 8:12; 2 Tim. 4:1). It will also be a time of rejoicing and feasting in the Messianic banquet (Matt. 26:29; Luke 22:28–30).

The Kingdom is at the same time a heavenly as well as an earthly reality. Our Lord left this earthly scene to occupy his throne and to sit at the Father's table. For the believer the Kingdom as a heavenly reality is no more than one generation away. Jesus said to the penitent thief, 'Today you will be with me in paradise' (Luke 23:43). Paul expresses his assurance to Timothy, 'the Lord will rescue me from all evil and take me safely into his heavenly Kingdom' (2 Tim. 4:18).

The coming of Christ was therefore to inaugurate the Kingdom in a provisional form. Its final consummation still lies in the future.

This future emphasis of the Kingdom is most strongly present in the Apocalyptic books of the Bible. In the Old Testament the eschatological expectation is elevated to a transcendental level (Dan. 7:13f, 27), while the book of

Revelation represents the Kingdom as final consummation (Rev. 11:15; 12:10). The coming glorious age co-exists with the present evil age. In other words, 'The Age to Come has overlapped with This Age' (Ladd 1974:42) which results in intermingling and close combat. Thus in his embodiment of the Kingdom Jesus confronts demonic powers which openly manifest their opposition. We therefore find ourselves living in disputed territory. 'The Kingdom has come, but is not yet perfected' (Mark 9:1; 13:26); 'The enemy is stricken, but not yet destroyed' (Stauffer 1975:125).

There is one further related problem which we must now briefly consider, namely our temporal distance from the events described in the New Testament. In the Gospels there is a powerful sense of imminence regarding the Kingdom. Then it seemed that the consummation would follow soon on the heels of its inauguration. Indeed it would come within the lifetime of Christ's hearers (Matt. 24:34; Mark 9:1). Whatever the intended meaning of those words, there is strong evidence in the New Testament that many of the early Christians expected the Lord's return at any moment.

The German theologian, Wolfhart Pannenberg, emphasises this impact of the future on the present in Jesus' teaching. 'God's Kingdom does not lie in the distant future but is imminent. Thus, the present is not independent from that future. Rather does the future have an imperative claim upon the present, alerting all men to the urgency and exclusiveness of seeking first the Kingdom of God. As this message is proclaimed and accepted, God's rule is present and we can even now glimpse the future glory' (Pannenberg 1975:54). The Kingdom is not and cannot be relegated to an appendix which follows the turning of the last page of world history.

This is an attitude of life which the twentieth-century Church urgently needs to recapture. We must avoid the temptation to project time-spans from the past into the future. We need to 'feel' time as well as measure it. 'The *eschaton* is a future event but, to the extent that our lives are determined and qualified by it, it is also a contemporary event, an event that can be seen in the signs of the times' (Nolan 1976:76). 'Now' is not a panic word, but one which conveys the idea of both opportunity and urgency. It is not a command from God to advance on all fronts, but is a strategic word identifying and emphasising his order of priorities.

THE SIGNS OF THE KINGDOM

The signs of the Kingdom are clear pointers to the coming Kingdom. The sign contains sufficient of the content of the thing signified to be more than a symbol. But the sign acts as shield as well as pointer. It shows enough to reveal the nature and genuineness of the reality, but not so much as to overwhelm. Thus the sign can be ignored or disputed.

The clearest most powerful 'sign' of the Kingdom is the presence of Christ himself. In much recent talk about the Kingdom Jesus' centrality has been overlooked, or refuge has been taken in the concept of his anonymous presence which does not square well with the New Testament Kingdom emphasis. The Kingdom of God is equally described as the Kingdom of his dear Son or the Kingdom of Christ (Eph. 5:5; Rev. 11:15). The verdict passed on men in the final judgement will be determined by the attitude they adopted to Christ during their lifetime (Matt. 10:32 cf. Luke 12:8). The unrepentant cities will be condemned because they did not turn from their sins despite his mighty works (Matt. 11:21; Luke 10:13). Christ himself will appear as the judge of all men to separate the sheep from the goats (Matt. 25:31). He will discern between those who say 'Lord, Lord' as an empty profession and those who yielded their lives to the service of God (Matt. 7:23; Luke 13:27). He will plead before the Father the cause of those who confess him (Matt. 10:32; Luke 12:8). The presence of the Kingdom in the person of Jesus faces the individual with a clear-cut decision (Matt. 5:30; 15:8f; Mark 9:43–48; Luke 9:62).

The signs of the presence of God are various. It is to be seen in the *healing* ministry of Christ (Matt. 4:23; 9:35; Luke 9:11) and of his disciples who healed in his name (Luke 9:2; 10:9). These healing acts follow directly on from his teaching about the Kingdom. Yet these signs in themselves emphasise the provisional nature of the Kingdom, because all of those who were healed in the New Testament subsequently became sick and died. In the subsequent experience of the Church in exercising this ministry there have been many instances of failure, partial, delayed and temporary healing, reminding us that we live with the tension of the 'now' and the 'not yet' of the Kingdom.

Tom Smail, writing from a charismatic perspective, maintains a healthy balance. 'Within that tension of the already given and the still to come all Christians have to live – including charismatic Christians. God gives enough evidence of Christ risen to call to faith, but not enough to compel to acceptance . . . In the realm of healing much happens to authenticate Christ's present will and power to heal the otherwise incurable, and yet, often distressingly, enough fails to happen to serve to remind us that we are not yet at the last day, and to leave the mystery of the "not yet" all around us' (Smail 1975:124).

Closely linked with healing is the *casting out of demons*. This ministry was also exercised by Christ and his disciples. Deliverance provided proof that the Kingdom of God had already come (Matt. 12:28; Luke 11:20). This was especially significant for a society in which demonic possession was so prevalent and feared.

Such miracles constitute more than signs and wonders. They are 'mighty works' demonstrating the powers of the Kingdom in operation. They show that 'Satan has met his match (Luke 10:18; Mark 3:27); the cosmic end-struggle has begun' (Bright 1953:218).

Instances of *dead people brought back to life* (Matt. 10:8; Luke 9:2; John 11:44) were also a sign of the life in abundance which Christ came to bestow (John 10:10).

When Jesus began his public ministry he made his manifesto the prophecy of Is. 61:1–2 which he selected and read in the synagogue at Nazareth (Luke 4:18, 19):

> The Spirit of the Lord is upon me,
> because he has chosen me to bring
>   good news to the poor.
> He has sent me to proclaim liberty to the
>   captives
> and recovery of sight to the blind;
> to set free the oppressed
>   and announce that the time has come
>   when the Lord will save his people.

Such promises were meant to be fulfilled in the life of Israel in the provisions of the year of Jubilee scheduled for every forty-nine years. However, there is no evidence for that provision of the law ever being implemented. If this is indeed the case the significance of Jesus' words to the congregation as he gave back the scroll, 'This passage of scripture has come true today, as you heard it being read' (Luke 4:21) is even more poignant. Jesus liberated not through a programme of political activism, but simply through his spoken word. His word conveyed power and achieved results as it had from the time of creation itself.

Western commentators have frequently 'spiritualised' this prophecy in the sense of individualising and internalising its application. The 'poor' become the spiritually impoverished, the 'captives' those who are enslaved to sin, the 'blind' those who are unaware of their spiritual plight. On the other hand, there are those who turn this prophecy into a programme for political and economic emancipation: the poor are the exploited proletariat, the captives are the prisoners of conscience and the recovery of sight to the blind is achieved through 'awareness building' so that the exploited recognise the factors which have contributed to their plight and come to realise that their situation is not inevitable. The victims can become victors by taking power forcibly in their own hands.

Neither of these interpretations does full justice to the text. There can be no separating of the vertical from the horizontal dimensions of reconciliation. The preaching of the Good News brings reconciliation with God and makes reconciliation possible with our neighbour. Repentance includes turning away from social as well as personal sins. Salvation is not simply individualist and other-worldly. It means God's saving grace working through individuals and communities of people who know him as Saviour and Lord to influence a wider society. But I fail to see how we can talk about the 'redeeming of structures' without an effective Christian presence. This is not to say that there are not many people of good will who are working conscientiously for a more humane society, but such efforts inevitably succumb to the demonic. They are like the newly swept house of which our Lord spoke which was then taken over by more spirits than before (Matt. 12:43–45).

Poverty and prosperity are both characteristics of the Kingdom. *Poverty* is the recognition that we possess nothing to buy privilege with God, and *prosperity* results from our readiness to receive from God.

A characteristic of the Kingdom is an attitude of *forgiveness* which further should pervade all our relationships. It comes about as a result of our gratitude to God for his wiping out of a colossal debt that we could never have paid back (Matt. 18:22ff). We are able to forgive because we know what it is to be forgiven, and the love of God shed abroad in our heart gives us a new capacity to do so.

The Kingdom also demands *willing obedience to the law of*

God (Matt. 5:19, 20). This is not the keeping of the letter by escaping through the loopholes which we have opened up through clever casuistry. This is a joyful response to the spirit of the law, as we see its deeper meaning and wider application. For 'every teacher of the law who becomes a disciple in the Kingdom of Heaven is like the owner of a house who takes new and old things out of his storeroom' (Matt. 13:52). The new does not cause us to discard the old, but to see its contemporary worth.

Lastly, but by no means least, the Kingdom is characterised by *suffering*. This comes inevitably to those who belong to the Kingdom precisely because it is 'not of this world' and presents such a challenge which arouses hostility. 'Happy are those who are persecuted because they do what God requires; the Kingdom of Heaven belongs to them!' (Matt. 5:10), Jesus assures the children of the Kingdom. Such was the experience of the believers through subsequent years (2 Thess. 1:5; Rev. 1:9). The faithful Church has been described as the suffering form of the Kingdom of God (Snyder 1977:30).

ENTERING THE KINGDOM

Life in the Kingdom presented a challenge to the status quo. Where the gospel of Christ is faithfully proclaimed it is always subversive. It undermines the power-seeker, the affluent materialist and the self-righteous. It comes with equal challenge to the religious as to the irreligious. Many wealthy people will be prevented by their love of money from entering into the Kingdom. Although entrance is free we have to lay aside everything to enter through the narrow gate, so that it costs us everything. The Kingdom of Heaven belongs to the poor who have nothing to bring in with them. The 'poor' in Scripture does not simply refer to those living at or beneath subsistence level – it 'can be extended to cover all the oppressed, all those who are dependent upon the mercy of others. And this too is why the word can even be extended to all those who rely entirely upon the mercy of God – the poor in spirit' (Matt. 5:3) (Nolan 1976).

Whatever our position in society, the Kingdom makes an absolute demand; we either seek it first or not at all (Matt. 6:33). Having accepted the prior claim of the Kingdom, we then discover the generosity of God. We no longer have to worry about what we eat or drink or wear, for we will know his provision. However this is only a practicality within the economy of the Kingdom, where God's will reigns. For the adequacy of God's provision is dependent on our corporate responsibility, including our stewardship of resources and equitable distribution. Individual saints may testify to God's supernatural provision, but their experience cannot be universalised. Among the millions who die each year through malnutrition there are many children of the Kingdom. For we still live with the tension of the 'now' and 'not yet' of the Kingdom. This is allowed to happen not only because of the sin in the world, but also because of sin in the Church. To quote a Christian Aid slogan, because we refuse 'to live more simply that others may simply live'.

It is difficult for the twentieth-century, non-Jewish reader of the Gospels to appreciate just how radical Jesus appeared to his contemporaries, and especially to the religious establishment, who held such a powerful position in Jewish life. He completely disregarded strictly enforced social conventions and religious restrictions in order to contact the outcasts of society. He was not afraid to be seen deep in conversation with a Samaritan woman who he knew was cohabiting with another man after having gone through five husbands. He accepted the devotion of a prostitute who anointed his feet with costly perfume, and he dined out on a number of occasions with tax collectors and sinners, who represented the social outcasts – the 'untouchables' of the day.

Within an eastern culture, table-fellowship and the sharing of a meal is regarded as a particularly intimate form of association. The fact that Jesus was prepared to act in such a fashion, and to be *seen* doing it, communicated as powerfully as any pronouncement, both to his friends at the table and his enemies at the window (Matt. 11:19; Luke 15:2; Mark 2:15ff; Matt. 9:10; Luke 5:29). For a man who claimed and was popularly acknowledged to be a man of God, such behaviour was extraordinary to say the least.

His actions were deliberately intended to demonstrate the present reality and radical nature of the Kingdom. In contrast to contemporary society which denied social misfits and those deemed 'irreligious' their civil rights and spiritual privileges, such people are especially welcomed into the Reign of God. 'By accepting them as friends and equals Jesus had taken away their shame, humiliation and guilt. By showing them that they mattered to Him as people He gave them a sense of dignity and released them from their captivity. The physical contact which He must have had with them when reclining at table (compare John 13:25) and which He obviously never dreamed of disallowing (Luke 7:38, 39) must have made them feel clean and acceptable' (Nolan 1976:39).

Such socialising had significance not just at the time but for the future, for table-fellowship was, in Jesus' thinking, an anticipation of that great feast which will mark the consummation of the Kingdom. Those in company with Jesus, therefore, occupied seats which represented a future inheritance as well as present fulfilment.

Jesus pressed home the truth that the Kingdom breaks through all social and religious barriers not only by his startling personal actions which sent shock-waves through society, but also by a story with a sting in its tail. To that representative of the religious élite who by his bland statement, 'How happy are those who will sit down at the feast in the Kingdom of God!,' revealed that he counted on a reserved seat, our Lord told the parable of the Great Feast.

In the story, those invited to attend made excuses; a response which so infuriated the host that he ordered his servant to 'Hurry out to the streets and alleys of the town, and bring back the poor, the crippled, the blind, and the lame. . . .' 'I tell you all that none of those men who were invited will taste the dinner' (Luke 14:15–24). The implication is clear. Those who were rejecting Christ's ministry were thereby refusing their invitation and relinquishing their place.

However, Jesus' free association with the poor and despised should not be interpreted to indicate their automatic admission into the Kingdom by virtue of their downtrodden position in society. In addressing them he utters no words of condemnation as he does in the case of the scribes and Pharisees, yet he nevertheless looks for a life-changing response from them. Having assured the woman caught in the act of adultery of forgiveness, he tells her, 'do not sin again' (John 8:11). It is after Zacchaeus has stood up and said to God, 'Listen, sir! I will give half my belongings to the poor, and if I have cheated anyone, I will pay him back four times as much', that Jesus exclaims, 'Salvation has come to this house today . . .' (Luke 19:8, 9). Of the two thieves crucified with Jesus, it is only to the one who expresses his penitence that Jesus responds, 'I promise you that today you will be in Paradise with me' (Luke 23:39–43).

Entry into the Kingdom is not automatic. It is not a consequence of heredity privilege. Neither is it a reward for human effort. Indeed Jesus warned that those who came with an attitude of exclusive nationalism or spiritual complacency were in danger of being thrown out (Matt. 8:11, 12). The New Testament makes abundantly clear that the key to entry into the Kingdom is the acceptance of Jesus as Saviour and Lord. Taking this step demands genuine repentance and a baptism which signifies cleansing from sin and death to the old way of life and resurrection to the new. It is not simply a matter of a verbal profession but of whole-hearted, life-yielding response. Matthew and Luke record our Lord's solemn reminder, 'Not everyone who calls me "Lord, Lord" will enter the Kingdom of heaven, but only those who do what my Father in heaven want them to do. When Judgement Day comes, many will say to me, "Lord, Lord! In your name we spoke God's message, by your name we drove out many demons and performed many miracles!" Then I will say to them, "I never knew you. Get away from me, you wicked people!"' (Matt. 7:21–23) (cf Luke 13:25–27).

Peter was given the keys of the Kingdom when he came to the point of confessing Jesus as the 'Messiah, the Son of the living God' (Matt. 16:19). But his profession was deficient at the time in that he failed to recognise the necessity of suffering.

Entering the Kingdom is by invitation only, and that invitation must be given top priority. Other commitments must be held over (Matt. 22:1–4).

Some people stumble across the Kingdom without looking for it, like discovering a hidden treasure while turning over the soil in the field (Matt. 13:44). Others, only enter the Kingdom after a prolonged and intense search, like the pearl merchant who sells his entire assets to buy one pearl which was everything (Matt. 13:45).

Membership of the Kingdom is non-transferable. No one can shift responsibility on to others or trade off their resources. The five foolish virgins with no oil for the lamps could neither buy nor borrow from those who had supplied their own lamps. Life in the Kingdom is one of constant readiness (Matt. 25:1–13). There are no gate-crashers; it cannot be taken by storm.

To enter the Kingdom of Heaven one has to come as a little child, with an attitude of trust, and prepared to be teachable and flexible (Matt. 18:1).

This same point was made to Nicodemus who came to consult with Jesus cautiously and privately under cover of darkness. The Lord told him plainly that entering the Kingdom demanded a new start. He had to be born of water – that is, new life after the burial of baptism – and of the Spirit. Kingdom membership was only possible through an act of God. The work of the Spirit cannot be predicted or controlled by the religious profession! (John 3:1–13).

GROWTH OF THE KINGDOM

As we noted previously, 'Kingdom' is a dynamic concept which might better be rendered 'Kingly rule or government'. Its growth, therefore, does not come about by territorial gains, but by individuals and groups submitting their wills to that of their Heavenly King. While entry into the Kingdom has an essential personal and individual element, it also has profound and extensive community ramifications. Individuals make their response not as one man islands, but within a framework of family, group, community and national involvements. Dr McGavran has drawn attention to the corporate dimension of conversion in describing 'people movements' to Christ, which we will be considering later in greater detail.

At this point I simply want to underline the fact that Scripture demonstrates clearly that it is God's intention that the Kingdom should grow and not merely remain static.

The manifestation of the Kingdom often starts with *small and seemingly insignificant beginnings*. It is like the tiny mustard seed which grows into a sizeable bush that provides sufficient shade for the birds to come and shelter in its branches (Matt. 13:31; Mark 4:30; Luke 13:18, 19). At first many people may have been tempted to discount it. The opponents of Jesus were unimpressed by his followers. 'If he really had a divine mission, ran the objection, he would not be surrounded by this rag-tag band, but by the best and the brightest. . . . Appealing for faith and confidence, the parable invites the hearer to see in Jesus' followers the seed of the vast communion of the saved . . . out of this unprepossessing band of disciples is destined to come the restored people, not only the lost sheep of Israel's house, but the nations, as well' (Meyer 1979:164).

The spread of the Kingdom might be *unobtrusive* like yeast in the dough (Matt. 13:33) which causes the whole mixture to rise, or like salt rubbed into the meat to preserve and flavour it (Luke 14:34). On the other hand the Kingdom might appear like a *blaze of lights* from a city located on high ground which can be seen from miles around (Matt. 5:14).

Although the Kingdom may have its origins in small beginnings in the majority of places, it is none the less capable of surprising growth. The seed planted in the good soil produced thirty, sixty and even a hundred times the original sowing. Even by the standards of modern high-intensity farming this is a remarkable yield (Mark 4:3–8).

John Kessler writing in the *International Review of Missions* in qualified support of Dr McGavran comments, 'The parables of the mustard seed and of the leaven (Matt. 13:31–35) give an implied warning of the dangers attending numerical growth, but at the same time they confirm that such growth is characteristic of the Kingdom of God' (IRM July 1968:299).

Other imagery, apart from husbandry, is also used to illustrate the growth of the Kingdom. It is represented as a net full of fish (Matt. 13:47, 48), and as a banquet in which all the places must be occupied (Luke 14:21–24).

In our concern for church growth it is imperative that we discern the relationship between the growth of the Church and the realisation of the Kingdom. Too close an identification will blind us to the shortcomings of the institutional Church, so that church growth becomes denominational aggrandisement. As soon as our focus of attention moves from Christ to the Church we move towards ecclesiastical deification and our evangelism is in great danger of degenerating into proselytism.

On the other hand to disassociate the Church from the Kingdom breaks the nerve-cord of hope and destroys the community of commitment to Christ as Saviour and Lord.

'Christ points the Church toward the Kingdom of God that is beyond the Church. To the degree that the Church follows his pointing and heeds his reminder, the Kingdom of God will manifest itself through the Church' (Pannenberg 1975:77).

'But note that this is quite different from attributing to the Church in its established structures the dignity of being the Kingdom of Christ. The rule of Christ is effected wherever man becomes aware of the coming Kingdom of God and lives in accord with that awareness. . . . Precisely because the Church mistakes herself for the present form of the Kingdom, God's rule has often had to manifest itself in the secular world outside, and frequently against, the Church' (Pannenberg 1975:78).

The New Testament provides strong evidence that the Church occupies a central place in God's redemptive purpose for the world. We have already noted that entering the Kingdom entails a personal, saving relationship with Christ. When Peter made his profession of faith at Caesarea Philippi, Jesus declared that this was the rock foundation on which he would build his Church, which realisation provided the keys of the Kingdom (Matt. 16:17–19).

At the time of his ascension, how does Jesus respond to the question put to him by his disciples, 'Lord, will you at this time give the Kingdom back to Israel?' The way they phrase the question reveals the fact they are thinking in the old materialistic and nationalistic terms. His response is to impress upon them that the time is not now, that only God knows when it will be, and in the meantime they are to concentrate on the number-one task of world-wide witness for which the Holy Spirit would equip them (Acts 1:8). This is in line with his earlier command. When Jesus appeared after his resurrection to his disciples in Galilee, he told them, 'I have been given all authority in heaven and on earth.' In other words, has assumed the throne of the Kingdom. The consequences for his followers are clear. He commands them, 'Go, then, to all peoples everywhere and make them my disciples . . .' (Matt. 28:18–20).

When Philip is preaching in Samaria and the residents believe his 'message about the good news of the Kingdom of God and about Jesus Christ', their immediate response is to be baptised in his name (Acts 8:12). Paul, in presenting the gospel to Jews during his missionary journeys, equated his message about the identity and saving work of Christ with the Kingdom (Acts 19:8; 20:25; 28:23; 28:31). In his letter to the Colossians Paul describes Aristarchus, Mark and Justus, his companions in evangelism and church planting, as those who 'work with me for the Kingdom of God' (Col. 4:11).

Finally, the Epistle to the Ephesians, looking forward to the consummation of the Kingdom, with Christ ruling above all heavenly rulers, sees him given 'to the Church as supreme Lord over all things. The Church is Christ's body, the completion of him who himself completes all things everywhere' (Eph. 1:23).

SUMMARY

Yes, the Kingdom is a much broader concept than the Church. God's activity is in no way restricted to the Church. His arena is the world he came to save. Outside the Church are to be found signs of the Kingdom in the form of his image, recognisable, though sadly disfigured, in the lives of all men. These traces not only witness to a sad history, but also hint of glorious possibilities. God, by his unpredictable and uncontainable Spirit, is guiding the destinies of nations and individuals who do not know him, or deny his very existence. Without such works of grace the world would rush even more rapidly towards the abyss. But such divine activity does not obviate the urgent need for witness. It makes it all the more opportune.

I believe that there may be many true children of the Kingdom outside of the institutional churches. Some have dissociated themselves because the churches have turned them off through their disobedience and indifference. Others are isolated individuals with no church within miles of where they live. Still others throw themselves on the mercy of God without being able to name the name of Christ because they have never been told about him. But such responses are inadequate, being less than the best that God intended, and has provided for.

While evangelism may not represent the totality of mission, it rests at its heart. 'How can they hear if the message is not proclaimed?' (Rom. 10:14). Having looked at the broader canvas of mission in these first two chapters, we now focus our attention without apology on the need for 'church growth'. In using this phrase I identify with the popular definition offered by Dr Peter Wagner of the School of World Mission, Fuller Seminary. 'Church growth means all that is involved in bringing men and women who do not have a personal relationship to Jesus Christ into fellowship with him and into responsible church membership' (Wagner 1976:12). This narrowing of focus does not mean that we are laying to one side the issues raised in these two chapters as now dispensed with. On the contrary, they form the foundation blocks to all that follows, and serve as a constant reminder of the need to ensure that we are building on the right foundation and that the materials with which we build have spiritual survival capability (1 Cor. 3:12). The emphasis of the book from now on is of a pragmatic nature, but I hope it is a sanctified pragmatism applied to operating within and shaping the contemporary manifestations of the Church of Christ. We recognise that the Church is a divinely constituted organism and not merely a human institution. Its task is to point beyond itself and not to indulge in self-glorification. If it is to be truly the Church it must submit to the Lordship of Christ and live its daily life in dependence on the presence and resources of the Holy Spirit. It must be incarnated in the world Christ came to redeem, in which he is already present, and for which he has prepared a transformed future. When such growing churches manifest the marks of the Kingdom of righteousness, peace and joy (Rom. 14:7) both in their own lives and in engagement with the world, then we will be able to pray less wistfully and more hopefully 'thy kingdom come, thy will be done on earth, as it is in heaven.'

CHAPTER THREE

Gospel and Culture

Effective communication of the gospel depends not only upon a thorough understanding of the content of the message, but also on an ability to relate that message to the contemporary situation. Most Christian communicators have been more message than receptor oriented. They have not been sufficiently sensitive to the fact that the message received may differ substantially from that which they imagined they had delivered. When it comes to evangelising, Michael Green reminds us, 'Evangelism is never proclamation in a vacuum; but always to people, and the message must be given in terms that make sense to them' (Green 1970:115).

In the case of a Christian communicator seeking to convey the essence of the gospel and establish a church in a culture other than his own, the communication process becomes still more complex. The missionary who has lived with a cultural expression of the gospel adapted to his own context has to divest the message of that cultural adaptation and seek to introduce the gospel in a form which is culturally appropriate to the community with which he is then seeking to communicate. Once the gospel has been received by a group and a church formed, the next question which must be faced is, 'How should this Christian community live and organise itself to most authentically express the new life of the gospel within that cultural context.'

These are some of the complex issues which will be our

concern in this chapter. It is the author's conviction that this subject is highly relevant not just to the overseas missionary situation, but to many sectors of society in this country which as yet have remained unreached and resistant to the traditional approaches of the institutional churches.

During his time as Bishop of Woolwich, responsible for an area stretching from the inner-city boroughs of South London to the Surrey commuter belt, David Sheppard conducted a survey of 150 parishes to show the electoral roll members of the Church of England as a percentage of the total population. The results, based on the revised figures of 1972, were as follows:

Surrey	9%
Blackheath and Dulwich	4%
Outer suburban	3.25%
Inner suburban	1.8%
Working class	0.9%

(Sheppard 1974:45)

This pattern is also repeated in an unpublished survey conducted by Richard Whatmore on Church of England parishes in Brighton and Hove. His research showed that the electoral roll membership per percentage of population was 5.6% for upper middle-class areas, falling to 0.9% in working-class parishes consisting mainly of council housing.

Such statistics clearly show that the Church of England has a more widespread appeal in middle-class than in artisan areas. Many people still regard it as the Tory party at prayer. But have the Free Churches succeeded where the Church of England has failed? Regrettably the answer is 'No'. They too failed to make any significant impact, and many struggling churches have either been forced to close or to relocate in the suburbs following the migration pattern of their members.

Bishop David Sheppard raises the question, 'If it can be shown that visible response to the Church is on a totally different scale in working-class areas from middle-class areas, who can we blame?' He identifies four possibilities:

1 *Working-class people* – presumably for being harder-hearted than others.
2 *God* – for not sending revival to those areas of society.
3 *The Church* – for not learning how to be an effective vehicle of the gospel.
4 *Society* – for what it has done to those who are trapped by the forces of the big city.

(Sheppard 1974:42)

Few would deny that the answer to the bishop's question lies with alternatives 3 and 4. Although the Church was slow off the mark following the population migration and concentration in the expanding towns during the Industrial Revolution, her failure has not been for want of trying. The root of the problem is located in the culturally inappropriate methods which were adopted in response to this evangelistic and pastoral challenge.

Not only have the churches significantly failed to appeal to those within artisan cultures, they have also been unsuccessful in attracting those of other races from among the West Indian and Asian communities. As the majority of the latter are either Moslem, Sikh or Hindu, it is understandable that the Church has encountered severe problems in trying to communicate her message, either with a view to attracting them into their fellowship or to see the significance of the gospel of Jesus Christ within their own cultural context. The same problem did not exist, however, in the case of the West Indian communities, as the majority of these were members of churches in their home countries, but lapsed on migrating to Britain.

DEFINING CULTURE

When we speak of 'culture' we are not thinking about high-brow music, or good table manners. We understand the term in the more technical anthropological sense. Paul G. Hiebert offers the following definition of culture 'as the integrated system of learned patterns of behaviour, ideas and products characteristic of a society' (Hiebert 1976:25). For Dr Eugene Nida 'culture' is 'all nonmaterial traits which are passed on from one generation to another. They are both transmittable and accumulative, and they are cultural in the sense that they are transmitted by the society, not by the genes' (Nida 1954:28).

The Willowbank Report – Gospel and Culture helpfully expands Dr Eugene Nida's definition to show its comprehensive coverage of all aspects of life. 'Culture is an *integrated system of beliefs* (about God or reality or ultimate meanings), of *values* (about what is true, good, beautiful and normative), of *customs* (how to behave, relate to others, talk, pray, dress, work, trade, farm, eat, etc.), and of *institutions* which express these beliefs, values and customs (government, law courts, temples or churches, family, school, hospitals, factories, shops, unions, clubs, etc.), which bind a society together and give it a sense of identity, dignity, security, and continuity.' (Willowbank Report 1978:7).

CHRIST IN RELATION TO CULTURE

When the gospel is proclaimed and the Church begins to emerge there is an inevitable interaction with the cultural milieu which surrounds and permeates this activity. We need, therefore, to understand the relationship of gospel to culture in general terms, and then go on to examine in detail its engagement with the specific culture in which we are involved.

H. R. Niebuhr has shown the range of thinking with regard to the relationship between Christ and culture adopted by theologians at various times (Niebuhr 1951). He categorises five views:

Christ against culture

This is the radical position which sets the Church against the world. When the individual turns to Christ he rejects the world, for the world 'is in the power of the evil one'. Support for such a position can be found in the Gospel and Epistles of John. The 'world is under judgement' (John 12:31), it is a place of tribulation for believers, which has to be 'overcome' by the Lord (John 16:33). His Kingdom does not belong to this world (John 18:36). Believers are not to love the world, and one day it will pass away (1 John 2:15, 17). The 'Christ against culture' position was adopted by Tertullian in the fourth century and Tolstoy in recent times. It is represented by the thinking of Anabaptists and many fundamentalist and Pentecostal groups, who regard the Church as a rescue post from the world.

Charles Kraft exposes three fallacies in this approach:

(i) 'it equates the concept "culture" with only the negative use of the Greek word *kosmos* in the New Testament.' He points out that when John uses that term in a negative sense it is with 'specific reference not to the whole of culture, but to a particular *use* of that culture by the forces of evil.'

(ii) 'it assumes that it is possible by "running" to escape from one's culture. However, this is to misunderstand the nature of culture as something external to us. Culture is within as well as surrounding us.'

(iii) 'it assumes that since Satan is able to use culture to his ends, all of culture is evil. As we shall see shortly, the Scriptures employ "kosmos" in a positive as well as a negative sense' (Kraft 1979:105, 106).

Christ of culture

In this view, Christ is regarded as the inspirer and perfecter of culture. The best ingredients of each culture are selected

which most express his values and purposes for mankind.
This was the position held by many of the Gnostics, Abelard,
Ritschl and those who express syncretistic sentiments within
the ecumenical movement.

Some would turn the argument around and claim that the
concept of deity is the product of that culture, being no more
than an idealisation and personalisation of cultural elements,
without any objective existence. In the case of the Judaeo-
Christian concept of deity this can be strongly challenged on
the grounds of the historical basis of divine revelation. For,
while the Scriptures speak within particular cultural contexts,
they present a constant challenge to the concepts of deity and
morality which are generated by the cultures addressed. God
is no sense an idealised self-image to be possessed and mani-
pulated. Israel is constantly reminded of the 'otherness' of
Yahweh. He dwells in the unapproachable light of the *shekinah*
glory, and reminds his people Israel that his thoughts are not
their thoughts or their ways his ways (Is. 55:8).

Christ above culture

This is the position of Justin Martyr, Clement of Alexandria
and Thomas Aquinas, who see Christ as 'the fulfilment of
cultural aspirations and the restorer of the institutions of
true society. Yet there is in him something that neither
arises out of culture nor contributes directly to it. He is
discontinuous as well as continuous with social life and its
culture' (Niebuhr 1951:42). Christians who adopt this con-
ceptual framework recognise that within culture there are
laws additional to those expressed by Jesus Christ which
are also from God. They must therefore seek to achieve a
synthesis of those God-imposed requirements rendering 'to
Caesar the things that are Caesar's and to God the things
that are God's' (Matt. 22:21).

Christ and culture in paradox

This view accepts the 'Christ above culture' position, but

fails to achieve a workable synthesis. It therefore places them in a paradoxical relationship and leaves the believer to live with the tension of relating to the world. This dualistic position can be detected in the writings of the apostle Paul, a view endorsed by Luther, where the Christian is described as 'under law, and yet not under law but grace; he is a sinner, and yet righteous, he believes as a doubter; he has assurance of Salvation, yet walks the knife-edge of insecurity. In Christ all things have become new, and yet everything remains as it was from the beginning . . .' (Niebuhr 1951:156, 157).

In its negative assessment of human effort it is akin to the 'Christ against culture' position, yet differs in response to that situation. Recognising that man cannot escape, it leaves him to cope with the paradox and frustration, content to walk by faith, not by sight, believing that one day all things will become new and be reconciled in Christ.

Christ the transformer of culture

This represents a more positive attitude towards culture than the previous three positions, although it is more critical than the second position listed here. While culture remains under the judgement of God it is also subject to his saving rule. This view is sometimes seen as represented in the Gospel of John. In support of this view are the positive responses of John to the world. 'God so loved the world that he gave his son' (John 3:16). John regards him as Saviour of the world and records Jesus' declaration to be the light of the world (John 8:12). Augustine, John Wesley and F. D. Maurice have identified with this emphasis. For them culture is there to be converted rather than replaced by something entirely new. 'Culture, therefore, is seen as corrupted but convertible, usable, perhaps even redeemable by God's grace and power' (Kraft 1979:113).

To Nida's original five categories we venture to offer a sixth.

Christ above but working through culture

This is the alternative accepted by Kraft. He argues 'though God exists totally outside of culture, while humans exist totally within culture, God chooses the cultural milieu in which humans are immersed as the arena for his interaction with people' (Kraft 1979:114). Such an approach represents a deliberate self-limiting on the part of God in order to speak in understandable terms and with perceived relevance on the part of the hearer. He acts redemptively with regard to culture, which includes judgement on some elements, but also affirmation in other areas, and a transformation of the whole. We will trace in this chapter the significance of the 'Christ above but working through culture' model in terms of God's revelation and the Church's communication task and structural adaptations.

Despite the mixed benefits, man cannot dispense with culture. For culture helps to explain and evaluate the realities of life. It provides the stability of psychological reinforcement. It establishes a commonality of understanding on which to build a community. It weaves the societal framework which serves as a bridge to the next generation, preserving continuity, and a wall against encroachment and disintegration.

No one lives outside a cultural context. We are all to a great extent the product of our culture. As we have noted, there are good and bad, strong and weak elements in each culture. The cultural framework in which we have been raised and within which we have been taught to operate provides both security and significance within its frontiers. But beyond those frontiers are alien cultures which impinge on our own for good or ill. Sometimes the relationship is one of *co-existence* – two cultures exist side by side but in separate compartments. At other times they may exist in *competition*, each endeavouring to gain influence in a third area. Yet again, they may give rise to *conflict*, with one seeking to dominate the other either through conquest or infiltration. At other times they serve to enrich each other through the mutual benefit of *cross-fertilisation*. These options indicate something of the complexity of relationships between cultures.

Eugene Nida argues that humans are 'culture-shaped and culture-transmitting beings' (Nida 1954:28). Each transmits culture down to the next generation and out through his network of relationships. He cannot help but notice the presence of other cultures when they come into contact with his own, because their influences are all-pervasive. Having become aware of the difference, his deep-seated bias is to consider his own as not only different but preferable. He is prone to regard his own pattern of belief and behaviour as normative and all others as deviant. 'To view other people's ways of life in terms of our own cultural glasses is called ethnocentrism' (Keesing and Keesing 1971:21–quoted by Kraft 1979:48).

In the early days of the development of anthropology it was the fashion to place culture on an evolutionary ladder ranging from primitive to developed. The fact that Western cultures were placed by the anthropologists on the upper-most rungs reflects their ethnocentric perspective! This evolutionary model has subsequently been replaced by a relativistic one; this maintains that 'an observer should be careful to evaluate a culture first in terms of its own values, goals, and focuses before venturing to compare it (either positively or negatively) with any other culture' (Kraft 1979:49). Patterns of behaviour which appear strange or even wrong from the standpoint of the outside observer interpreting what he sees in terms of his own cultural frame of reference, may, when understood in their broader cultural setting, be perfectly reasonable and even commendable. This is easier said than done. But to highlight the problem helps us to identify and confess our bias. It requires special gifts of insight and patience to move from a mono-cultural to a cross-cultural perspective.

CULTURE AND BIBLICAL REVELATION

The biblical perspective of divine revelation is of God speaking at specific times addressing himself to particular situations. He uses language and imagery which communicate most precisely the truths he wishes to convey to a specific audience. 'He reveals Himself in a receptor-orientated fashion' (Kraft 1979:169). Though God is totally free of culture he chooses to clothe his message in cultural form so that people will immediately see its relevance and feel its impact. By the way it is expressed it becomes a word from God to *them*, at their level of understanding, indigenous and applicable to their times and struggles.

Kraft, in Part IV of his book *Christianity in Culture* entitled 'The Dynamics of Revelation' introduces a new perspective to the debate on the inspiration of Scripture among evangelicals. He sees the Bible as containing a section of classic case studies of the ways God deals with mankind in a variety of situations across a considerable period of time. As such, it emphasises that God's revelatory activity is a dynamic process rather than a static product. The completion of the canon of Scripture by the early Church does not signify that they thought the Lord had stopped speaking or that he had nothing fresh to say. The purpose of Scripture is to act as a 'yardstick' and 'tether' by which to assess any claim to contemporary revelation, and to regulate its interpretation. The Holy Spirit continues to operate in revealing the mind of Christ to his Church. 'But the nature of his teaching ministry has changed. We believe that his work of "inspiration" is done in the sense that the canon of Scripture is closed, but that his work of "illumination" continues both in every conversion (e.g. 2 Cor. 4:6) and in the life of the Christian and the Church' (Willowbank Report 1978:9). He speaks in the life situation as well as through the sacred page.

Yet God still speaks by his Spirit to throw fresh light on his word so that we might see its relevance to the contemporary world, and he speaks to his servants to guide them through the perplexities of life. Though he may say things to them that have no exact parallels in Scripture, his word does not contradict Scripture, neither does it have the same normative quality. It is a specific word for a particular situation.

The Bible is no academic tome with an esoteric appeal to those with scholarly minds who can handle abstract concepts. It is a record of events, with interpretative comments woven into the narrative. Kraft records that 'even the most theological portions (e.g. Romans) participate in the "eventness" of the facts that they were written as letters from specific persons to specific persons to meet specific needs' (Kraft 1979:128).

The literary combination of narrative content and picture-language commentary make for powerful communication. No wonder the Bible has such a universal appeal, and its potential impact so alarms political and ideological leaders antagonistic to its message that its production and distribution is severely restricted in half the world.

Our emphasis on the culture-conditioning of revelation poses some problems which must be squarely faced.

Firstly *it must not lead us into a relativist position regarding Scripture as but one of many revelations of God*. The Bible occupies a unique and normative position by which to judge the statements of other sacred writings, be they from other religions or Christian devotional classics.

Lesslie Newbigin expressed the problem in terms of two dogmatic systems. 'According to one dogma, world history is in some sense a coherent whole, and it is therefore possible to affirm that certain events have a unique significance for the entire story. According to the other dogma, there are no events which have such unique significance and therefore no universally valid affirmation can be made about the

meaning of history as a whole' (Newbigin 1978:174). The
acceptance of the former dogma rather than the second
depends on an acceptance of the unique salvation history
expressed by God through his people Israel which has
significance for the whole of mankind.

However, such acceptance does not extend to a recognition 'that the cultural forms of the semitic world have
authority over all other cultural forms' (Newbigin 1978).
Paul firmly resists the strenuous efforts of the Judaisers
to demand cultural conformity from the Gentile converts
(Gal. 2:11–14).

Newbigin cites the evidence of not one but a variety of
Christologies in the New Testament reflecting 'the attempts
of that community to say who Jesus is in terms of the
different cultures within which they bore witness to him.'
The *variety* of Christologies actually to be found in the New
Testament is part of the fundamental witness to the nature
of the gospel; it points to the *destination* of the gospel in all
the cultures of mankind. The *unity* of the New Testament,
the fact that it contains not every Christology, but only
those which were judged to be faithful to the original testimony, reflect the *origin* of the gospel in the one unique
person of Jesus (Newbigin 1978:176).

Secondly *the fact that God's personal self-disclosure in the Bible
was given in terms of the hearers' own culture inevitably means that
misunderstanding may arise and points be missed when read by people
of another culture who are unfamiliar with the cultural milieu of the
Bible.* If questions are put to the text which the particular
passage was not written to answer then wrong conclusions
can easily be drawn. This is a problem with which Bible
translators constantly have to battle. They recognise that
it is inadequate and sometimes completely misleading to
translate the text word for word, or phrase by phrase from
the Hebrew, Aramaic and Greek into their mother tongue.
Their task is to so translate the text that it speaks with the
original intention and force as it did to those originally

addressed. In order to achieve this they may from time to time have to change the form in order to preserve the meaning. This translation principle is called the 'dynamic equivalence' as distinct from the 'formal correspondence' method.

Dr Eugene Nida has a fund of examples to illustrate the need for 'dynamic equivalent' translations. 'One cannot say to the Zanaki people along the shores of the sprawling Lake Victoria, "Behold I stand at the door and knock" (Rev. 3:20). This would mean that Christ was declaring himself to be a thief, for in Zanaki land thieves generally make it a practice to knock on the door of a hut which they hope to burglarise, and if they hear any movement inside, they dash off into the dark. An honest man will come to the house and call the name of the person inside, and in this way identify himself by his voice. Accordingly, in the Zanaki translation it is necessary to say, "Behold, I stand at the door and call"' (Nida 1952:46).

The translation problem is even more difficult when faced with presenting Jesus as the 'Good Shepherd' (Ps. 23 and John 10) in parts of Africa where the care of sheep is relegated to children or the mentally subnormal. It is the care of cattle which is regarded as man's work. Therefore, simply to represent Jesus as the Good Shepherd without any explanatory note would convey entirely the wrong impression.

We Europeans are equally prone to misunderstand because of our cultural distancing. For instance, we can easily miss the point made by our Lord when he set a child in the midst of the crowd and declared to the surrounding throng that if they wished to enter the Kingdom of Heaven they would have to become as a little child (Matt. 18:4). He was not here primarily teaching the need for simplicity and trust, though this is within the range of permissible inter-pretations according to Kraft's 'tether model'. His main point, which his immediate audience would not fail to grasp, was that the 'little child' had not yet reached the age of the 'bar Mitzvah' ceremony, or 'coming-of-age', which within the Jewish culture meant that the 'little child' had no rights before the Law of God. He was in fact confronting the self-righteousness of the scribes and Pharisees.

Such illustrations lead to a third problem: *Does the culture conditioning of God's self-revelation mean that the Bible cannot be understood by ordinary people without the help of theologically trained interpreters?* The foregoing illustrations emphasise problems of interpretation across cultures, however much of the teaching of Scripture is so plain and obvious that no great intellectual capacity or specialist training is required. Enlightenment comes through spiritual perception which results from the work of the Holy Spirit in the individual's life (1 Cor. 2:10–13). 'The reader interprets the text as if it had been written in his own language, culture and time. . . . For God intended his word for ordinary people; it is not to be regarded as the preserve of scholars; the central truths of salvation are plain for all to see; Scripture is "useful for teaching the truth, rebuking error, correcting faults, and giving instruction for right living" (2 Tim. 3:16); and the Holy Spirit has been given to be our teacher' (Willowbank Report 1978:10).

One does not need to acquire hermeneutical skills to appreciate the significance and personal challenge presented by the great truths of salvation. If a point is missed because it is too deeply embedded in its cultural setting in one place, it stands out prominently and unequivocally in another. In many places the cultural context of the original account may bear sufficient likeness to our own to enable us to interpret what transpires without much difficulty. The exhortations of Scripture which relate to personal qualities and Christian virtues require little adaptation when transposed from one culture to another. The command to 'love one's neighbour', for example, is a cultural universal. Furthermore, despite the diversities of cultures there remains a great deal of commonality. It is chiefly in the realms of social customs and economic arrangements that we must have specialist knowledge of the context to enable us to interpret the passage accurately.

Yet, notwithstanding the problems generated by a culturally conditioned revelation, it has enormous value. 'Because of their specificity to the cultural agreements of the original hearers, these materials communicated with maximum impact to them. This is a major part of the genius of God and of his Word – that it speaks specifically to people where they are and in terms of the culture in which they are immersed. At the same time this fact enormously complicates the task of the person immersed in another culture who seeks to interpret the Scripture' (Kraft 1979:134).

CULTURE AND CONTEMPORARY COMMUNICATION

In the preceding section we emphasised the fact that revelation in Scripture is 'receptor-orientated', not in the sense of affirming the hearers by telling them only what they want to hear, but by speaking specifically to their situation so that they cannot miss what they need to hear.

In both the Old and New Testament people are addressed through concepts which are already familiar to them. The Old Testament alluded to 'leviathan' the Babylonian sea-monster. It takes up the concept of 'covenant' already familiar in the ancient world. In the scriptural usage of that term there is both continuity and discontinuity with that wider understanding. The Old Testament also alludes to a three-tier universe. Within the New Testament concepts from the Old Testament are taken up and spiritualised, for example 'messiah', 'Son of Man' and 'Kingdom of Heaven'. The teaching and life-style of John the Baptist identifies him with the prophetic tradition in Israel. Our Lord's ministry was styled along the lines of the rabbinic model, with the itinerant teacher followed by a group of disciples who learned by listening, questioning and working under supervision. Yet at the same time there was discontinuity, for Jesus taught 'not as the scribes', for unlike them his message was self-authenticating. He did not flinch from declaring 'I say to you' and then made astounding claims about himself.

As soon as the Church spread from Jewish into Gentile cultures further adaptation was required. Michael Green writes, 'Once Christianity took root in Hellenistic soil, it became necessary to do a tremendous work of translation. Not only words, but ideas had to be put into other dress. Without such a task of translation, the message would have been heard, perhaps, but not assimilated' (Green 1970:115). The terms Logos (Word), Lord, Kingdom, Adoption were meaningful to pagan ears, so the person of Christ and the nature of his mission is expressed in those concepts.

As for initiatory rites, while circumcision was peculiar to Judaism in the Roman world, baptism was widely practised. 'For in the first century water initiation rites were used to induct people into a number of different groups. Among these were Judaism (for proselytes) and the Greek mystery religions as well as the Church' (Kraft 1979:68). The one form is given a new meaning in its Christian context in which the initiate is identified with the death and resurrection of Jesus Christ.

In the communication process the one who speaks and the one who hears each formulate their ideas within their own frame of reference. Each frame of reference is constructed largely through cultural influences. Broadly speaking there are four possible approaches:

Isolation. This describes the process of non-communication. The speaker expresses his message in terms of his own perceptions and within his own frame of reference without making any attempt to relate what he wants to say with what the other person is likely to hear. His hearers completely fail to comprehend because the message is couched in unfamiliar vocabulary and does not make contact with any of their felt needs. His speaking is no more meaningful than the conversation of adults as portrayed in the televised version of the Charlie Brown cartoons. These adults never actually appear on the screen and their speech is represented as no more than an incoherent buzz of verbal static, because adults are irrelevant to the world of Charlie Brown, Lucy, Linus, Snoopy and Woodstock.

Extraction. This describes the classroom (and frequently also the pulpit) approach to communication. The teacher (or preacher) establishes the lines of communication by educating the pupils (or congregation) into his terminology and concepts.

Such a method introduces two serious inhibitions to the communication process. The person being processed into the speaker's frame of reference may in so doing lose contact with his own, so that he cannot relate his new knowledge to his life situation; neither can he communicate it to others.

'Extraction' applies to the form of the communication as well as to the content. A Bible translator in one of the Andean republics recounted the following story to the author. The particular tribe among whom he was working couched their teaching in story form, and the main story-line was always the same – the events were set in the context of a journey, for they were a nomadic people. He noticed that when local church leaders had been away for Bible School training, they ceased to tell stories in their preaching. They had been trained at college to preach Western-style sermons based on abstract thinking arranged in linear form. As a consequence they were 'extracted' from their culture and failed to communicate to their own people. He decided to adopt a different approach and to try and teach the Bible through story-telling. He soon realised that the Bible was full of journeys! What better way to describe God's dealing with Israel in the Old Testament, than with the stories of Abraham, the Exodus and the Exile. In the Gospels Jesus is for ever on the move. The Acts is a non-stop travelogue. Paul's letter to Philemon tells how he has urged Onesimus to stop running and return to the scene of his crime and seek reconciliation with his master.

Identification. In this communication process the speaker explores his hearers' frame of reference, seeking to identify areas of common ground between them. He then couches his message in terms with which his hearers will be familiar, seeking to move from the known to the unknown. Thus, Paul in Athens uses language and concepts with which the Stoics in his audience can identify and before the Sanhedrin, the Jewish supreme court in Jerusalem, he establishes common ground with the Pharisees among the council members.

Reciprocation. In a mature relationship imitation is replaced by reciprocation, in which the parties frankly recognise their differences while resisting the temptation to think that 'because my ways are different from yours they are therefore better'. The reciprocal relationship embodies two-way communication, with each open to be influenced by the other. Through such cross-cultural pollination the ideas of each are challenged, affirmed, enriched or modified.

THE COMMUNICATION PROCESS

The human sciences of anthropology, psychology and sociology have thrown much fresh light on the complexity of the communication process in recent years. Much of this insight has a valuable application to the communicating of the gospel. The Christian communicator is never the primary source of his message in the sense that he is not the originator of that which he is seeking to convey. His *primary source* is the written word of God through which the Spirit of God speaks to him. The prophet and apostle fulfil the role of *secondary sources* when they speak in God's name prefacing their message with an introductory 'Thus says the Lord . . .'. To a lesser extent the preacher and the witness stand in the same relationship to their message, as they declare what has been revealed to them or that which they have personally witnessed. A degree of interaction between themselves and their source is required for them to act in this capacity. What they are seeking to share with others must have become true for them. The communicator who has not interacted with his material and is merely passing on what he has read or been told functions as a *tertiary source*. He is often more of a blockage to communication than a channel. One has to get behind him to appreciate the significance and 'impact' of the message.

In the process of transmission the message does not have an independent existence. It is encapsulated in the mind of the speaker who sends a complex pattern of signals which enable the receptor to build up his perception of the message in his own mind. In the ideal communication event the result is that the receptor's understanding corresponds exactly with the intention of the communicator, but this ideal is seldom achieved. In most instances the communicator must settle for an approximation within acceptable limits. This state of affairs causes no surprise when it is recognised that 'what is understood is at least as dependent on how the receptor perceives the message as on how the communicator presents it' (Kraft 1979:148).

The transmission of a message inevitably involves first that the message be encoded by the communicator and then that it be decoded or 'translated' by the receptor. It is in this complex procedure that 'slippage' occurs. The extent to which this is likely to occur is compounded when there is a wide cultural gap between those involved in the verbal exchange.

One does not have to be a missionary in a remote situation to become aware of the communication barriers. Many

Christians experience them whenever they attempt to communicate their faith to their non-Christian friends. The longer they have been Christians and the more they have been preoccupied with their Christian activities, the more difficult it becomes to relate their beliefs to the perceived needs of their friends. The new convert, on the other hand, has no such problems because his pre-Christian experience is still fresh in his mind and he communicates his faith in an everyday language because he has not yet learned a new jargon.

The communicator 'encodes' his message by the concepts he uses, the language he employs, and the communication format he adopts, whether that be monologue, dialogue, question-posing, or a dramatic presentation, prose, poetry or song.

The encoding process will also include what Abercrombie describes as *paralinguistic phenomena*. 'Paralinguistic phenomena are non-linguistic elements in conversation. They occur alongside spoken language, interact with it, and produce, together with it, a total system of communication. They are not necessarily continuously simultaneous with spoken words. They may also be interspersed among them or precede them, or follow them; but they are always integrated into a conversation considered as a complete linguistic interaction' (Abercrombie:65). They include sounds such as 'tut tut', 'phew', 'ugh', 'shshsh', 'ahem'; gestures (shrugs, nods, winks, hand and arm movements); posture (sitting, standing, leaning forward and back, crossing and uncrossing legs) and facial expressions (smiles, frowns). They are expressed in voice control. The *ways* in which we say things convey as much as *what* we say. This is reflected in how loudly we speak, texture of voice, use of pauses, etc. Eye contact is also an important element. 'In the mutual look the participants express their involvement with one another. The longer the periods of eye contact, the greater the level of this mutual involvement, other things being equal. But in any situation there is a limit to the amount of mutual involvement that may be tolerated, and too much mutual looking may arouse anxiety' (Argyle and Kendon 1972:39). When the preacher looks at the ceiling before long his congregation look at their shoes and then their watches!

Yet another element in 'paralinguistic phenomena' is the distance between those engaging in face-to-face interaction. These vary between cultures and in accordance with the nature of the communication in the scale: intimate, casual, social, public or frozen. In the communication process a change of distance can signal a change of relationship. I have noticed that when older people put out chairs in preparation for a church meeting they will tend to place them in straight rows and arrange them further back from the speaker. This reflects the emphasis on 'status' and the formal school classroom layout which was more prevalent in former years.

When the receptor receives and decodes the message in order to uncover the meaning, the operation is no less complex. He will be concerned with the status of the source; statements may be accepted quite uncritically from a peer whom the receptor admires and emulates. He will examine the credibility of the source to ensure that he is genuine and sincere. As we have previously noticed, he will perceive the message within his own frame of reference and proceed on the basis from the known to the unknown. He will assess the person on his voice quality, mannerisms and dress. If the message is to influence him it must have an appropriate degree of impact (Kraft 1979:149). Due to the fact that we are all constantly being bombarded with stimuli, we have learned from an early age to be very selective in our response. Our listening ability is related to the relevance of the communication, its intelligibility, and a level of predictability. We listen more quickly than we speak, and when we can anticipate what is coming next then we switch off. Often what we 'hear' is not what is said, but what we think we are going to hear! Where there is a high level of predictability then there is a low impact. One gifted preacher known to the author frequently resorts to the shock statement to break through the 'selective hearing' of his audience. He began one address with the statement that, '1 Corinthians chapter 13 is *not* about love . . . it's about the need to exercise gifts in love.' In another he riveted the attention of his hearers with the statement, 'Samson was the weakest man in the Bible!' Sometimes what we expect to hear is predetermined by cultural influences as well as the ways in which facts have previously been presented to us. At every stage in the communication process we can detect the powerful influence of culture.

Up to this point in our discussion we have been preoccupied with the *mechanics* of the communication process. We must now turn our attention to the spiritual *dynamics* which operate in relation to the communication of the gospel. In addition to the cultural blocks there is a spiritual blindness in the hearts and minds of people which prevents them from hearing the Good News. Paul explains to the Corinthians that those who do not believe have minds which have been kept in the dark by the evil god of this world. 'He keeps them from seeing the light shining on them, the light that comes from the Good News about the glory of Christ.' (2 Cor. 4:4).

Therefore, the application of communication techniques, no matter how skilled and imaginative, will not of itself ensure the effective transmission of the gospel message. The Holy Spirit is the essential communicator. If he is absent, the message will not get through. The Old Testament prophets knew the impossibility of making any impression on those who were stiff-necked and hard of heart (Is. 6:9, 10; 29:10). Even our Lord experienced the frustration of trying to communicate to those who did not have ears to hear (Luke 10:16; Matt. 13:14; Mark 6:52). He taught his disciples about the role of the Holy Spirit as communicator, who would lead them into all truth (John 14:17; 16:13) and would 'convince the world concerning sin and righteousness and judgement' (John 16:8 RSV).

Paul the missionary, that master of cross-cultural communication, admitted that the message about Christ's death on the cross was nonsense to those who were being lost (1 Cor. 1:18). For God in his wisdom made it impossible for people to know him by means of their own wisdom (v. 21). How, then, are they to know him? Paul replies, 'by means of His Spirit'. He continues, 'So then, we do not speak in words taught by human wisdom but in words taught by the Spirit, as we explain spiritual truths to those who have the Spirit.' (2:13).

If the New Testament witnesses were truly to communicate, they had to speak in the 'power of the Spirit' (1 Thess. 1:5; Rom. 15:19; Acts 1:8; 4:33; 6:8; 1 Cor. 2:4). At the same time the Holy Spirit was at work on the receptor's end of the communication process (1 Thess. 1:6; Col. 1:9).

The Christian communicator's awareness of the essential role of the Holy Spirit does not provide him with a short cut to achieve instant impact. Rather the role of the Holy Spirit is to heighten his awareness of the problem and enable him to identify with those to whom he is called to speak. There is no true communication without genuine incarnation. And the incarnational route is always costly intellectually and emotionally. It requires a special gift of the Spirit (Eph. 3:7).

CULTURE AND CHURCH STRUCTURE

The relationship between conversion and culture is of enormous importance to the task of evangelism and church planting. These activities inescapably take place within a specific cultural context, which may be a clearly defined mono-cultural situation, or, more frequently, within a multi-cultural environment. As we have seen, culture permeates the whole of life and has a profound influence on the meaning which people attach to the messages they hear, the way

they make decisions and the social and institutional structures which they build around their creeds and values.

The insights of the church growth movement in showing
the impact of culture in these areas has been a major
contribution to the Church's understanding of its missionary task in recent decades. These perceptions are as
relevant to the mission of the Church in the United Kingdom
as in Asia, Africa and Latin America.

The spread of the gospel through homogeneous units
In his examination of the working of the Great Commission,
McGavran draws attention to the significance of *ta ethne*
in the phrase translated in most English versions as 'all
nations', but rendered more accurately as 'all peoples' in
the Good News Bible. 'Go, then, to all peoples everywhere
and make them my disciples . . .' (Matt. 28:19). McGavran
and Arn point out that *ethne* does not mean 'modern nation
states' such as India, the United States, or China. *Ethne*
means the castes, tribes, peoples, ethnic units of mankind
(McGavran and Arn 1970:38). This distinction has been
widely overlooked in modern missionary strategy to the
extent that when a church has resulted in a particular
country, it has been assumed that an adequate base for
evangelisation has been established. However, the extent of
the command in the Great Commission is not simply the
spread of the gospel outwards territorially but down
through the cultural layers.

McGavran describes society as honeycombed in a 'cultural mosaic'. Individuals need a social identity – a sense of
peoplehood – if they are to identify, develop and function in
society. They therefore form themselves into various groups
in which they identify themselves as 'we', as distinct from
those who are outside and described as 'they'. He defines
such sociological groupings as 'homogeneous units', which
he admits 'is an elastic concept, its meaning depending
on the context in which it is used' (McGavran 1970:86).

Simply stated, the homogeneous unit is a group in which all the members have some characteristic in common. The homogeneity may be represented by a political unit, a culture or a language, a tribe or caste or tribal sub-unit. Within western society it might represent a socio-economic group, people in a particular employment, a young people's counter-culture, etc. These are groups which share a particular life-style, language, and assumptions so that they feel at home with one another. Each develops its own behaviour pattern. 'Thus, within each homogeneous unit, individual action is considered typical or atypical as judged in the light of the social roles determined by the group' (Wagner 1979c:59).

In Britain denominational planning has depended too exclusively on the 'geographical map'. Within the Church of England this has been influenced by the parish structure inherited from rural society with a feudal structure. While the geographical map may be helpful to ensure a measure of blanket coverage, it can at the same time be very misleading if used as the only planning model. The homogeneous unit concept provides a valuable alternative map by which to gauge the Church's effectiveness in relation to the 'mosaic' of peoples which make up the population of the British Isles. When applied to particular urban or rural situations it will reveal the dynamics which, while attracting some into the fellowship of the churches, are at the same time excluding others.

Church growth theorists have observed that churches tend to grow within homogeneous units. Peter Wagner claims that between ninety-five and ninety-eight per cent of churches are basically homogeneous (Wagner 1978). While it is impossible to either prove or disprove this estimate, as a matter of observation it is true that a high proportion of churches seem to attract 'their kind of people'. The reason for this is stated by McGavran as, 'men like to become Christians without crossing racial, linguistic or class barriers'

(McGavran 1970:198). If people outside the Church can see people among its membership like themselves, they are more likely to want to identify. On the other hand, when people outside the Church see no one within the Church with whom they can readily identify, they will not be so easily attracted. They will conclude, as people on a South London council estate expressed it when they observed the middle-class congregation going into their local church each Sunday, 'That church isn't for the likes of us.'

The other major contribution to missiological thinking by McGavran has been his stress on the corporate dimension of the decision-making process. He has provided a much needed corrective to the over-individualistic approach to conversion which has been characteristic of many western evangelists and missionaries. Such strategy he describes as 'one by one against the tide' (McGavran 1970:299). Against this, McGavran points out that historically in the Christianisation of Europe individuals have come to Christ in great numbers through 'people movements'. 'People become Christians as a wave of decisions for Christ sweeps through the group mind, involving many individual decisions but being far more than merely their sum. This may be called a chain reaction. Each decision sets off others and the sum total powerfully affects every individual' (McGavran 1970:12).

People movements take a number of forms. In the first place, there is the '*follow-my-leader*' model, in which groups respond to peer pressure. We also read of *crowd conversions* through the preaching of the Christians in Jerusalem after Pentecost (Acts 2:37–41; 4:4). There are a number of instances of *household conversion*. The extended household of the centurion Cornelius (Acts 10) and the business woman named Lydia in Philippi (Acts 16) were all baptised, presumably following family deliberation. This pattern can be extended to become a *community decision*. The villages of Lydda and Sharon turned to the Lord (Acts 9:35). The fifth pattern is that of a *web movement* when the decision of one person triggers other people with whom he is in contact. In this way Andrew influenced his brother Peter (John 1:40–42) and Philip found Nathaniel (John 1:45). This is perhaps the most common pattern by which the gospel spreads. To this list we might also add a sixth, *media movement* which is seen in the rise of the 'television church' through congregational sponsored televised services in the USA (Olson 1979:133–142).

Dr. McGavran first introduced the people concept in *Bridges of God* written in 1955. Fifteen years later he provided further elucidation in response to his critics. 'The kind of conversion on which people movements are based is the root of the difficulty. The crucial question is: Do people movements rest on group conversion? The answer is No. There is no such thing as group conversion. A group has no body and no mind. It cannot decide anything whatever. The phrase group conversion is simply an easy inexact description of what really happens.' He then decides what actually takes place is 'multi-individual, mutually inter-dependent conversion' (McGavran 1970:302). Although there is a powerful chain-reaction or 'knock-on' effect, each individual is personally responsible for his decision within the total group dynamic.

Whenever there is a widespread turning to Christ there is a very real danger of superficiality leading to nominality. Steps must be taken to ensure that each decision is genuine, and adequate post-baptismal (or post-conversion) counsel and care must be provided to ensure a good environment for the nurturing of the new life (McQuilkin 1973, 74:48).

Values of the homogeneous unit concept
This concept heightens the Church's awareness of the un-reached groups within a nation, county, or local district. It provides an alternative map to complement the geographical one most commonly used, which, when exclusively,

may mask as much as it reveals. It also helps congregations understand why they are finding it so difficult to reach 'resistant areas' for which they feel a responsibility. As we noted at the beginning of the chapter, white, middle-class churches in Britain have a poor 'track record' in relating to artisan, West Indian and Asian cultures. It underlines the need to adopt methods appropriate to the group which is to be reached. Part of their resistance may be explained in terms of the inappropriate methods pursued in the past by well-meaning people who were 'foreigners' to the area.

It also helps to sensitise the Church to the dangers of cultural imperalism. Earlier in the chapter we outlined the various views on the relationship of gospel to culture. Here I would identify with the position held by Charles Kraft, namely that God, whilst being above culture, chooses to work through culture (Kraft 1979:113–115). In such instances the Church can become more of a barrier than a channel in the communication of the gospel.

THE IMPACT OF THE GOSPEL ON CULTURES
The gospel redeems cultures. Every culture represents a mixture of good and bad, of ennobling and degrading elements. We must, therefore, seek to discover what the gospel has to say to our culture. What elements does it affirm, what does it reject, what does it accommodate, and which need to be redeemed? Wagner states that 'cultural integrity is part and parcel of human identity, and any system of thought or behaviour that denies cultural integrity is dehumanising' (Wagner 1979:97). He is strongly opposed to an extractionist approach in evangelism. 'When a gospel is presented that explicitly or implicitly teaches that becoming a citizen of the Kingdom of God requires a denial of peoplehood, its authenticity must be called into question' (Wagner 1978). The same point is emphasised by Tippett: 'Church growth theory believes that the Lord wants converts who can live the Christian life within ther own social structures – be they

industrial, nomadic, or subsistent. We ask the question: what does it mean to be a Christian in this or that kind of society? If our missionary methods extract converts from their society and leave them as social isolates or misfits, there is something wrong with our missioning' (Tippett 1970:34). The Christian communicator tries to avoid this unfortunate outcome by seeking reference points in the other's frame of reference. There must be an open dialogue as a result of which the participants will not only enter each other's world-view, but will as a result have re-evaluated their own position. An American Indian proverb cautions, 'One man should say nothing to another until he has walked in his moccasins'.

The gospel does not impose a cultural uniformity. From a Christian perspective cultural diversity is not simply the result of the interplay of sociological and environmental factors, it is a demonstration of the creative ingenuity of God. In 1978 an international group of evangelical theologians gathered in Pasadena under the auspices of the Lausanne Committee for World Evangelisation. They declared, 'We are unanimous in celebrating the colourful mosaic of the human race that God has created. This rich variety should be preserved, not destroyed, by the gospel. The attempt to impose another culture on people who have their own, into a colourless uniformity, is a denial of the Creator and an affront to his creation. The preservation of cultural diversity honours God, God respects man, enriches life, and promotes evangelisation. Each church, if it is to be truly indigenous, should be rooted in the soil of its local culture' (Pasadena Consultation 1978:3).

Such cultural diversity we should expect to find expressed in the structures and institutional life of the churches. Overseas too many missionary-planted churches are over-influenced by their imported histories, which reflect controversies and emphases which may be irrelevant to their environment into which they have been transplanted. Here at home there are denominations which, while they may boast a doctrinal comprehensiveness, manifest a cultural exclusiveness. They impose liturgical traditions, organisational structures, communication methods and leadership models which are alien to their environment. This is not to say that the world dictates the pattern for the Church to adopt, but to point out that the Church must be constantly examining itself to ensure that it is remaining true to the gospel and that the only barrier is the inescapable offence of the atoning message of the cross which stands at the centre of that gospel.

The gospel brings reconciliation. Sometimes the common traits of homogeneity which bind people together are evil; these may be expressed in the form of hostility or antagonism to those outside. This is reflected in the attitude of the National Front towards new commonwealth citizens in the United Kingdom at the present time. At other times cultural groups regard themselves in a superior relationship to other cultures. In the New Testament the gospel is depicted as a power of God to deal with enmity and superiority. 'For Christ himself has brought us peace by making Jews and Gentiles one people. With his own body he broke down the wall that separated them and kept them enemies.' (Eph. 2:14, 15). The Jews had to accept the fact that Gentiles could become Christians and that in so doing they did not have to come to Christ via Jewish cultural conditioning. They did not have to take on board the Jewish ceremonial Law. When Paul was writing to the Galatians he was confronting the Judaisers who were trying to act as cultural imperialists. Their attitude is firmly rejected by Paul as 'another gospel' which was in reality no gospel at all. In protecting the minority rights of the Gentile believers he states, 'there is no difference between Jews and Gentiles, between slaves and free men, between men and women; you are all one in union with Christ Jesus' (Gal. 3:28, 29).

The gospel brings about a reconciliation between groups

which were formerly antagonistic to one another. Yet the unity for which Paul strongly argues is not a uniformity. He is not urging the Jews to become more Gentile, or the Gentiles to become more Jewish. If such were his meaning here, it would make a nonsense of his other statement that 'there is no difference . . . between men and women'! Rather he is declaring the abolition of enmity and favouritism.

The gospel encourages mutual support and enrichment. Negatively, the New Testament says that believers should take care not to offend one another (Gal. 2:11, 16) and positively that they should recognise that they belong to one another and take active steps to welcome and support one another (Rom. 15:7).

The supracultural dimension of the gospel must be demonstrated in the strife-torn world of today. The Church should not simply reflect the divisions and distancing present in its social context.

This attitude is reflected by the Pasadena Consultation at which the delegates agreed 'that in many situations a homogeneous unit church can be a legitimate and authentic church. Yet we are also agreed that it can never be complete in itself. Indeed, if it remains in isolation, it cannot reflect the universality and diversity of the Body of Christ. Nor can it grow into maturity. Therefore, every Homogeneous Unity church must take active steps to broaden its fellowship in order to demonstrate visible unity and the variety of Christ's Church. This will mean forging with other and different churches creative relationships which express the reality of Christian love, brotherhood, and interdependence' (Pasadena Consultation 1978:4, 5).

At every level of church life, international, interdenominational, intercongregational and intracongregational structures must be developed to express both the unity and the diversity of the Body of Christ (1 Cor. 12:12, 13). In this search the closer one gets to home the more difficult it becomes. Where white and black churches exist side by side, some congregations are now meeting to worship together on a quarterly basis. This has resulted in a great deal of mutual education, and most would not want to worship together any more regularly than that! Other churches have endeavoured to build effective congregational structures to express both homogeneity and heterogeneity. The main congregation is divided into ethnic groups for time of worship, study and fellowship. This is sometimes done as part of Sunday worship, or, more frequently, in mid-week fellowship. The groups come together regularly for acts of celebration worship, cultural interchange (a Caribbean evening) joint action over community concerns, and to share and challenge each other's perception of the gospel and understanding of contemporary Christian discipleship.

SUMMARY

In this chapter we have opened up some of the complex issues raised by the impact of the gospel on culture. My purpose has been limited to increasing a level of awareness, rather than attempting to supply solutions. In reality there are no pat answers, for each situation has its distinctive cultural milieu and must, therefore, be approached with as open a mind as we can achieve. Such open-mindedness is an essential part of the missionary gift which the Church needs in order to function effectively in any cross-cultural situation.

As we engage with the culture in which we are located or which we are seeking to reach, we need to keep a whole range of questions continuously in mind: What elements in this culture reflect gospel values and should consequently be highlighted and affirmed? How does the gospel relate to those areas with which the culture is least able to cope, or which have a dehumanising influence? What practical steps are we taking to discover how the Church appears from the outsider's perspective and how its message is being interpreted; remembering it's not what *we say* but what *they hear* which really counts? What aspects of our ecclesiastical tradition facilitate and what create a barrier to our communication attempts? What are the most effective communication channels in this culture, and how can the Church gain access to them and speak authentically through them? If we were starting from scratch what would we do differently? And even after years of existence here, should we now start doing any of those things?

CHAPTER FOUR

Measurement and Meaning

One of the great services which McGavran has rendered to the missionary enterprise has been his insistence on the need to gather objective and accurate data in order to disperse the fog in which it has operated for so long. He argues, 'The numerical approach is essential to understanding church growth. The Church is made up of countable people and there is nothing particularly spiritual in not counting them. Men use the numerical approach in all worthwhile human endeavour' (McGavran 1970:83). The persistent tendency to cover up for our lack of effectiveness by using vague language must be strongly resisted. Such head-in-the-sands mentality is particularly evident in areas such as Britain, where prolonged and serious church decline is the prevailing trend.

James Scherer, writing in the *International Review of Missions*, makes the following appreciation of McGavran's emphasis on data-gathering. 'So rigorous is he (i.e. McGavran) in dispelling romantic notions and false theological rationalisations of non-growth that he may be said to have de-mythologized this subject. His own interpretation stresses measurable environmental factors and insists that situations be weighed in terms of their social and cultural complexity. The rigour and honesty brought to the task will put students of church growth in Dr McGavran's debt. Much to his credit, the author is even-handed in his criticism of conservative evangelical and ecumenical groups for the rationalisations (theological and promotional) which both employ in justifying or covering up non-growth situations' (IRM 1971:127).

Church growth data-gathering needs to be undertaken at least at two levels, national and local. The accuracy of the former will depend on the quality of the information gathered by the individual churches and their readiness to make their results more widely available. Denominational headquarters also need sound data-handling methods to ensure an accurate national picture. At both national and local levels trends can be analysed not only within churches and denominations, but across denominations, to learn from those who appear to be exceptions to the general rule. Only by painstaking research are we able to paint an accurate picture of what is really happening. Without such essential information we cannot plan responsibly for the future. We must take account of the cause and effect relationship which God has built into his created order, by unearthing and facing facts.

What are the most basic areas of research which the Church needs to undertake if it is to take growth seriously? McGavran identifies the following:

1 Church membership and attendance totals and the rate at which they are changing.
2 Homogeneous unit totals (to determine the degree of penetration into the different sub-groupings of society).
3 An analysis of the kinds of church growth, to identify how much represents conversion growth from the world into the Church.
4 A family analysis to determine how many full families, partial and singles.
5 A leader and worker analysis to ascertain the proportion deployed in extending the Church's witness in the community.

At this stage we merely introduce them in passing; we will return to them in greater detail later on. Demographic and social characteristics are also important in the interpretation of all the above data.

Before delving into the practicalities of the subject we must first examine four of the main questions about data gathering in the context of church life which lurk in the minds of many committed Christians.

ANSWERING OBJECTIONS TO DATA-GATHERING

'Data-gathering is unscriptural'

On the basis of 1 Chronicles 21, where it is recorded that David incurred divine displeasure because he ordered a national census, some Christian leaders refuse to gather statistics of their membership. They feel that to embark on such an undertaking might spiritually jeopardise their work. But the incident recorded in Chronicles must be balanced by other parts of Scripture. For instance in the Book of Numbers (sic!) Moses is expressly commanded to count the people upon entering the Sinai wilderness to ensure that they can subsequently be accounted for. He is told, 'You and Aaron are to take a census of the people of Israel by clans and families. List the names of all men twenty years old or older who are fit for military service' (1:1–3). He needed to know both the size of the total community for which he was responsible and the strength of the army he would soon have to deploy (see also Num. 2:32–34; 26:1–4, 63–65).

Why then is David punished for counting in 1 Chron. 21? On this occasion we are informed that the idea was prompted by Satan and not by God, who did it 'in order to bring trouble on the people of Israel' (v. 1). David insisted in proceeding with his intentions despite the opposition of Joab, his commander-in-chief, who sensed the wrong motivation for the exercise. Tippett suggests that, 'Such temptation was possible because David was now proudly aware of his kingdom and his military strength and organisation. The numbering was a sin because it was self-glorification' (Tippett 1970:15). At this time David failed to recognise that his strength lay in the arm of the Lord rather than in his own military capability.

The principle of counting to ensure pastoral care and effective deployment of manpower is carried over into the New Testament. In our Lord's parable of the lost sheep (Luke 15:3–6) we see that it was as a consequence of counting his sheep into the fold each night that the shepherd discovered that he was one short. If he had failed to take this action he would probably have been unaware of the emergency. But as soon as his regular check brings to light the absentee he is able to take prompt and appropriate action.

From the gospel record we know the precise number of Jesus' select team of disciples and that on one occasion seventy were sent out two by two on a mission to prepare villages for Christ's coming (Luke 10). Other ancient manuscripts give the number as seventy-two which shows that even then there was some confusion about statistics!

In his account of the performance of the Church in the Book of Acts, Luke displays no inhibitions in speaking about numbers. We are informed that there were a hundred and twenty believers meeting in Jerusalem (1:15). Three thousand were added to the Church on the day of Pentecost (2:41), and before long the number of male believers grew to about five thousand (4:4). Paul likewise informs us that on one occasion our Lord appeared to more than five hundred believers at once (1 Cor. 15:6).

While it must be conceded that the New Testament displays no great preoccupation with data-gathering – which is not surprising considering the complexity of numeration in both the Hebrew and Roman world! – there is no positive evidence to suggest that Christ's mission should be pursued in ignorance of obtainable facts.

'Data-gathering is inappropriate'

Many people discount the value of statistical analysis by saying that what matters is quality, not quantity. This viewpoint is upheld by no less a missionary statesman than Max Warren. He speaks of 'the strictly limited value of all statistical assessments of the value of missionary work. Scripture provides no justification whatever for taking statistics seriously. This is one of the quantitative fallacies of far too much missionary thinking. Quality is undefinable and known only to God' (Warren 1979:155).

While Max Warren is right to caution against an obsessive preoccupation with numbers, I believe that he overstates the case when he is so dismissive of all quantity measurement. McGavran highlights the fact that, 'Luke did not scorn numbers. He rejoiced in the large numbers becoming Christians and carefully recorded them. The early churches did not scorn numbers. When they heard that multitudes in Samaria had received the word of God, they gladly sent them Peter and John; and when they heard that in Antioch a great number had believed and turned to the Lord, they at once despatched Barnabas who, when he came and saw, rejoiced' (McGavran 1959:25).

The task of mission, while depending on the empowering and guidance of the Holy Spirit, also requires human planning. The interventions of God do not set aside the need for careful evaluation. The surprises of God are not intended as a substitute for strategy. Responsible decision-making requires well-researched data. Such research does not set aside the need for divine guidance, but the evidence produced by investigation forms some of the ingredients. The Holy Spirit guides us through discernment as well as by signs. McGavran and Arn spell out the attitude which should characterise the Christian in his decision-making. 'Father, I've endeavoured to gather all the facts available, and still I'm uncertain which is the best decision. I need your guidance and direction. I'm asking for your leading. I am listening for your instruction' (McGavran and Arn 1977:29).

Baptismal, confirmation, membership and communicant figures do not tell the whole story. They constitute only some of the ingredients in the evaluation and diagnostic processes. When a doctor takes the temperature of a patient, his reading gives him no more than one item of information. Neither will his examination alter the situation, for the thermometer has not yet been invented which can bring down the temperature of the fever-stricken patient. It does, however, provide helpful data which, when combined with the results of other investigations, reveals the state of health of the patient.

The point to emphasise is that the data is only of help to those who know the patient and can build up a case history. McGavran, in addition to emphasising the importance of data-gathering, balances this statistical emphasis by underlining the need for careful and competent interpretation. 'It cannot be over-emphasised that statistics, if these are to have any meaning, should be gathered by those who know the churches well and who are concerned that the statistics reveal the truth. They should also be accompanied by a full description of the churches, their natural groupings, and their geographical, social and spiritual environment. Statistics are a summary of significant information and care should be taken that they convey true meanings' (McGavran 1959:27, 28).

'Data-gathering is unnecessary'

This may be the case in a small house fellowship, or of a small church in a face-to-face village community where everyone knows everybody else. In such locations the leader who knows both his congregation and community and is aware of the facets of growth to keep under surveillance may not need to do a formal count. However, most churches in today's world, with its high population density, complex relationship networks and mobility will need to take a more sophisticated approach to alert themselves to the significant trends.

This is part of the explanation of the lack of statistical concern to be found in the Scriptures. There churches were just beginning. For the most part they consisted of small groups of people meeting in homes. Individuals were also part of extended households so their absences would immediately be noticed. This is a very different situation from many churches today which meet in large buildings and with eclectic congregations, the members of which are unlikely to meet unless they plan to do so.

It is inadequate and misleading to rely on general impressions in such churches. We need to isolate significant measuring points to assess current trends and the influences at work which produce them. Time after time, ministers who thought they knew their churches inside-out discover new factors relating to their growth or lack of it, of which they would have remained blissfully unaware if they had not taken the trouble to investigate.

Ministers as a professional group tend to be averse to data-gathering because they are more people than organisation orientated. Another hesitation arises in the minds of some ministers who are men of action and feel that data-gathering and detailed long-term planning are simply a cover-up for procrastination. They want to get on with the job, and are afraid of what the Archbishop of York, Stuart Blanch, has described as 'analysis paralysis' setting in. This needs to be said, because some churches feel more competent at the analysis than the action. So any activity which serves to postpone involvement in a church growth programme is to be welcomed!

'Data-gathering is uncomfortable'
Some denominations and local churches reject data-gathering because they are not prepared to face the truth

about themselves. They are like patients, who, suspecting that something is seriously wrong, steadfastly refuse to see a doctor in the hope that their troubles will clear up without the need to be told the truth about themselves or undergo painful treatment.

Some growing churches which have broadcast their 'success' do not want to look too closely at where their new growth has been coming from. They rejoice that their pews are full, without facing the sobering fact that they are only filling them by emptying someone else's. One further aspect needs to be mentioned for churches which have experienced prolonged decline. Their data-gathering can be a disheartening exercise. If they merely project their ski-slope profile membership and attendance graphs, they will plan for continuing decline. Retrenchment will be the order of the day, with the result that we get what we have planned for. In the knowledge that so much of the central and parochial planning has been based on these kinds of projections, many ministers want to ignore the evidence from the past and present, and work in the hope that God will do a new thing.

THE VALUE OF DATA-GATHERING

Having considered the objections, we now turn briefly to outline the advantages of collecting relevant statistical information about the progress of the Christian Church in a locality or nation. These have been mentioned in passing in the previous section, but they are summarised here for the sake of convenience and for added emphasis.

To be aware of general trends

As situations grow in size and complexity it becomes increasingly hazardous to rely upon hunches and rule-of-thumb measures. Furthermore, it is likely that trends will be well advanced before they begin to become apparent. The more entrenched unwelcome developments have become, the harder it will be to reverse them. Data-gathering provides an early-warning system so that the situation can be analysed soon after the trend has begun to take shape and plot a course.

To evaluate their significance

It is frequently said that you can make statistics say what you want them to say. This is a half truth. You can use them arbitrarily when you are speaking to those who can neither verify the accuracy of the data, nor have insufficient knowledge of the situation from which they are drawn to appreciate their significance. However, when the data are studied by a group of people who are all intimately involved in and have detailed knowledge of the situation they describe, they become an invaluable tool.

If you want to put this to the test, simply present your membership, attendance and income and expenditure figures to the church committee in graph form without comment beyond that of simple clarification. Then divide the committee into groups of three to spend twenty minutes drawing out their significance and listing questions to which they give rise. On a blackboard or overhead projector write the heading 'WHAT THE FIGURES SAY ABOUT US' and list the points identified by each group.

To allocate resources to responsive areas

In marketing terms you sell where you are selling best. In terms of the mission of the gospel you put your human and financial resources to reap where God has prepared a ripe harvest. Many a temporary gain has been lost because the significance of the development was recognised too late in the day and additional resources could not be made available. As we will describe in the final chapter, we should plan from strength and not from weakness.

Effective planning for mission in Britain has been

hampered at every level by lack of reliable data. In 1972 the report of the Committee on Mission for the British Council of Churches entitled 'Stand Up and Be Counted' expressed the conviction 'that a fresh approach to the collection and use of statistical information is the basic prerequisite of any realistic planning for mission in the United Kingdom' (p. 1). For future planning the report recommended the regular collection and review of statistics at four levels:

(a) At the *national* level, by improving, standardising and centralising the categories of data collection so that these provide a more reliable basis for research in depth and reflect changes in the work of the Church.

(b) At the *regional* level, by relating material to demographic and socio-economic statistics and deriving projections as a guide to strategic forward planning.

(c) At the *local authority* level, by the constant monitoring and adjustment of resources to meet changing needs and the changing social situation.

(d) At the level of the *local church* to enable them to formulate their missionary task in the area and assess their work in a creative manner.

To draw up long-term plans for resistant areas

Emphasising the responsive does not mean neglecting the resistant. So what was said under the previous heading needs to be counter-balanced. McGavran argues that resistant areas should be occupied lightly. While this strategy may be appropriate for a 'mission area' where only a few pockets of Christians are to be found and they have to decide between going to one place at the expense of another, it must be applied rather differently in a situation where the Church has extensive geographical coverage. Here in England there are identifiable resistant areas of society, representing particular kinds of people. Each will require a distinctive approach, which will take much prayer, research and expertise to develop. We must seek to discover through the experimental work of small teams which approaches have the best chances of success, before committing the battalions. Such schemes require adequate data-gathering, otherwise we will continue to hear ingenious theories unsubstantiated by facts.

DATA-GATHERING AT LOCAL CHURCH LEVEL

In many ways this is the most important level of data-gathering. People are intimately involved in the situation which they are endeavouring to analyse so they are well placed to assess the accuracy and relevance of the information and also to interpret its significance. The local church also plays a strategic role in building up a regional and national picture, the accuracy of which will depend upon the quality of the data which churches have amassed and are willing to divulge.

Before embarking upon data-gathering exercises some of the potential pitfalls must be recognised so that as many as possible can be avoided. People's suspicions are quickly aroused, so from the outset the congregation must appreciate the purpose and significance of the exercise and be assured that confidentiality will be preserved. This latter point is not easily achieved, especially when questionnaires are used with small numbers. Individuals may be identified by their handwriting, or their answers to the range of questions may serve to point clearly in their direction. If such a possibility is likely to arise, then the analysis of the actual forms must be confined to one person who will act in complete confidence, destroying the forms as soon as his analysis is complete and there has been adequate discussion of the data; or preferably, an outside person should be invited to undertake the task.

In most situations it is advisable that the research project be given a 'low profile', with the actual work of data-gathering and analysis confined to a small group of four or five suitably qualified people. By this means the church is preserved from 'analysis paralysis', with the church curtailing its activities and returning its plans to cold storage while it contemplates its navel. The church should resist the temptation to merely tick over. Once programme momentum is lost it becomes twice as hard to generate it again. Church leaders should gather data much as an airliner pilot reads his instrument panel during flight. There is a comprehensive range of information before him and his practised eye quickly detects any malfunction. He does not then relay all the information to the passengers, for to do so would serve no useful purpose. On the contrary it would merely increase their anxiety level, even if there was nothing to worry about. The information is mostly of concern to the crew in the pilot's cabin, who will then make the necessary course, altitude and speed corrections, and note items of equipment which may need a maintenance check, once the aircraft has reached its destination.

In a larger, more complex church, the minister should receive relevant information such as worship service attendance, Sunday School, Youth Fellowship and Home Group attendance on a monthly basis. The church committee may need a concise report every three or six months, and the congregation a pictorial summary once a year. This ensures adequate data for the decision-makers and a general awareness of the situation through the membership so that they can reassess their level of commitment.

In communicating with the congregation emphasis should be placed on the positive and encouraging aspects of the data. Those which give cause for concern are primarily the responsibility of the leadership to ensure prompt and effective action.

A further point to remember in the presentation of data is that most people cannot 'take in' lists of figures, so ensure that they are always presented in a diagrammatic form to show clearly proportions, relationships and trends. While a plain line graph may be adequate for the church committee, it is advisable to re-present the information to ordinary church members in terms of concrete symbols of people for members, and pounds signs for financial graphs. These communicate far more effectively.

Membership

This is the most readily available statistic in most churches. It is of most value as an indication of commitment in Free Churches, especially where the membership roll is kept up to date. However, it does present problems for Episcopalians and Roman Catholics, who think of their 'membership' as their total community. To illustrate the problem let us pose the question as to who are members of the Anglican Church in England? Are they the 39 per cent of the total population who are baptised as infants? Or the 16 per cent who are confirmed, or the 5 per cent who take the trouble to obtain and return a completed electoral roll form, or the 4 per cent who fulfil a basic 'membership' requirement of taking communion at Easter? (1979 figures). For historic reasons the infant baptism figure most accurately represents the 'external constituency' of the Church of England, that is, those who are favourably disposed, but most of whom do not bother to attend.

If we are to speak meaningfully in terms of membership it is probably better to define it in terms of communicant or active membership. How this is measured will vary from denomination to denomination. In Catholic and High Anglican circles it may be done on the basis of weekly attendance at Mass. In Presbyterianism it will be by attendance at the quarterly communions, and in Anglican Churches with a central or evangelical tradition the most accurate measure will be the numbers at Easter and possibly Christmas communion, although in some churches these two seasons will present difficulties if there is a tradition of members going away for holidays or to visit relatives at these times. Therefore, each church must work out for itself the best way and time to measure 'membership' which most accurately and helpfully reflects their situation. The important thing to ensure is that the measure is done in the same way each year so that true trends can be discerned by being able to compare like with like.

A revealing refinement in collecting membership data is to take notice of the number of full families (where husband and wife are both Christians) in the total as distinct from part families (where only one partner is Christian) (McGavran 1970:92). If you then discover that of your part families a high proportion consist of the wife in membership to the exclusion of the husband, this should lead to some questions being raised about your programme which is obviously proving more effective in one area than another. And what about the children in adolescent years? What proportion have neither one, nor both parents as members of the church? What do these results indicate you should be doing to minister to the situation?

Once you have established the rule of taking a membership count each year, after a period of time you will be able to represent these figures on a graph to compare one year with another. Having displayed in this clear format what has been happening, you will then be able to interpret the general trend, and raise questions regarding those years which proved to be exceptions to the overall picture.

Attendance
At first glance this might seem to be a more straightforward operation than gathering membership statistics – after all, attenders are visible on church premises and therefore easily counted. On further thought it is soon evident that it is not as easy as that, because the same people are not at church every week, some come more than once on Sunday

and will, therefore, be counted twice, and there is an attendance fluctuation depending on the state of the weather and
the time of year!

While smaller churches may be able to count every week,
this may prove impractical for large churches, especially
with more than one exit, without some fairly elaborate
means of arriving at a total for each service. One of the
simplest means is to buy a tally counter. Alternatively in
churches where hymn books are given out is to note the
empty spaces in the shelves where they are stacked or count
those that remain and deduct them from the total. Many
large churches, however, provide hymn-books in the pews.
An alternative scheme is to keep a record of the service
sheets which are frequently distributed in churches of this
size.

In order to compare one year's attendance with another,
it is important to count at the same time each year. For
England I suggest the best time is between late September
and the end of November, avoiding Remembrance Sunday.
This is when the new annual church programme gets under
way after the summer holidays, and is before the bad winter
weather sets in (hopefully!). Choose four typical Sundays
during this period, i.e. excluding festivals and other special
occasions, and divide your total attendance on those
Sundays by four. This figure will be inflated by those who
have attended more than once on a Sunday, but, providing
churchgoing habits do not change, you will still have an
accurate trend measure over a number of years, which is our
primary interest. If, over the years, you suspect that there
has been a swing to or away from attending more than once
a Sunday, you may want to take the trouble of further
refining your data. You can do this each year on a percentage basis which you set for that year on the basis of your
knowledge of the churchgoing habits of the congregation.
Alternatively on the 'count' Sundays you can ask people to
register their attendance by placing a disc in a box just *once*

during the day. The total number of discs will give you the total number of different people who have attended church that day.

Another way of tackling the problem is completely to separate morning and evening attendance figures so that you can evaluate churchgoing and the appropriateness of your morning and evening programme of services.

In addition to the 'four typical Sundays' measure, we recommend that churches keep a record of attendance at the most popular services on the major festivals of Easter, Mothering Sunday, Harvest and Christmas. It is these occasions which attract the 'fringe' members or the 'external constituency'. Growing churches tend to be those with the widest circle of 'fringers'. If your church is one which succeeds in attracting the crowds for special occasions, these people should constitute your prime target for deeper Christian commitment and church membership.

Churches with an active membership in excess of two hundred should also keep a record of those who attend primary and secondary groups (these are defined in Ch. 6) in order to identify those who only attend Sunday worship and are involved in no other activity. These people will constitute those who are at greatest risk, in that such people can easily go missing from a large church without being missed until it is too late to recover them.

Finance

The weekly offering is one of the most sensitive indicators of the extent of the commitment of the membership to the local church. Of the total annual income this figure should be separated from money which comes through legacies and other sources of income such as the hire of the hall and investments. Churches which achieve inspiring worship and operate a meaningful programme seldom have insurmountable financial difficulties. The level of giving is a barometer of church health. But as you graph your annual giving year by year, remember that to give an accurate impression you will need to correct for inflation. Many churches, in comparing their giving with previous years, neglect to take this sufficiently into account, thus giving a false picture, which may breed complacency if the church is succeeding in paying its bills.

Having represented the giving for a number of years on a graph, next ask what the figures have to tell you about the relevance and quality of your programme.

Trends

Establishing trends from the past is of enormous help in determining precisely where we are at present and where we should be going in the future. Year by year we should be concerned to know precisely the *rate* of growth or decline. This can be done on an annual basis with a bar graph which reveals the annual growth rate. The annual growth rate can be calculated by subtracting the earlier year's membership from the later year's. Divide the answer by the earlier year. Then multiply this answer by a hundred, which gives you the percentage figure.

One word of caution. A new church with a rapid initial growth rate should beware of an over-optimistic future projection. This is not to limit faith, but to recognise that it is increasingly difficult to maintain a high figure based on small numbers. The normal pattern is for the initial expansionist phase to give way to a marginal state, which eventually leads through recession to the residual phase. This sequence is not inevitable, but is highly likely to occur eventually unless adequate steps are taken to prevent it.

Gains and losses

In their church growth analysis, Currie, Gilbert and Horsley distinguish between *autogenous* and *allogenous* growth (Currie, Gilbert and Horsley 1977:80). The former represents those accruing from the families of those already members, while the latter represents those recruited who are from families of non-members. In simpler language, autogenous growth may be described as *biological*, that is the children of church members coming to Christian commitment or church allegiance, while allogenous growth we may describe as conversion from the world.

Growing churches should seek to identify where their growth is coming from. Biological growth of itself will not increase the size of the congregation, at least in the case of white Protestant churches, for the simple reason that white Protestant families tend to have fewer children.

A second classification is *transfer* growth, which means people are leaving other churches in order to join ours. It therefore represents a tidal flow, without any overall increase. One church is growing at the expense of another.

A third possibility is *conversion growth*, which is the most important category in terms of church growth. A church must regularly identify those coming to faith in Christ from a non-church background or with minimal previous church contact (McGavran 1970:87).

To these we may add a fourth, *restoration* growth, which is a significant category in areas which have witnessed serious church decline. These are people who have been restored to membership after a lapse of some years. They have usually been caused to reconsider their position vis-à-vis the church through contact with a zealous Christian friend or by the church demonstrating a quality of life which was previously unknown to the disillusioned 'back-slider'.

Not only does a church register gains, it also experiences losses. These too should be classified and measured. There are three possibilities; people can be lost through *death* (which may be a high proportion in an elderly congregation located in a retirement area), *transfer out* (high in an old community due for demolition, or where people move in search of employment or as they are relocated or promoted), or *reversion* (may be high where the social pressure is hostile to the church, or where church morale is at a low ebb).

Charting the gains and losses will help to give a more accurate picture of the church's growth profile.

Let us briefly consider the profiles of four hypothetical churches, whose gains and losses during a given year are represented in the bar graphs below.

Membership gains and losses

Church 'A' is Green Acres Estate Church. It is seven years old and located in a new development area of detached houses. Their prices are such that they are beyond the means of most first-time buyers. The estate is just five minutes drive from the motorway and fifteen miles distant from an international airport. It therefore attracts men in middle and upper management positions. The development is now four-fifths complete. When the final group of houses is occupied it will have a total population in the region of ten thousand. Through its attractive worship, effective publicity, well-planned visitation campaigns and interest groups it has attracted 375 worshippers.

Looking now at the gains and losses bar graph for the year we see that the main explanation for their growth has been the addition of thirty-two members through transfer. The fact that Green Acres is an expanding and highly mobile community with a high percentage of nominal churchgoers means that it is relatively easy to bring them into church services. As they were mainly couples who had been married for a number of years and were now able to move to a larger, more expensive home, their children ranged in age between seven and nineteen years. Thus the church added twelve through 'biological growth' as they became of age for church membership. The most dominant age group among the adults was thirty to fifty years. They were fairly set in their ways, committed to a particular life-style, and anxious to climb the promotional ladder. The non-churchgoers in the community proved hard to win, and those who had lapsed from church attendance some twenty years previously saw no need to reconsider at their time of life. The church, consequently, only added four through conversion from the world. These people had been contacted by a couple who had opened their home for evangelistic supper parties. The two restored to Christian commitment and active church membership were brought back through the testimony of their teenage son and daughter.

During that year the church had lost seventeen members. As they were a new and active church they lost no one through reversion. There were few elderly people in the congregation as people moved away at retirement, so they only lost two through death. The major loss was through transfer out as fifteen people were relocated or moved abroad on promotion or on changing to a new firm.

One suburban Anglican church in Surrey discovered on doing this exercise that they had to gain on average thirty-four new members each year just to stay where they were in terms of membership, such was the high level of mobility in their community.

Church 'B' is located in Perivale, an urban area of mixed housing, some of which is a pre-war estate owned by the local council and the remainder older semi-detached houses constructed between 1900 and 1920. The Perivale Church is a hundred and twenty years old. From the post-war years until the mid 1960s it had experienced steady decline. But in the mid 1970s things began to look more promising, with the arrival of a young new minister which coincided with movement into the area of young couples who found that older properties were the only type of house they could now afford as a first buy.

Young marrieds represent one of the most responsive groups in Britain today, as is witnessed by the popularity of family services. The Perivale church had grown to a Sunday morning attendance of two hundred. During the year twelve people had been converted, eight of whom were young wives brought to Christ through a young wives' group. A further two mothers from single parent families had been brought into the fellowship through the understanding and practical help offered by the group.

Among the young couples moving into the area were those who had dropped out of church life when they had left home to go to university, or when they got married. However, now that they had family responsibilities and were beginning to put down roots, they returned to their former churchgoing. This occurred when they had their children baptised or mothers came into contact with other Christian young mums through the play group organised by the church. As most of these young people would move on before their children reached their teens, the church experienced little 'biological growth' in its adult membership. Some of the older properties were occupied by elderly couples, and, as the life expectation of women is seven years longer than for men, there were a number of widows in the area. Many of these had had church links in the distant past, and were brought into the church's fellowship by elderly members of the Women's Bright Hour group.

During the year the Perivale church lost seven through death, nine moved out of the area, four of whom were elderly people who transferred to an old people's home in another part of the town, and five to a 'better neighbourhood'. In addition, four people in the fifty to sixty-five age bracket left because they didn't like the family service and other changes which the young new minister had introduced.

Church 'C' we will call Station Road Mission. It is located in a run-down, vandalised, inner city area which is due for redevelopment. The old terraced houses are being demolished to make way for a new shopping precinct. The church no longer has a Sunday evening service and the morning worship is attended by about thirty-five 'old faithfuls'. Although few people now reside in the immediate locality, it is a gathering point for young people in the area, who hang around the shopping area and occupy the bench seats located in a landscaped approach to the precinct. A local evangelist working with a youth mission saw the potential of the Station Road Mission premises for coffee bar evangelism. He gained the permission of the elders to occupy and renovate a section of their hall, and enlisted the support of Christian musicians from other churches in the town.

The coffee bar saw thirteen young people converted

during the year, who were baptised on profession of faith. The coffee bar evangelist had identified with the Station Road Mission to the extent of becoming a member, but as a newcomer he was not able to influence the traditional pattern of Sunday worship. In consequence, many of the young people drifted off. Other factors contributing to the high loss rate were lack of parental support, ridicule by their peers, and no examples of maturer Christians with whom they could identify. As there was no movement into the area, the church was unable to grow through either transfer or restoration.

Church 'D' is a black independent church, now seventeen years old. It is located in an inner-city residential area. Originally it met in the hall of the local Anglican church. Five years ago the host church was made redundant and was purchased by the independents. This church added sixteen members through restoration. These had been regular churchgoers in the Caribbean but had not felt at home in the more restrained worship of the British churches, and some had felt cold-shouldered by the white members. However, once there was a church in the area which reminded them of life 'back home' and with black leadership, they were restored to membership. This opened the way to twenty conversions from the world, through the extended family network to those who had no previous church connections. On the debit side the church also witnessed a high proportion of reversions, particularly among their young people through the secularising influence of their English education and the fact that they did not share their parents' nostalgia.

Of all the areas of local church data-gathering the identification and classification of membership gains and losses is one of the most important. To understand the dynamics of the situation, one must be aware of *who is joining*, where from and why, and *who is leaving*, where to and why. A church with a static membership may equally describe a stable community or a church in rapid transition which is just managing to hold its own. The water level and dip-stick don't tell you everything. We need to know if the tap is on and whether the plug has been removed from the plug hole!

Having identified who has joined the church in the past year we need to know what were the main influences which caused them to make their decision. In this way we can learn more clearly about the strengths of our church in order to improve on them further. Information can be gathered by means of a questionnaire which new adherents are either invited to fill up themselves, or which can be completed in an interview by one of the church leaders.

When you have analysed a number of completed questionnaires you will probably discover that the most influential factor in introducing people to your church is the personal invitation of a friend. One of the greatest impediments to effective out-reach on the part of local congregations is their lack of meaningful contact with non-Christian people. But when the church breaks through this isolation it has created a potential for growth. A recent Gallup survey of church-goers reveals that '58 per cent of those who now go to church regularly, first began going when they were invited by someone they knew. Conversely, 63 per cent of those who do not go to church report that none of their friends or acquaintances has ever invited them' (McGavran and Hunter 1980:33, 34).

On the other side of the picture it is also instructive to know who has left the church during the past year and their reasons for leaving. We are particularly concerned to iden-tify whose who have lapsed while continuing to live in the locality. Such people obviously cannot be approached to fill up a questionnaire! But they will almost certainly have friends and perhaps relatives who are still church members who can be approached to discover the real reasons for their departure. Most churches, when asked, claim that they are friendly churches. But the committed membership are not those best able to give an accurate assessment. Their very 'friendliness' towards each other may have excluded others by its exclusiveness.

Once you have collected the data from those who have joined the church and about those who have left, then decide what action you will need to take to correct any deficiencies in attracting and holding people. In subsequent years when you prepare your gains and losses bar charts you will then have objective data on which to evaluate the effectiveness of your plans.

QUALITY OF COMMITMENT

McGavran cautions that numerical increase 'is not adding mere names to the roll or baptising those who have no intention of following Christ. Roll padding, aside from being dishonest, is useless. The numerical increase worth counting is that which endures from decade to decade. Roll padding and dishonest baptising will never produce lasting growth' (McGavran 1959:16). As we emphasised in the opening chapter, church growth is far more than increasing the head count of those who profess to be Christians.

In developing measuring tools for the local church we are concerned with quality control as much as quantity performance, to use commercial language. Responsible leaders want to know how people are growing in their understanding of the Christian faith, whether relationships are deepening and extending throughout the church-fellowship, and to what extent the Christian presence is evident in the community outside. Such information cannot be gathered with such precision as numerical data, but it is essential that each area be investigated to ensure that there is a balance between worship, fellowship, learning, evangelism and service. Healthy organic growth is proportionate, with each area and function developing in relation to the other.

Quality of church life can be measured in the following three ways:

Continuous assessment

The true shepherd knows his sheep. This becomes increasingly difficult as the flock increases in size. The time comes when under-shepherds will need to be appointed to maintain growth in numbers and quality. We must be observant to detect what is happening and continually be asking questions to test knowledge and measure reactions.

Sample interviews

From time to time draw up a questionnaire on some aspect of Christian truth or church life or community concerns and use those in contact with different segments of the congregation to interview selected individuals in order to sample opinion and collect suggestions. This method might be used to gather ideas for the next course of sermons, for example.

Congregational questionnaires

Such questionnaires have been used extensively in the Leighton Ford's Reachout campaigns in Vancouver and Melbourne. But congregational questionnaires can be very threatening to the individual and should only be used in churches where there is a high degree of cohesion and commitment to agreed goals. Otherwise they may prove divisive and generate defensive attitudes. They are best used in an inspirational setting as part of a total church-life conference. For the responses to be regarded as in any way representative of the views of the congregation, there should be at least a seventy-five per cent response rate.

USE OF FACILITIES

Our buildings are an asset to be used to the full. In some areas the church premises represent the only public amenities; they must, therefore, be utilised to meet the needs of that community to which God would have his people minister. How many hours a week is each room, the hall and the church, sanctuary used, and by how many people each week? In what ways can their use be rightly extended? What alterations need to be made to our programme and the structure and decor of the building to make them more adaptable and attractive? Again, by measuring each year, we can determine what progress we are succeeding in making.

COMMUNITY PROFILE

At the outset the church needs to identify the geographical area or kind of people it is seeking to reach with the gospel. For the city-centre Anglican church this will mean working with a map of the entire city, in recognition that the majority of their congregation will be living in someone else's parish! Estimate how many people live in the area you cover, and then describe the different kinds of people within those boundaries in terms of socio-economic levels, race, employment, age groups and interests. Describe and quantify each group as accurately as you are able.

Next locate the other churches in the community and identify the kinds of people they appeal to and the numbers they are successful in reaching. Such an exercise is, therefore, best done not in isolation but in co-operation with the other churches. This reduces the workload and helps in the production of a more comprehensive and accurate picture. Having worked together in the area of analysis, it is then more likely that you will be able to co-operate in developing a corporate strategy. In such an exercise we should be especially alert to identify the unreached, contact new arrivals and respond to unmet needs.

Such a community profile must have an eye to the future. The churches should seek to discover the community trends and local authority plans for the coming years. This will save the church from planning for yesterday rather than tomorrow. As a generalisation it is a fact that new churches grow better than old. So growing communities need new churches to develop within them.

FUTURE PROJECTIONS

Data-gathering should only be undertaken if we intend to act upon the informaton which has been accumulated. One of Murphy's Laws states that if the statistics don't prove your point then you obviously need more statistics! We might extend this in many church investigations to state that even when the statistics prove your point, your next course of action is to gather yet more statistics. James Engel defines research as 'the gathering of information for use in decision-making' (Engel 1977:13). Thus research must be phased into strategy. The consistent failure to implement findings has given rise to cynicism regarding research. Engel explains, '. . . research must be undertaken for the right reasons. It is especially essential that those who are responsible for implementation must have a thoroughgoing commitment to change if research is to be anything other than counterproductive' (Engel 1977:176).

Our efforts in data-gathering are to maximise our chances of making right choices and decisions. Having drawn up our membership, attendance, financial and other relevant graphs, we can then project them forward not simply as an extension of the existing trend, but as a 'faith projection'. This will represent what we believe it is possible, by God's grace, to achieve. It is called a 'faith projection' because it relates to the measure of faith which God has granted as we have analysed our performance, related these to biblical priorities, and prayed through our response.

If we simply allow events to take their natural course it is likely that the church will follow the life phases of most other institutions. The rapid-growth *progressive* phase, characterised by conversion growth and a high loss rate due to instability and immaturity, will eventually settle in the *marginal* phase, in which the institution is maintained by a high level of biological growth and a lessening appeal to non-members. This in turn will give way to the *recessive* phase as the external constituency from which the institution recruits its membership dwindles and biological growth declines. Eventually the institution will find itself in the *residual* phase, in which the external constituency has ceased to exist and the biological growth is eroded by the loss to the movement of the uninterested children of the members.

To prevent such a sequence of events the church must seek continual spiritual renewal; deploy a high proportion of its members to work in the external constituency; in McGavran's terminology, to turn them into class two leaders and workers, i.e. 'members whose energies are primarily directed to serving and evangelising non-Christians in their ministry area in an effort to bring them into the Body of Christ', and to establish new groups and plant new congregations.

SUMMARY

One of the drawbacks in presenting such a wide range of analytical exercises in quick succession is that we become so overwhelmed by the options that we end up by doing nothing.

In a one-off data-gathering exercise the results are a highly perishable commodity; they date immediately. Therefore, before embarking on any research project we must make clear that we intend to act on the results.

Review your situation in the light of the preceding pages asking yourself, 'Are there areas of church life where we are operating in the dark, and where hard evidence would help us do things better?' The responses to this kind of question should help you pin-point where to begin.

CHAPTER FIVE

Medium and Message

A number of excellent books are available on personal evangelism, dealing with the one-to-one and small group situations. One of the best to appear in recent years is *Out of the Saltshaker* by Rebecca Manley Pippert (IVP). She describes how she was 'turned off' by the way evangelism was presented as a stereotyped technique. It appeared to be an assembly-line processing methodology. Consequently, she admits, 'There was a part of me that secretly felt evangelism was something you shouldn't do to your dog, let alone a friend' (Pippert 1980:16). The book goes on to describe, in a reflective and anecdotal way, an approach to evangelism which is true to our experience, moulded by our personality and sensitive to the needs of the individuals with whom we believe it right to share openly our faith. For personal evangelism to be effective it must be spontaneous, flexible and sensitive.

When we turn from personal evangelism to community-focused church-based evangelism there are far fewer books which provide practical help in this area. This is a serious omission because the church is both medium and message in the process of gospel communication. Evangelism does not simply happen through persuasive individuals, but through communities of believers, who give credibility to the proclamation, by demonstrating something of the reality of what they speak. Our concern in this chapter is, therefore, to highlight a number of considerations which a local church should bear in mind in pondering its evangelistic effectiveness and over-hauling its strategy. In our concern that evangelism should happen spontaneously we cannot ignore the need for planning and structure. The church is intended to facilitate, not hinder, growth.

Our purpose in this chapter is not to offer a blueprint, but to outline basic requirements which are applicable to almost any evangelistic programme. When a church has established the prior requisites, then it will be in a position to consider and experiment with a number of alternative approaches maximising their potential.

MAKE PRAYER MEETINGS THE POWER HOUSE

The concern of this book to provide practical guidelines to assist churches in developing growth-enabling strategies must not be pursued to the neglect of the spiritual dimension. No matter how helpful some of the tools presented seem to appear, they will prove useless and even harmful if taken up by those with eyes which are spiritually blind and whose hands lack spiritual strength.

As one studies case histories of growing churches there is one recurring factor – they are all *praying* churches. The Pentecostal movement in Chile was born in a prayer meeting. The Lord spoke to a nightwatchman in the port of Valparaiso in a dream, instructing him to go to his pastor and tell him to gather his most spiritual people together to pray every day. For the Lord revealed, 'I intend to baptise them with tongues of fire' (Wagner 1973:16). Within months revival began, and overjoyed Christians overflowed into the city streets. Seventy years later the Pentecostals of Chile, now numbering over a million, regularly meet for their *vigilias* – their nights of prayer.

Presbyterian ministers from South Korea have told me of their daily dawn prayer meetings, many of them attended by thousands. And around the British Isles ministers of growing churches in all denominations testify to the fact

that it began as they met with those in their churches
burdened by God to confess their spiritual apathy or im-
potence and to seek his power to heal their defeated lives
and divided churches in order to become the people he
intended them to be, not only in the Church, but in the
world.

Yet prayer meetings for the renewal of the church and
for revival in the nation are not an automatic answer to
decline. I have sometimes been saddened by encapsulated
groups praying along these lines. They are nostalgic rather
than expectant, thinking only in terms of God doing a
'repeat performance' rather than a new thing. Although
their sentiments sound very pious as they earnestly cry,
'Lord, send revival', what they are in fact engaged in is not
so much a prayer meeting as a spiritual buck-passing session. For coupled with the voiced appeal for revival is the
unspoken rider, '. . . and until you do we are not budging'!
One learns to grow suspicious of cosy, predictable and
sentimental prayer meetings.

Effectual prayer is 'in the name of Jesus', which ascrip-
tion means, 'according to his character and purpose' – and
we are part of that purpose! If, while we are praying for
the Lord to do a new thing, we are failing to take action in
areas where his intentions are perfectly clear and his resources for their implementation guaranteed, then he is
unlikely to respond to our appeals to do more. Indeed, if he
were to accede to our request, we would probably become
so alarmed by the manifestations of his power that you
wouldn't see most of us for dust!

Expectation is generated not through the effervescence
of the enthusiasts, but through the intercession of the people
of God. We plead not simply that God will change our
circumstances, but that he will change *us* so that we can
become catalysts, through whom his plans can be implemented. We must be prepared to face the cost of being a
part of the answer to our own prayers. Such an attitude

underlies all of the strategy described in this chapter and those that follow.

ESTABLISH A POSITIVE ATTITUDE

In some churches a casual visitor gets the impression from the mournful atmosphere of the service that the congregation must be rehearsing their own funerals! Where such an atmosphere of gloom persists it needs to be dispersed by affirming the Christian hope. This was delightfully expressed at the national Roman Catholic Pastoral Conference held in Liverpool in 1980 where Christians were described as 'Easter People'. The people of God should never consider themselves as being the people of yesterday. The authentic Church is part of a Kingdom which is not on the way out, but on the way in. The people of God, therefore, have a stake in today and an inheritance for tomorrow. No matter how unpromising the immediate situation may seem, they have an unshakable hope that the best is yet to come. Nostalgia needs to be replaced by expectancy.

'Remnant theology' exercises a powerful influence in the Protestant churches of Western Europe. When the future seems to be filled with storm clouds, it may appear that the Church has no other recourse but to batten down the hatches and attempt to ride the storm. Our Lord did indeed warn of persecutions, heresy and growing violence in the last days. These 'last days' have in measure been with us since his crucifixion two thousand years ago. The Church was born in troubled times. In many places it advanced in the teeth of opposition. But the policy then was not to lie low until a more favourable climate developed. When the Jerusalem authorities, both Jewish and Roman, attempted to gag the Christian witnesses by threats and the token arrest of Peter and John, the Christians responded by taking the matter to the Lord in prayer. They placed the facts before God, declared their faith in his complete control over circumstances, and resolved to carry on despite the dangers, and requested that the Lord should continue to authenticate their testimony through signs and miracles (Acts 4:27–31).

We are not abandoned waifs or orphans, but adopted sons in a growing family. The future is not a blank wall to line up against, but a way to be walked. Establishing a positive self-image does not depend on a cheery morale boost, but on appropriating the promises of God and praying and planning expectantly for their outworking in the situations in which God has already placed us or challenged us to become involved.

BUILD AN ADEQUATE BASE

In missionary strategy people come before buildings and equipment. On a new housing estate the priority task is to establish Christian cells rather than launch into a brick-by-brick building scheme. New residents are at their most receptive during the first six months. If the opportunity to reach them is missed through a preoccupation with building plans and bricks and mortar, then a never-to-be-repeated golden opportunity has been lost.

From the four Gospels we can see the extent to which our Lord invested his time in people. In addition to addressing the crowds as he journeyed through Galilee and around Jerusalem, he drew aside to be with his closest associates. They represented his investment in the future. The twelve disciples were the core of the new people of God which had originally been organised in its twelve tribes. The writers of the four Gospels show their awareness of this strategy by the emphasis they place on his relationship to the twelve and the teaching he shares with them.

The need to build an adequate base is not only relevant to the pioneer missionary situation, but also to many run-down, inner city locations – only here the problems are even greater because of a history of decline, premises which are impossible to maintain in good order and totally unsuitable for the task in hand, and demands made upon inadequate resources by the needy people in the community and over-stretched social services trying to meet their needs. Sometimes the building is a major stumbling-block to progress. Its maintenance costs can absorb a major proportion of the available funds. It is more of a liability than an amenity.

Some of the Victorian monstrosities are less inviting as a place of worship than a cold-store warehouse. I remember visiting one such on a freezing winter's day. Clouds of vapour formed as we sang the opening hymn and three people walked out before the sermon from sheer cold. To heat the building to a reasonable temperature would have cost so much that they would have needed to charge a two pound entrance fee! I read the account of an architect who was consulted by a church with unsuitable premises which they wanted to adapt. After his inspection, he tried to think of something positive to say. His only comment was, 'Well, at least it's militarily defensible!'

Another church suffered from a lack of adequate base not in terms of buildings, but of people. This was a Non-conformist church in an inner city area with a modern dual purpose building surrounded by high-rise local authority dwellings. From the outset the denomination planned that the church should serve the local community in two principal ways: through an open youth club and by providing sheltered accommodation for elderly people housed in purpose-built flats alongside the church. However, the new minister on arrival soon found that he was faced with a seemingly impossible task. On the one hand he had to contend with a tough gang of young people attracted to the youth club, and on the other to care for the elderly people who made up a considerable proportion of his congregation. The local authority had provided half the capital for the dual purpose church and the salary for a youth leader, so the church had obligations to maintain the club open despite continuous vandalism and verbal abuse directed at the elderly people, who became understandably reluctant to attend church. To sustain the ministry among the youth and elderly people demanded a substantial core of local leadership. It was this vital element which was lacking.

Most run-down inner city churches need more than an isolated minister, however devoted, to get things running again. They require a missionary team, which, in addition to having a gifted leader, comprises a task force with an allocation of funds. Experience of urban mission in other areas of the world needs to be applied to the British situation. If there is little or no local Christian presence, then a team from outside needs to be brought in. Ministers for such tough assignments need pioneering gifts (i.e. they need to be made in the apostolic mould) and cross-cultural training if a church is to put down local roots. Unfortunately, theological colleges give little specialist training in the area of new church planting or moribund church rejuvenation.

AGREE ON YOUR EVANGELISTIC GOAL
Before it embarks on the task of proclaiming the gospel of Jesus Christ the local church must have a clear idea as to the hoped-for result of such an undertaking, and should make appropriate plans to maximise the chances of achieving it.

Of the four activities mentioned in the Great Commission recorded by Matthew – going, baptising, making disciples and teaching – the objective of these activities is to 'make disciples'. The going is in order to establish effective contact. The baptising is the act of initiation into the community of the redeemed. 'Teaching' is about the personal life-style, ethical standards and world-view consistent with discipleship. The content of that teaching is to be found in the discourses of our Lord recorded in the Gospels. No new word is added by the Lord after his resurrection. His relationship with his disciples prior to the crucifixion provides a model for the fellowship that believers are to enjoy in subsequent centuries.

A disciple is one who hears the call of Jesus and joins his company. In its Jewish context it means much more than in secular Greek. For the Greek it meant student, pupil or apprentice. In the New Testament it means total allegiance. This is reflected in the teaching emphasis in making disciples. Such teaching is not simply with the object of enlightening the mind or to satisfy curiosity, but to mould the personality and give direction to life. Our Lord's teaching is presented to us not as information to be sifted, but as guidelines to be followed. It welds together understanding (Matt. 13:52) and commitment (Matt. 27:57).

In any assessment of evangelistic effectiveness the church growth movement stresses the need to focus attention not so much on decisions registered but on disciples made. This is a healthy shift of emphasis, although in itself it does not completely clarify the goal. Discipleship is far more than initiation into a particular congregation or even accepting the terms of membership prescribed by a particular denomination. The significance of the individual's decision in terms of 'responsible church membership' will depend on the congregation's understanding of 'discipleship' and its quality of life and breadth of vision in working that out in practical terms in today's world.

A. W. Tozer makes this timely and uncomfortable reminder:

Many of us Christians have become extremely skilful in arranging our lives so as to admit the truth of Christianity without being embarrassed by its implications. We arrange things so that we can get on well enough without divine aid, while at the same time ostensibly seeking it. We boast in the Lord but watch carefully that we never get caught depending on him (Tozer 1955:49).

The man of pseudo-faith will fight for his verbal creed but flatly refuse to allow himself to get into the predicament where his future must depend on that creed being true (Tozer 1955:50).

Perhaps it is because we are so aware of the unsatisfactory nature of so much of contemporary church life that we are so reluctant to define our evangelistic goal in terms of disciples made. We are not convinced that the object of the exercise is to make yet more people to become like ourselves! If there is little to distinguish the Christian from his non-Christian neighbour, then discipleship can have little significance. This is a further reason why the renewal of the Church cannot be divorced from evangelism. By inviting people to follow Christ, we must also be in a position to include the invitation to join us in the pilgrimage. The Church is more than the herald announcing the message, it is a demonstration model which gives credence to the effectiveness of that message.

IDENTIFY THE EVANGELISTS

Peter Wagner has described the ineffectiveness of attempts to mobilise the whole Church by putting the entire membership in the front-line of evangelism (Wagner 1971: Chapter 7). Such a strategy, he says, rests upon the mistaken premise that every Christian is called to exercise the gift of evangelism. To attempt to dragoon people to fulfil a role for which they are not equipped by God is to invite frustration and instil feelings of guilt as Christians become aware of their inadequacies and ineffectiveness in this area.

Every congregation is none the less called to fulfil the evangelistic mandate. It must, therefore, ensure that it has the means within its membership to fulfil this inescapable obligation. Accepting that evangelism is no optional extra, the church must seek to identify, train and deploy those with the evangelistic gift. And while not everyone has the gift of the evangelist, everyone must be prepared to contribute their gift and fulfil the role of witness in the church's evangelistic programme.

At this point it may be helpful to try and distinguish between a witness and an evangelist. A witness is someone who can and is ready to speak from personal experience of what Christ has done in his life. This verbal testimony stems from the silent witness of a quality of life which demands an explanation. When questioned he should, therefore, be able to give adequate and appropriate testimony. 'Be ready at all times to answer anyone who asks you to explain the hope you have in you, but do it with gentleness and respect' (1 Pet. 3:15, 16). He should be able to interpret his experience and assurance in the light of the revealed truths of the gospel. All Christians are called to fulfil this role without exception. Our Lord heavily underlines this responsibility. 'If anyone declares publicly that he belongs to me, I will do the same for him before my Father in heaven. But if anyone rejects me publicly, I will reject him before my Father in heaven' (Matt. 10:32). A witness must be clear and open about his own position, but this does not necessarily imply that he will be effective in convincing and persuading others. To do this requires the particular gift of the evangelist.

Peter Wagner defines the gift of the evangelist as 'the special ability that God gives to certain members of the body of Christ to share the gospel with unbelievers in such a way that men and women become Jesus' disciples and responsible members of the Body of Christ' (Wagner 1979:173). It is clear both from Scripture and in the long experience of the Church, that some Christians can do this much more effectively than the majority.

Accepting the fact that not all Christians have the gift of evangelism, it is important to know those who do, and by what means they may be identified, especially when such persons might seem in very short supply or completely non-existent in the local church. On the basis of extensive research in a number of congregations in the United States, Peter Wagner has postulated an estimate of ten per cent who are either effectively or potentially gifted as evangelists. If this percentage potential could be considered to hold true outside the U.S.A., we would certainly have to ask of the great majority of congregations, 'What has happened to your ten per cent?' If it exists at all, their efforts must be going unrecognised, or have been rendered inoperative, or were never activated in the first place. The fact that there is little or no evidence that a gift is operating does not necessarily mean, however, that it is not present. Gifts can atrophy. Timothy was admonished by Paul to reactivate the gift which has been bestowed upon him (2 Tim. 1:6).

For the evangelistic gift to emerge within the life of the local church, evangelism must be placed high on that church's list of priorities. It must be the concern of the minister, the church council of board of deacons, the range of organisations, the home groups and the membership as a whole.

What kind of people are evangelists? They are likely to be fairly extrovert personalities, who are clear and confident in their approach to people and can easily relate to a stranger by establishing immediate contact. We all have people in our churches who have this sunny disposition, who can chat unselfconsciously with the shy and defensive newcomer, and so relax them that quickly and imperceptibly he takes them from small talk on to more serious matters. These people may either develop into evangelists or degenerate into gossips. Perhaps some of our gossips are unemployed, untrained and unrecognised evangelists!

In pleading, however, for home-grown evangelists we are not excluding the role of the itinerant evangelist. It is always helpful to have a fresh voice with a different approach from time to time. And there are those with an exceptional gift which the church has recognised and set apart to serve the Church at large. They either operate through independent organisations or, as is becoming increasingly the case today, are based in a local church, which anchors them, provides a support team, and keeps them in close touch with the need for post-evangelistic care and of the difficulty widely experienced of integrating the convert into the life of the local church. Such gifted people will, however, be most effective in churches where there is a prayerful concern and sense of expectancy and which have an ongoing programme of evangelism. Unless the inviting church can show that it has the capacity within itself to attract and retain the outsider, it is unlikely to do so as the result of a brief visit from an itinerant evangelist, no matter how gifted.

TRAIN THE CHRISTIAN COMMUNITY TO COMMUNICATE

The character of the members, the priorities and performance of the organisation and the appearance of the premises all communicate something. The question is, do they enhance or impair the church's evangelistic ministry? There must be a correlation between the medium and the message, for the medium is an essential part of the message in the communication process.

Within the evangelical tradition there has been a strong emphasis on the need for clear proclamation in evangelism. It draws attention to the centrality of preaching in the New Testament. This form of communication must not, however, be equated with the formal, structured monologue which may reflect classical Greek influence rather than the Judaic – Christian tradition. In addition to 'heralding' the gospel the New Testament mentions discussing (Acts 17:2, 17; 18:4, 19; 19:8) and arguing and debating (18:28). Communicating, then as now, was a two-way process.

In his monograph *Communicating The Good News in a Television Age* Tom Houston has an important section on the Bible as Media. There he writes:

It is clear that many media underlie the revelation we have in the Scriptures. The progressive dominance of print since the invention of the mechanised production of books in the fifteenth century has given us a very prosaic and flat image of the Bible that hides its true nature. If we try to identify the media pressed into the service of God's revelation of himself in the Bible, there is an astonishing variety (Houston 1978:7).

He then goes on to list and classify a lengthy and diverse list: visions, dreams, voices, discussions, parables, speeches, proverbs, rituals, laws, songs, drama, poetry, letters, ciphers, anthologies, history, records and stories, and for each he gives chapter and verse. In the unimaginative and uniform way that we present this exciting range, we give the impression that God's appointed way of gaining our attention is by throwing a book at us! Tom Houston reminds us that 'it takes a community to communicate' (Houston 1978:12). The task cannot be handed over to the superstar preacher and those with 'the gift of persuasive oratory'. The message has to be presented in a multitude of ways, recognising that different people respond to different approaches. In addition to the sermon, others will be reached through song, drama, dance and mime, poetry, or dialogue. Monologue is certainly not the only medium.

When one begins to take passages of Scripture and to ask how those can be so presented that they speak with equal force and with the same intended meaning as when they were originally communicated, all kinds of possibilities emerge. These will involve a wide range of communication from skills supplied by teachers, writers, interviewers, dancers, actors, artists, photographers, electronic experts, as well as the preacher. Of course, too much should not be attempted at any one time, and the ideas should not run ahead of our abilities to put them into effect. It is better to keep things as simple as possible and to avoid mere gimmickry. The style of presentation must be suited to the audience. A gimmick is a communication attempt which has failed.

A group should be organised to take charge of these presentations, representing a range of skills, and preferably including someone with some knowledge of communication theory. In order to experiment without threatening the Sunday services, some churches have found it profitable to hold 'creative worship' services on a week-night. Those attending can choose between a number of groups, electing to do either music, drama, poetry, collage or banner work, etc. This helps to identify the hidden talent and to capture a vision of the wide range of communication possibilities.

IDENTIFY RECEPTIVE GROUPS AND INDIVIDUALS

In Church growth thinking the distinction is made between three kinds of evangelism. These are Presence Evangelism, Proclamation Evangelism and Persuasion Evangelism. Consideration of the first of these categories will hold over to the next section. With regard to proclamation and persuasion one of the major difficulties in urban society is, how do you bring together those who want to tell with those who want to find out? The sharer needs to be brought into contact with the seeker (Reid 1979:32–36).

Within Western societies what are the most likely responsive sectors (these may also apply in some measure to North America and Australasia)?

New residents

When people move house to take up residence in a new community they are likely to be more open to change in other areas of their life. Their old behaviour pattern has been interrupted, while they adjust to their new neighbours, work, school, shops, recreational centre, etc. Churches located near areas where new housing estates are being

built or where there is a high population turnover should be
alert to this fact. It is significant that most of the growing
congregations in Britain are located where there is a new and
growing population. As a general rule, the older and more
stable the community, the more difficult it is to penetrate.

The church should make contact with new residents as
soon as possible after their arrival. Some operate a 'welcome
wagon' scheme consisting of a pack of information about
the locality – half-day closing of shops, local schools, doctors
and dentists, bus times, recreational amenities and information about the church. In many areas such schemes are
operated by the local chamber of commerce or residents'
association. When this is the case the churches can ask to
provide their material to add to the pack, and then ensure
that they follow up with a personal call.

Many churches which have area-based house groups give
them the task of contacting new arrivals. As soon as the
removal van is spotted by a neighbourhood group member,
the new family is welcomed into the area with a few pastries
and an offer of practical help. This initial contact can then
be followed up through subsequent casual encounters in the
street or at the local shops, and through an invitation to a
coffee-chat or meal to meet other neighbours.

The Rev. Jess Yates of Bamford Chapel, Rochdale
(United Reformed Church) reports that, 'Just over a year
ago a visitation was carried out on the newest estate in the
community. Before the visitation not one family came to
our church from the estate. One good contact was made
and followed up. Now twelve couples and their seventeen
children are integrated into our fellowship. They were
strangers to each other before, now there is a real sense of
community amongst them. They open their homes to each
other and are always seeking to bring new friends to "their"
church.' Within a four-year period Jess Yates has seen two
hundred and fifty people join Bamford Chapel, seventy of
whom had never been church members before. This is a

measure of the responsiveness of a new residential, middle-class area in Lancashire.

Such a ready response needs to be contrasted with that of the Rev. Martin Gooder in an inner-city redevelopment area in Manchester. His church's faithful, year-long, door-to-door visitation covering two thousand homes resulted in just one family joining the church. But their dogged determination has brought its rewards. From thirty worshippers seven years ago, they now have a multi-racial congregation of over two hundred, meeting each Sunday for family worship. Many other churches in the inner city have been equally faithful without as yet seeing anything like this level of response.

The people visiting your church
This is so obvious that at first sight it might seem superfluous to state it. Yet experience shows that such people are frequently both overlooked and mishandled. When people do cross the threshold of the church, do we make it easy for them to do so? Many church buildings are so austere and fortress-like from the exterior that the visitor not only has to pluck up a great deal of courage, but also has to exert considerable effort to force open the creaking, heavy door.

What can we do to make it easier for the potential visitor? Can the entrance be 'opened up' in any way? Do we need a strategically placed welcoming notice outside? Does the lighting need to be improved? And when people step inside, what will happen to them? First impressions are of enormous importance.

As regular, well-known members of the church it is difficult to put ourselves into the shoes of the first-time visitor. To find out what it is like, why not arrange for a member of another church to come unannounced one Sunday morning, playing the role of a visitor. Then get him to recount his experiences and suggestions to the church

council. It is salutary to learn how we appear not simply
through our own eyes, but through the eyes of an objective
assessor.

It is important that the visitor be made welcome on the
way in rather than left until he is on the way out. Practical
arrangements for the conducting of public worship should
be finalised as far as possible before Sunday, leaving the
minister free to welcome people as they arrive. In addition,
the stewards handing out the hymn books require alerting
and training to their responsibility in making the visitor
welcome. Some churches with large congregations find that
they have to make additional arrangements. The minister
gets waylaid by members of the congregation who want
to discuss urgent matters or exchange pleasantries. The
stewards are also preoccupied stacking books, inserting
leaflets and handing them out. They cannot hold up a
stream of people to talk to an unfamiliar face.

Those experiencing a major crisis in life
There are specific occasions in life when we are more open
to God:

1 At the birth of a baby when we marvel at the appearance of new life.
2 During adolescent years when we face the responsibilities of adulthood and the prospect of choosing a career
   and making a living in the world.
3 When facing the prospects of marriage, bringing personal adjustments and added responsibilities.
4 Serious illness and the prospect of death and what lies
   beyond.

To these we might also add:

5 The threat of unemployment and the prospect of retirement.

The church must seek to develop its spiritual and personal resources to minister imaginatively and responsibly in all of these situations in its care of people from the cradle to the grave.

One Anglican vicar in a church on a housing estate in the Coventry area concluded that his methods of dealing with families bringing their babies for baptism and couples coming to make wedding arrangements needed radical reappraisal. His sincere and careful counselling was ineffective in introducing them to the life of the church. After the 'great event' they were not seen again in the church until the next 'rite of passage' came along. He decided on an entirely new approach. Instead of seeing them individually in the privacy of his study, he arranged regular 'Sharing Jesus' evenings to which the baptism families and wedding couples were invited. There they met an equal number of members of the congregation, people like themselves, who would be invited to share their experiences. This new policy has paid dividends. Some of the couples coming to the church respond to the claims of Christ upon their lives as they see the evidence in the lives of the church members.

With increasing unemployment and early retirements, the Church will need to do fresh thinking in the area of ministry to those with time on their hands, opening up opportunities to learn new skills and engage in spheres of community service. In the United Kingdom perhaps churches have been too ready in the past to leave such concerns to the local authorities. The current serious cutbacks in adult education and the social services due to economic difficulties are perhaps an indication that the Church should step in to make available its local resources in building plant and volunteer personnel.

EMPHASISE A BIBLICAL THEOLOGY OF CONVERSION

Growing churches recognise the radical nature of conversion

to Christ and preach the need for a decisive commitment to him. They are not prepared to accept an 'easy believism' by baptising the status quo. They require a genuine allegiance to Christ demonstrated by a new quality of life. While churches may differ in their understanding of the timing and mode of water baptism, they must emphasise the decisive spiritual reality depicted by the sacrament. It represents both the *washing* from the stain and defilement of sin, and also *death* to the old way of living and the beginning of a new resurrection life.

Conversion

This is the act of turning by the individual. It represents a complete turnaround rather than a minor course correction; a turning away from sin to salvation and service in Christ. As an initial act it is a once-for-all, unrepeatable experience. It is a turning from darkness to light, from the domain of Satan to the Kingdom of God, from slavery to sin, to freedom, to service and worship of Christ as Lord (Matt. 18:3; Acts 3:19; 4:15; 26:18; 1 Thess. 1:9).

However, conversion does not refer exclusively to the initial act of reorientation. For as we mature in the Christian life so we come to recognise that there are still unconverted areas in our life which need to be repented of and handed over to God. As Keith Miller has pointed out, 'all a man does when he commits his "whole life" is to commit that of which he is conscious. . . . So the totally committed Christian life is a life of continually committing one's self and problems day by day as they are slowly revealed to his own consciousness' (Miller 1965:60).

Conversion, which emphasises the human response, would be impossible without the accompanying initiative-taking and power-enabling act of God. There are five key theological terms: Reconciliation, Redemption, Justification, Regeneration and Adoption, which express God's involvement in the total process.

'*Reconciliation*' means the ending of a quarrel by which former enemies become friends (Rom. 5:10f; 2 Cor. 5:18f; Eph. 2:13; Col. 1:20). The New Testament clearly teaches that man in his natural fallen state is opposed to God (Rom. 5:10; Col. 1:21; James 4:4). The seriousness of this condition should not be minimised. Until people are unequivocally taught this unpalatable truth there can be no preaching of good news. If they are left unaware of impending judgement they will not appreciate the significance of salvation.

So Paul calls upon all men everywhere to be reconciled to God (2 Cor. 5:20). Our acceptance is not represented as a reward for good conduct. No probationary period was required before the prodigal son was received by the waiting father. He ran towards him as soon as he came in sight, and he was still a long way from home when the father first spotted him (Luke 15:20). It was while we were yet sinners that Christ died for us (Rom. 5:8). Furthermore, we are not left in any doubt as to whether we are fully accepted. Reconciliation is not an event in the future to be anticipated but to be received now, because it is offered now (Rom. 5:11).

'*Redemption*' expresses the means by which reconciliation is made possible. It describes how deliverance from evil is achieved through the payment of a price. Thus prisoners of war may be released or slaves freed on the payment of an agreed sum being received. In the New Testament those who do not enjoy salvation in Christ are regarded as slaves of sin (John 8:34; Rom. 7:14). Christ's atoning death on the cross is regarded as the price paid to release the slaves and free the condemned (Eph. 1:7; Rom. 3:24; Heb. 9:15; 1 Cor. 6:19f; 7:22f).

The cost to God of his redemptive act is underlined by the fact that it was only achieved through the death of his Son. In other words it was on the basis of *substitution*. The innocent one stood in place of the guilty (Gal. 3:13; Mark 10:45). While the concept of substitution is not the only way in which the atonement may be understood, it is an essential feature as represented in Scripture.

'*Justification*' is a legal term meaning to 'acquit' or declare righteous. God, in Scripture, is represented as judge of all the earth. And because he is at the same time King, he is also responsible for the executive as well as the judicial aspect. He not only passes the verdict, but also implements the sentence. In the New Testament it is Paul who develops the concept of salvation in terms of justification.

> Justification means to Paul God's act of remitting the sins of guilty men, and accounting them righteous, freely, by His grace, through faith in Christ, on the ground, not of their own works, but of the representative law-keeping and redemptive blood-shedding of the Lord Jesus Christ on their behalf (Lilley 1962:683) (Rom. 3.23–26, 4:5–8;5:18f).

Thus having passed the appropriate sentence, he then, through the atoning work of Christ, stands in the sinner's place and stead. The sinner is thereby declared righteous, not because he was innocent of the charges brought against him, but because of the righteousness which belongs to Christ and is bestowed on him. Technically this is known as 'imputed righteousness'. (See also Gal. 2:15–21; 2 Cor. 5:16–21; Phil. 3:4–11). The grounds of the sinner's justification is by faith, that is by placing his confidence in Christ for salvation, and not in his own good works. Justification is on the basis of God's grace not human merit.

'*Regeneration*' describes the new beginning and permanent change brought about by the presence of the Holy Spirit in the life of the person who has responded by faith to Christ. Indeed that very initial act was only made possible through the Spirit who bestowed the gift of faith (Eph. 2:8). The new birth (John 3:3–8; 1 Pet. 1:3, 23) has brought us into God's new creation (2 Cor. 5:17; Gal. 6:15). The new beginning has permanent and far-reaching effects, as individuals become part of God's plans for the future as citizens of his coming Kingdom.

'*Adoption*' is a concept closely allied with the previous one. The idea that all men are the children of God is not found in The Bible. To be able to call God 'our Father' is a covenant privilege, not a universal right. John, in the prologue to his Gospel, makes it clear that we do not become God's children by natural means, that is, by being born as children of a human father, but by receiving Christ as God's son and our saviour (John 1:12–13). Our adoption is only made possible through the exercise of God's grace and the operation of his Spirit (Eph. 1:5; Gal. 4:1, 3; Rom. 8:15; Gal. 4:6). The gift of Sonship does not come through our being born, but through our being born again.

Dr James I. Packer describes 'adoption' as 'the highest privilege that the gospel offers; higher even than justification' (Packer 1973:230). While 'justification' is the primary blessing it is not the highest blessing. 'Adoption is higher, because of the richer relationship with God that it involves' (Packer 1973:231). Because we have been made children of God, we carry the family likeness through the indwelling of the Holy Spirit, we want to live so as to please our Heavenly Father, and we enjoy his Fatherly protection and generous provision.

In these few paragraphs we have not been able to do more than provide a sketchy summary of these rich concepts. But it is only when we see conversion as a miraculous, radical and gracious act of God, that there is an adequate basis and motivation for church growth.

DEVELOP A LONG-TERM STRATEGY FOR RESISTANT AREAS

So much of Christian attempts at communication begin where we would like people to be rather than where they are actually at. Our minds are so full of the 'pre-packaged' message that we have not stopped to think how it relates to those for whom it is intended. George Hunter reminds us that 'Effective communication of the gospel begins with a demonstration of its relevance . . . the point of contact between people and the gospel is people's needs, hopes, yearning, fears, longings, and deepest motives' (Hunter 1979:39). This was the communication principle which our Lord himself used. With the adulterous woman who came to the village well to draw water, he spoke first of the water and then of the men in her life. When the impetuous wealthy young man rushed up to him, he turned the conversation to the subject of money. Surrounded by the crowd, among whom were many subsistence farmers, our Lord's opening words were, 'A sower went forth to sow.' They were with him immediately. With the demon-possessed, disintegrated personality, our Lord exposed the situation after the direct question, 'What is your name?'

An inductive approach to communication means knowing the audience, whether that audience is an individual or a group, and beginning in the area of their known or anticipated needs. If it is a group, then you will need to identify the elements of community. Whilst the Spirit is ready to help the prayerful communicator to guide him to hidden personal needs of which otherwise he would be unaware, he also expects us to take practical steps to discover the needs around us. Robert Schuller, of the Garden Grove Community Church near Los Angeles, built up his congregation on the motto, 'Find a need and feel it, find a hurt and heal it.' This, however, was more than a slogan – it was a strategy. He spent several weeks calling on the homes around his church to discover the needs of the community and the inhibitions which kept them from church attendance (Schuller 1974:81).

Nearer home this same strategy has been applied to good effect. An Anglican church in Cambridge recognised that there were a lot of elderly people around the church. The gospel touched their lives at the point of loneliness, so the church opened a day care centre providing a lounge with comfortable chairs and a hot meal as an alternative to depending on the local authority 'meals on wheels'.

We must begin at the point of the individual's, or group's, needs and perceptions. Abraham Maslow has drawn up a model of seven motivational needs, all of which are basic to human personality. He lists them as follows:

1 Physiological needs
2 Safety needs
3 Love and belonging needs
4 Esteem needs:
   a. self esteem,
   b. esteem by others
5 Need for self actualisation
6 Desire to know and understand
7 Aesthetic needs

While all these elements are continuously present, not all are to the forefront of our consciousness. At any given time one or more will emerge to motivate a particular train of action. Effective communication occurs when the relevant motivational need is identified and addressed.

But such a model must be applied with caution. Considered in isolation, it may lead us to tell people only what they *want* to hear, which may be very different from what they *need* to hear. Our Lord's ministry, for instance, provides examples to guard us against this danger. In identifying and responding to real needs he did not shrink from touching the painful spots. We may have to sound a warning note of challenge as well as minister a word of comfort. Beginning at the point of need does not imply changing the gospel to suit the situation. The gospel is changeless and is centred on the saving power of Christ and his lordship over our lives. Here we are focusing attention on the point of contact which will vary from person to person. But, by whichever door they enter they will then need to come to terms with the whole gospel, which applies equally to all.

RECOGNISE THE EVANGELISTIC POTENTIAL OF GROUPS

Most congregations are subdivided into groups of one kind or another. One of the most significant developments in English church life during the past fifteen years has been the mushrooming of home groups. Such groups may now number more than a hundred thousand, and represent potential launching pads for mission. The sad fact is that the vast majority are failing to realise their evangelistic potential, preferring to concentrate on spiritual nurture of the group members. They are locked in on themselves out of a sense of fear or inadequacy.

Where such nervousness has been overcome and groups have invited their neighbours along, they have often been surprised by the level of response (Gibbs 1977:13; 1979a:22).

For many groups this is an idea so novel and daunting that it is unlikely to happen spontaneously. It will need positive leadership and in many cases the provision of a skilled person to initiate and guide the home group evangelistic programme. We will, however, postpone further discussion of this important topic until chapters six and seven.

ACHIEVE VISIBILITY

While it is probably advisable for the church to aim for a low profile in the small, stable, face-to-face village community, the opposite is almost always the case in the urban and suburban scene. Where there is a high population density and a rapid population turnover, the church must achieve visibility. This is achieved not by headline-grabbing sensationalism, which method Jesus repudiated in confronting Satan (Matt. 4:5–7), but by its members being seen whenever possible in the community, contributing to its life and responding to its needs. The church will be seeking to serve, expecting nothing in return, which is an essential characteristic of self-giving love as described and demonstrated by our Lord. But in addition to the church's calling to be the invisible yeast leavening the whole dough and the salt savouring the whole meal, it is also called to be a light placed prominently and strategically upon a lamp-stand so as to light the whole house. It is to be as visible as a city built upon a hill. The illumination is not the neon-sign of self-advertisement, but the outshining of a spirit-filled life. The light is the Shekinah glory of God's presence which is not restricted to the Tabernacle and Temple as in Old Testament times, but shines through every believer and Christian community.

In modern urban life, prominence involves skill in handling publicity.

Most churches produce a *magazine or news sheet*. If we have such a periodical the key question to ask, and to keep on asking, is, 'Who is it written for?' Is it a domestic journal intended primarily for the church members? If so, then one would expect it to read like an extension of the church notices. However, if it is intended for the community, the contents must reflect the concerns of the community, with comments on the wider world and put together with a certain degree of journalistic skill. When church events are mentioned, they need to be 'angled' to the community, with plenty of human and local interest to catch the eye. Many church magazines attract a readership far wider than the congregation, so it is strategic that these be prepared as attractively as possible both in content and format to create a favourable response.

The next significant area is the *local newspaper*. While national newspapers have to work hard to increase their readership levels, the sales of local newspapers continue to rise. Their editorial resources are, however, limited, so the church will be welcomed if it can provide good story 'copy' and clear photographs, thus saving them the expense of sending their own paid staff along to the various functions. There is always the danger that if they do send someone, it will be a junior reporter who does not know how to handle 'religious' news or is unsympathetic. Newspapers welcome with open arms a regular, efficient news service on which they can rely.

In addition the church might consider placing paid *advertisements* from time to time, highlighting forthcoming events which could be made especially attractive to the outsider. The themes and wording should be related, not to the regulars who will be there anyway, but to the felt needs of the additional people you are hoping to reach.

IMPLEMENT NEW MEMBERS PROCEDURES

Most churches have membership classes which consist of a course to teach basic Christian beliefs and membership requirements. Usually such classes only run once a year, which may leave someone who has come to the point of decision too late for that year's class in limbo for several months. During the waiting period he may fade from the scene. A further problem arises in relation to those who return to church life after an absence of many years, or who transfer from one church to another. In many churches their arrival receives no public recognition. Individuals slip in and out without most people being aware of the fact. New converts and transfers in should be introduced to the church leaders and members of the congregation. They need to feel that they are part of the family. St Andrew's,

Chorleywood, has started an annual welcome evening which provides an opportunity for the Parochial Church Council to meet all those who have started coming to the church during the past year. Some larger churches can be so impersonal that to think in terms of 'joining' is as meaningless as joining the cinema! Do people have a clear idea how to become members and to transfer that membership? Are the procedures for doing so effective in practice?

Even in the case of the large church with a regular new members' class, this may need to be supplemented by a sponsorship scheme in which the convert is matched with a church member of the same sex and similar age and background, to help him find his feet and be introduced to the family. If such a scheme is implemented, there must also be procedures established to deal with any possible mismatch. Someone in charge of the scheme will need to establish contact with both parties to assess how things are working out.

Some churches have found it helpful to set out a few simple guidelines to indicate what is entailed in 'responsible church membership'. Here is a suggestion:

1 I will endeavour whenever possible to worship with God's people each Sunday.
2 I will endeavour to be a consistent witness to Jesus Christ in the way I live and speak.
3 I will join some group within the church so that I relate to others on a personal level.
4 I will become a functioning member by involving myself in a specific area of regular Christian service within my church.
5 I will contribute financially in a systematic and sacrificial way.
6 I will uphold my church and especially the leaders in my daily prayers.

SUMMARY

In this chapter we have looked at twelve issues relating to the church's task in communicating its message effectively. Not every point will be applicable to every situation. But pondering each may heighten awareness or trigger new avenues of thought to help us break through the double walls which arise around every church: one built by the members and the outer one constructed by the community. List the points you have identified as especially relevant to your local situation and keep them particularly in mind as you read through the remaining chapters. Let us think beyond the problems to the opportunities and potential which lie before us. To prevent our visions degenerating into day-dreams they will sooner or later need to be earthed in goals and plans.

CHAPTER SIX

Groups and Growth

The proliferation of small groups has been one of the most significant developments in church life in recent years. While no statistics are available of the percentage of churches in Britain which have encouraged the formation of groups, I would estimate that in England at least, it is probably in the region of sixty per cent. I base this estimate on my questioning of clergy and laity at many conferences and training courses. Every time I ask people to raise their hands if they have home-based groups as a regular feature of their church programme, over sixty per cent indicate that this is the case. In Wales, Scotland and Northern Ireland, however, the percentage appears to be rather less.

While no detailed research has yet been undertaken here in Britain there are clear indications that most growing churches would regard the establishing of fellowship groups as being a significant factor.

While the existence of groups does not in itself guarantee growth, their presence means there is a higher probability that the church is growing.

This chapter will mainly be concerned with groups which are linked with a local church. I have not complicated the discussion by dwelling on either ecumenical groups or the House Church Movement. The former have been omitted due to the fact that I have little personal experience of them to draw from. The latter is only mentioned in passing, not because the House Church Movement is of little significance, but in recognition of the fact that it is a complex recent phenomenon which, to do it justice, requires a detailed study of its own.

By a 'home group' I mean a small group, generally numbering between five and twenty persons, meeting in homes for the purpose of mutual encouragement, Bible study, discussion, prayer and sometimes including community service and evangelism.

God has not made man to live in solitude and independence. Neither does he intend him to be lost in a crowd and so made to feel a nonentity. From the very beginning of the Christian church small groups have played a significant role in helping Christians build up their faith and extend their witness.

GROUPS IN THE NEW TESTAMENT
Within the New Testament we can see the strategic significance of the small group at every phase of the development of the Christian Church.

The synagogue
The synagogue is a Jewish place of meeting. From the time of the Babylonian exile it has come to fulfil both a religious and social function. It was a place set apart for worship, study and interpretation of the law and prayer. It was also the gathering-point for the community to discuss important local affairs. Much of the early Christian preaching took place in the synagogue. Our Lord was instructed there and himself ministered both in the one at Nazareth (Matt. 13:54; Luke 4:16) and at Capernaum (Mark 1:21; John 6:59).

Synagogues began in a small way. A new one could be formed with ten men as charter members. According to various traditions, Jerusalem had between 190 and 480 in the year AD 70. Worship was informal in style, yet firm control was exercised by the elders who were empowered to exercise discipline and punish members. The synagogue provided a model for the organisation of Christian congregations within the Hebrew Christian culture.

Jesus and the twelve

Our Lord invested the major part of his three years of ministry in the training of a small team. These were to continue his ministry and to form the nucleus of the new people of God. The pattern on which they themselves had been taught would be influential in their own future ministries. They in turn would catch men in the same way as they had been caught by Christ. The disciples were commissioned to the mission of making disciples, and discipleship was a distinctive learning process. Although discipleship groups may take a variety of forms due to the changed circumstances, the principles of discipleship are true for all time and locations. This learning pattern has been analysed in an excellent book by Robert Coleman entitled *The Master Plan of Evangelism* (1963). He details the steps as follows:

Selection. Christ's concern was not with programmes to reach the multitudes, but with men whom the multitudes would follow. The decisive factor in his choice was not brilliance, but a readiness to learn, and to respond to his teaching. Their changed lives would in turn influence others.

Association. He stayed with them. He himself was the curriculum. They learned through being in intimate contact with him, and through rubbing shoulders with one another. Discipleship learning is learning in community, which provides an immediate point of reference for the application of principles learned.

Consecration. Our Lord required obedience. He exposed the impossibility of trying to be the slave of two masters – God and money (Luke 16:13). You will not survive for long if you have a divided loyalty. There is an all-or-nothing implication to discipleship.

Impartation. Our Lord gave of himself daily in ministry, and gave his all at the cross. But that was not the end of his self-giving. In the upper room discourses he encouraged his followers to expect 'another comforter', that is not someone different from himself but essentially the same. This same attitude of self-giving is seen in the missionary motivation of the apostle Paul. Writing to the Thessalonians, he reminds them that he not only gave them the gospel, but also gave them himself (1 Thess. 2:8).

Demonstration. Jesus showed them how to live. His classes were always in session, and there was nothing predictable about the timetable! They learned to pray, use Scripture, heal the sick, deal with objectors, and win individuals, not by hearing talks on the subjects, but through seeing Jesus in action.

Delegation. He assigned them work. They had to put their hands to practical jobs such as gathering food, rowing boats and arranging rooms. They were also sent out unsupervised, and with the minimum of provisions on preaching missions. The twelve were sent out first (Mark 6:6f), and then seventy-two disciples (Luke 10:1). They received specific instructions as to what to do and were given the spiritual resources and authority to carry out their mandate. These missions were a preparation for the global mission which Jesus entrusted into their hands at the time of his death, and burned into their souls with the flame of Pentecost.

Supervision. He also kept a check on their activities. They were accountable for their actions, so were required to report back at the conclusion of their missions. And throughout his ministry he continued to ply them with questions.

Reproduction. He warned them that, as branches, if they failed to produce fruit they would be cut away. When they bore fruit they would be cut back in order to bear more fruit. The followers of Christ who had spent two and a half

to three years in the school of discipleship were themselves
to go and make disciples.

We may summarise discipleship under three 'Cs':

1 Commitment – there is a yielding of oneself;
2 Community – learning is a corporate activity;
3 Communication – what is experienced is intended to be
   shared with the wider world.

The church in the home

Throughout the New Testament there is an emphasis on the
home. Jesus was teaching at his home base in Capernaum
where the paralytic was lowered through the roof. He visited
people's homes to heal the sick, raise the dead, converse
over a meal, and advise those who had begun to follow him.
When he sent out the twelve and the seventy-two they were
to go in pairs to people's homes (Matt. 10:14; Luke 10:5).

His intention was that they should find a welcome there
as their greeting of peace was received.

From its inception the Church took root in homes. In
Jerusalem the Christians met together for fellowship
in addition to attendance at temple worship. 'Day after
day they met as a group in the temple, and they had their
meals together in their homes, eating with glad and humble
hearts . . .' (Acts 2:46). Acts 5:42 makes clear that Christians
used their homes for more than eating. It was there that
'they continued to teach and preach the Good News about
Jesus the Messiah'.

When Peter was imprisoned with the fearful possibility
of execution, believers in the home of Mary, the mother of
John Mark, were earnestly praying for his release. Their
prayers were answered beyond their expectations so that
Peter through a miraculous deliverance was able to join
them briefly (Acts 12:1–17). At Troas Paul was making a
long after-dinner speech in the upstairs room of someone's
home when Eutychus fell out of the window (Acts 20:7–12).
Later in that same journey, when he gathered together the

elders of Ephesus he reminded them, 'You know that I
did not hold back anything that would be of help to you
as I preached and taught in public and in your *homes*'
(Acts 20:20).

Not only were homes used for preaching, they also became
the regular meeting place for groups of Christians. Aquila
and Priscilla made their home a base for the church both
in Ephesus (1 Cor. 16:19) and Rome (Rom. 16:3–5). In
Laodicea a group of Christians met in the home of Nympha
(Col. 4:15), and in Colossae they were given hospitality by
Philemon (Phil. 2). For the first two hundred years of the
Church's life, it was a home-based movement. No special
church buildings were constructed for Christian worship
until the close of the second century.

The home-based church enabled the Church in the New
Testament to expand at a phenomenal rate with the minimum of human resources. Commenting on Floyd Filson's
article on house churches and their influence in ancient
Corinth, McGavran writes, 'Lacking church growth insight,
Filson misses the most important influence of house churches:
that they enabled the tiny church to grow mightily. At one
stroke they overcame four obstacles to growth which the
church met as it liberated new populations. (1) *The cost
of a church building*. Without any cash outlay at all, house
churches provided as many places to worship as there were
groups of Christians. This first common obstacle to multiplying churches never appeared. (2) *The obstacle of the Jewish
connection*. House churches pushed the church away from the
synagogue into the Gentile population. (3) *The obstacle of
introversion*. Each new house church exposed a new section of
society – a new set of intimates and relatives – to close
contact with ardent Christians. (4) *The obstacle of limited
leadership*. Each house church thrust the responsibilities and
prestige of leadership on able men of the new congregation.
These, within the elastic bonds of the Old Testament, oral
tradition of the life of the Lord, and a letter or two of Paul's

were free to follow the leading of the Holy Spirit' (McGavran 1970:192, 193).

THE STRATEGIC IMPORTANCE OF GROUPS

The availability of church buildings does not do away with either the need for small groups or the continuing use of the home. As we have already demonstrated, the small group learning situation is essential for discipleship training. Alongside worship with the crowd at the Temple the believers in Jerusalem also met with one another in their homes for fellowship meals, prayer and teaching. Many churches today are likewise feeling the need to divide their congregations into home-based fellowship groups. There is a continuing need for small groups and there are aspects of our urban and rural society today which make them even more important.

Intimacy

Today's urban society combines many powerful depersonalising elements. We are strangers in the crowd on the streets, in the shops and on public transport. We make many casual contacts, but there are few abiding relationships because the crossroads of contact are constantly changing in our mobile, cosmopolitan society. There is in consequence a deepseated hunger for face-to-face contact; to know and be known. Yet, paradoxically there is also a hesitancy and reluctance to expose oneself or become too involved with other people. For some people the small group is so threatening that they don't feel able to cope emotionally. This has tactical implications which we will consider later.

Intimacy is essential for establishing an atmosphere of mutual trust, to the point where we are prepared to remove our masks. The primary group provides the structure for face-to-face relationships and accountability. I need to have confidence in people if I am to share a confidence with them without the fear of being betrayed. As we get to know one another so we are prepared to lower our guard and share our sorrows, joys, frustrations, feelings of rejection and perplexities. We do not minister to each other from any superior standpoint but as 'wounded healers' of others who also bear this same wound (Clemmons and Hester 74:38).

In Britain we are more nervous than most about becoming involved with others at a deep personal level. This is partly due to the national characteristic of reserve and maintaining 'the stiff upper lip'. In the USA there seems to be a greater openness and informality enabling churches to make use of the insights of the secular small group movement. Osmaston has observed that 'in England, the Church has tended to fall into the opposite error of feeling that close sharing groups are vaguely dangerous, probably immoral and certainly upsetting' (Osmaston 1977:7). While being alert to the dangers of over-intense relationships developing, we must find ways of expressing that intimacy and frankness which is assumed in the letters of the New Testament. These are addressed to groups of Christians who recognised their responsibility to encourage and admonish one another.

Flexibility
While urban society can keep people apart, it can also bring together people from a variety of backgrounds. Communities are made up of people who have come from all points of the compass, and from locations near and far. They will represent different personalities, social levels and types of employment. This variety of clientele can be catered for in groups. There is no need for an extensive church campus if fellowship activities are located in homes. This will not be a practical option for every group; it will depend on the group's size and the nature of their activity. Snyder comments that 'because the group is small, it can easily change its procedures or functions to meet changing situations or to accomplish different objectives. . . . It is free to be flexible as

to the place, time, frequency and length of its meetings. It can easily disband when it has fulfilled its purpose without upsetting the institutional seismograph' (Snyder 1975:140).

Community

Discipleship is not a claim to self-reliance and independence. It is a frank acknowledgement of our vulnerability and interdependence. Christian fellowship in the small group is designed to help counteract the extreme of diffidence on the one hand ('Because I am not a hand, I don't belong to the body' 1 Cor. 12:15) and arrogance on the other ('I don't need you' 1 Cor. 12:21). In pre-industrial society this sense of belonging existed in the village, face-to-face community and through the network of the extended family. Urbanisation, employment opportunities and housing availability have destroyed these relationship networks so that the Church in the city has the task of recreating community.

As far as those outside the fellowship of the Church are concerned the existence of a Christian community in their street or place of employment should ideally serve as a model of what the Church is seeking to demonstrate. Ron Trudinger likens them to an oasis: 'An oasis beckons by just being there; the greenness and water attract the thirsty desert traveller' (Trudinger 1979:88).

Mobility

As McGavran observed, home-based cells enable the Church to multiply economically and speedily. It can quickly move to where people are and put down local roots.

Home-based groups are a good way of 'soil testing'. If the ground proves to be productive, then the groups can meet together in a local schoolroom, community hall or other suitable premises. One 'daughter church' in a County Durham parish held its services in a local public house as an interim arrangement. Not every church will find this an acceptable solution!

Eventually, the time will probably come when the size of the work and the demands of ministry make it necessary for the group to obtain their own premises. This will bring added freedom, with the church able to arrange their activities to suit their own needs; this is frequently not possible in rented premises which are hired out to a variety of groups. Having one's own church building, however, is not all gain, as a number of new churches have discovered. In those areas where there is a wide cultural gap between church and community, the fact of having a distinctive building labelled 'church' keeps many people away who would be more likely to attend if services were held on 'neutral territory' such as a school or community hall.

Conversely, in middle-class urban areas in Latin America it has been discovered that a church building is a distinct advantage as a 'back-up' to home-based evangelism. Groups which do not have a church building to relate to are regarded with a certain amount of suspicion. There people are culturally conditioned to worship in church with the service conducted by professional clergy.

Sensitivity

Home groups enable the church to keep its ears to the ground. They are like detectors scattered around the area to pick up a variety of signals. Through the home groups the church can keep track on who is moving in or out, those who are sick or in trouble and those who have lapsed. They can alert the church to community concerns and can gauge how their image stands in the neighbourhood.

THE PURPOSE OF GROUPS

It is recognised that a healthy church will have a variety of groups. In this section we are confining our attention to the cell unit which is a primary face-to-face group. In the next chapter we will move on to consider larger groups which are less personal and more programme orientated.

To provide a learning situation
The home group circle provides an opportunity for Christians to air their doubts and voice their opinions. For obvious reasons this is not possible in the more formal context of a church service; consequently if no opportunity is provided for 'come back', people are left with their questions unanswered and their views unheard. As educationalists are eager to remind us, no one has taught anything until somebody has learnt something. There is no impression without expression. In the informal atmosphere of a living room and seated among friends, individuals become relaxed and confident enough to raise questions and invite the response of the others in the group to their ideas and concerns.

To develop meaningful relationships
Juan Carlos Ortiz, the Argentine pastor, has drawn attention to the fact that the object of discipleship is not simply the information of the mind but the formation of the life (Ortiz 1976:ch. 14). Faith in Christ entails a life of obedience. The truth of the gospel is made known 'so that all may believe and *obey*' (Rom. 16:26). It is designed to bring about a transformation in the way that we live in every department of life. Such a change is made possible by the work of the Holy Spirit in the life of the individual. But this does not imply that his operations are exclusively individualistic and privatised. The Holy Spirit speaks to a Christian community as well as to the individual. When we read the letters of the New Testament we have to remind ourselves constantly that when the recipients are addressed to 'you', the word used is second person plural and not singular. This simple, yet significant fact, is obscured in our modern English translations. The primary group provides both a context and a support group to implement our dedication.

An essential part of our development occurs as we respond

and relate to other people. Without the stimulus and challenge of other Christians we would be in danger of carving out a gospel to our own liking and which we found comfortable to live with; a gospel which confirms our prejudices without challenging our presuppositions. The Church today needs the constant stimulus to think and act. Che Guevara, the Marxist guerilla who was killed in Bolivia, was described as 'one of those ready to risk his skin to prove his platitudes'. This pinpoints the issue of credibility which faces us all.

To identify gifts

The small groups situation is the ideal context in which to begin to identify and develop one another's gifts. Opportunities to do so should arise naturally as the group responds to each other's needs and to those which arise within the community. Among the members will be those who reveal gifts of discernment and wisdom as personal problems are tackled or possible lines of action considered. There will be those with gifts of healing who will pray and lay hands upon the sick. Others will display a gift of hospitality in the way that they host the meetings, making everyone feel relaxed, comfortable and cared for. People from the neighbourhood will feel inclined to pop in for a chat, to ask for help, or to share a confidence, because it has become known as a warm and welcoming home. There will be those with practical skills who will be delighted to make and mend in the home and garden. And there will be some who are especially effective as witnesses who will be introducing new people to the group.

Within the confines of a small group latent gifts can bud and flower in modest and unobtrusive ways. Such blossoming of life is frequently inhibited by the more formal structures and public worship services where people feel they have to be polished performers before they can contribute acceptably. Shy and diffident people are easily overlooked in the crowd, whereas in the small group they can be coaxed along to reveal their hidden talents for the immediate benefit of the group, and in preparation for a wider context.

To train new leaders

Another highly significant aspect of the cell group for church growth is that it provides an ideal structure for leadership training. Whereas the centralised pyramid structure severely limits the number of leaders who can be usefully incorporated, the cellular structure can multiply infinitely, continually creating a growing number of leadership vacancies. This is most dramatically illustrated in the growth of the Full Gospel Church in Seoul, South Korea, which in September 1984 had a membership of 395 thousand divided among over 20,000 house groups around the city. A similar pattern is also to be found in the Jotabeche Methodist Pentecostal Church in Santiago, Chile. It has now a membership of eighty thousand distributed in a large number of house groups or shack churches. The pressure of numbers is so great on the central place of worship that groups are only allowed to attend on one Sunday in four!

To ensure greater pastoral care

As a congregation grows so the pastoral demands increase upon the minister. If the church relies upon a one-man ministry then experience shows that his effectiveness will begin to tail off beyond the 80–150 member bracket. Pastoral care then increasingly comes to mean occasional contact and emergency calls. If no special needs are detected then you are left to drift on. When the flock becomes too large for one man to care for, the shepherd finds himself becoming little more than a vet! This is a far cry from the kind of pastoral care envisaged in the New Testament. A growing church needs a growing number of pastoral elders who will act as undershepherds of the flock. While larger congregations may be able to provide such training resources themselves, this is not the case in the majority of smaller parishes. A high proportion of clergy who received their training over fifteen years ago have themselves had little training in group work, so they are in need of help themselves before they can facilitate others.

To demonstrate concern for the neighbourhood

Christian cells do not simply exist for the nurture of their own souls, they are there to try to recognise and then help meet the needs of the neighbourhood. They should be alert and responsive to domestic emergencies – doing the shopping and taking care of the washing for a sick housewife, driving the elderly to hospital appointments or to the departmental stores when public transport is unreliable, looking after children when they cannot be met at school. The home group should also keep a look out for the arrival of removal vans to welcome new arrivals into the district and help them with their orientation. They should be prepared to spend time listening sympathetically to tales of domestic troubles without reprocessing the information as gossip with a high retail value! A broken confidence can mean a loss of credibility for the whole group. And, when appropriate, they should give assurance of prayer either personally or on behalf of the group. The Christian cell provides a means of showing that someone cares. And it is good when Christians can be numbered among those who put themselves out for neighbours in need.

To establish a base for neighbourhood evangelism

There is increasing evidence from the United Kingdom, the USA, Australia and elsewhere of the effectiveness of small groups for evangelism. They are particularly effective in those situations where the church is perceived as culturally distant from the community as a whole, or from sub-cultures within the community. Whereas people might be inclined to refuse an invitation to a church-based event, they are more likely to say 'yes' if the occasion is hosted in a home or arranged in a restaurant or club which they are accustomed to frequent.

Understandably, many groups feel nervous about responding to a challenge which is outside their previous experience. They may not in fact have anyone in their group with the gift of evangelism. They may not know what kind of programme would be appropriate in their circumstances, and they may be frightened of so mishandling the occasion that they lose the friendship of those people whom they have invited. Therefore the church leaders will need to provide guidelines for conducting evangelism in a small group context. They may need to offer programme suggestions. And for groups who feel they do not have anyone with the gift or experience to lead such an occasion, the church must be able to supply people skilled in group evangelism and suitable for the kind of people whom the group are intending to invite for the occasion.

DEALING WITH PROBLEMS LIKELY TO ARISE IN GROUPS

When a church decides to subdivide the membership into groups as an answer to the problems of the individuals' lack of a sense of identity and belonging, and to lift the congregation from its numerical plateau, it may soon discover that in solving one problem area it has exposed itself to new problem areas. Groups can create as many difficulties as they solve. This fact should be recognised from the outset. By the exercise of a little forethought, and by taking care to build in safeguards we can save ourselves a number of headaches. The following problems are those most likely to arise in a cell group structure.

Introversion

Groups of people can quickly develop an intense relationship. They form a clique which regards others who try to join the group as intruders. This is especially the case if that person is of a different age bracket or economic class, or holds views which are strongly at variance with the other group members. The other people in the group are unlikely to repel him overtly, but a number of subtle innuendos will signal to him that he does not really belong.

The ultimate purpose is not for groups to turn in upon themselves, but for the members to be activated to find and fulfil their mission in the world. The 'inward journey' must be accompanied by an 'outward journey'. To facilitate this two-way movement Elizabeth O'Connor has suggested the following structure. The first stage is to enlist in a school of Christian living which is designed to help members in 'three essential engagements: with God, with others, with self'. The programme involves personal assignments in learning to 'reach a state of inner attention', to establish personal growth disciplines, to discover and exercise new gifts, to relate to others so that we continue to be 'growing people' (O'Connor 1968: ch. 8). Having completed the school of Christian living, people have a wide choice of options in joining mission groups engaged in a specific activity, which may range from intercessory prayer, evangelistic visitation, to operating a coffee shop, or carrying out home improvements. People join a group which is in line with their particular gift and 'call'. If no group exists which corresponds to their leading a new group can be formed. Such mission groups are not simply activity-oriented. They also minister to one another, by appointing members whose main concern is the maintenance needs of the group itself. Thus work is not divorced from worship and mutual ministry.

Fragmentation
When groups become preoccupied with themselves, they begin before long to pull away from the centre and vie against each other. Many churches have been torn apart in

this way because almost from the outset the groups set themselves up as protest groups, to register their frustration at the irrelevance of the central acts of worship and traditional organisations. If the groups are then able to supply what was previously denied to the members, and if the central activities have no distinctive contribution to supplement and stimulate that cell life, then the main structure will lose cohesion and begin to fall apart.

To prevent this unhappy state of affairs developing, the distinctive roles of the cell groups and the congregational activities must be clearly defined and strong links between the two forged. Later, we will look at this in practical detail. The primary principle to be upheld is that the cell is a subdivision of the congregation and not a substitute for it. Therefore the group members' primary allegiance is to the congregation rather than the group.

Domination

Small groups can suffer through an overbearing leadership. Some leaders dominate through their strong personalities, others through their show of expertise. Their presence in the group is oppressive and inhibiting, rather than relaxing and enabling. The situation has arisen through an unwise choice at the outset, or because of inadequate guidance and supervision, or because no established procedures were devised at the outset to deal with such an eventuality.

This oppressive style of leadership has developed in some sections of the charismatic movement which have exercised 'oversight' or what they term a 'covering' ministry in a rigidly authoritarian and hierarchical framework. Discipleship training should be geared to making people disciples of Christ, not to the processing of individuals to become extensions of any human leader. Michael Harper observes, 'The master–disciple relationship is, of course, used frequently to describe the human relationship that Jesus had with others on earth, and therefore, can equally describe our relationship to the Lord today. We are still his disciples, and he is still our master. But it is never in the New Testament used to describe the relationship which Christians may have with one another' (Harper 1977:152). Such an emphasis is in response to the need to bring a highly individualistic spirit-led movement under some kind of authority and disciplined commitment to a body of believers. 'But if the language of "discipling" is used in place of "serving", it will simply be a way of replacing anarchy with tyranny' (Harper 1977:74, 75).

Dependency

This represents the other side of the coin to the problem described above. Some groups demand the complete subjection of the individual's will. They process people into a dull, predictable uniformity. Socially inadequate people may be especially attracted to such groups to provide them with support and a sense of identity. This may be beneficial up to a point, but there is a danger of such a strong sense of 'belonging' developing that 'the group becomes the source of an individual's identity, and he becomes dependent on it rather than on Christ. He lets the group become God for him, in making his decisions and planning his life' (Osmaston 1979:15).

Stagnation

Birds of a feather flock together, but after a time the feathers may begin to fly as disagreements develop, or the birds may resort to tucking their heads under their wings through boredom. Groups which begin well with members dropping their guards, getting to know one another, affirming each other's beliefs and challenging each other's opinions, may eventually lapse into lethargy. Individuals in the group begin to bore each other as they ride their hobby horses, and frustrate one another as they chase shoals of red herring. Eventually they may reach the stage when they only have to catch the opening sentence to predict with unfailing accuracy what is likely to follow. People then stop listening to one another, and merely wait for the person to finish speaking in order to add their contribution to the ritual conversation. When meetings become routine and predictable, the more resourceful members will begin to look for more stimulating activities to occupy their time.

Subversion

Groups are vulnerable to subversion by those who seek acceptance for ulterior motives. They may want to push a personal view point, or, more seriously, to disrupt the church by generating discontent and rivalry. Some have utilised the mutual support of the group for personal gain. They have made the group feel responsible for them, and traded upon their generosity. The New Testament letters which are addressed to small group situations, warned against such eventualities.

Our Lord warned against false prophets who would succeed in penetrating the Church's defences, like wolves in sheep's clothing (Matt. 7:15). Paul alerted the recent converts in Thessalonica to deal with the layabouts who were living off the earnings of the more industrious (1 Thess. 4:11; 5:14; 2 Thess. 3:6–15). When he met with the elders of the church in Ephesus he predicted that after he left, wolves would devour the flock and that 'some men from your own group will tell lies to lead the believers away after them' (Acts 20:29, 30). He constantly warned against those who preached another gospel (Gal. 1:6–8; 5:10; Eph. 4:14), posed as apostles (2 Cor. 11:12–13), stirred up envy and strife (Phil. 1:15) and worked evil (Phil. 3:2). He counselled the young Timothy to guard against those who would challenge his authority and undermine believers (1 Tim. 1:3; 4:1, 6; 2 Tim. 2:14; 3:6–9, 13). Titus was similarly warned (Titus 1:10–14; 3:10). This was not simply a hobby horse of Paul. The same line is taken both by Peter (2 Pet. 2:1f) and John

(2 John 7, 10, 11; 3 John 10). Such dangers have not
subsided with the passage of time; the Scriptures highlight
the fact that they will intensify 'in the last days'.

Overloading
This danger arises when the cell structure is superimposed
on existing, centralised organisational framework. As a consequence the committed church members are locked still
more tightly into a merry-go-round of church activities.
They find themselves committed to so many groups that
they are likely to become eventually spiritually as well as
physically exhausted! If home groups are to fulfil their twin
functions of building up the believers in their spiritual lives
and of becoming launching pads for mission, then there will
have to be a clearing of the decks of other organisational
clutter. From time to time every organisation (including
home groups) should be required to justify their continuing
existence and to review their programme.

Many church leaders have been all too aware of these
dangers, either because they have observed them occurring
elsewhere, or have imagined their possible development if
their own church were to set up groups. They have, consequently, resisted any moves in this direction. However,
where groups have been well-organised and managed as an
integral part of an overall strategy for Christian education,
pastoral care and evangelistic outreach, they have had a
transforming effect on church life. In all of my eleven years
of itinerant ministry I cannot recall any growing church
which does not encourage small groups.

LEADERSHIP FOR GROUPS
The larger the congregation the greater the percentage of
passengers and the larger the number of unused and frustrated leaders one is likely to find. This state of affairs,
although common, is not inevitable. It occurs and usually
indicates that the large church does not have an adequate

cellular growth structure. By multiplying cell groups the growing church creates leadership positions and an ideal training ground for future leadership.

Capable leaders of large congregations are sometimes slow to recognise the need to widen the leadership base. Moses, one of the outstanding leaders of the Old Testament, was no exception. He was a workaholic who was heading for a breakdown when Jethro, who was alert to the situation, stepped in. 'You are not doing it the right way. You will wear yourself out and these people as well. Now let me give you some good advice, and God will be with you. . . . You should choose some capable men and appoint them as leaders of the people: leaders of thousands, hundreds, fifties and tens. . . . That will make it easier for you, as they share your burden' (Ex. 18:17–22). At the base of this leadership pyramid were the leaders of tens – the primary group.

Leadership qualities

The personal qualifications required for leadership among the people of God are spelt out in a number of places. For example, the leaders appointed to assist Moses were required to be capable, God-fearing men who could be trusted and would not yield to offers of bribery (Ex. 18:21). Turning to the New Testament, the qualities expected in an elder, presbyter or deacon would apply equally well to a group leader with pastoral responsibilities for the members. He is to have a blameless reputation, to be faithful to his wife, to be trustworthy, self-controlled, discreet, disciplined, hospitable, able to teach, respected by his children, fair-minded, devout, well thought of by non-Christians, able to get on with people, reasonable, gentle and firm yet patient with difficult individuals (see 1 Tim. 3:1–17; 4:14; Titus 1:5–11).

In order to operate effectively in a primary group context he needs to be able to develop inter-personal relationships.

Therefore, he must be a person who is secure in himself, does not feel personally threatened by criticism and is able to evaluate himself and the group. In temperament he is relaxed and restrained; calm, poised and objective. He displays a loving concern for everyone in the group and has an understanding, generous attitude which covers the fault of others. He is sensitive to 'atmosphere'; able to display tact and apply 'antifreeze' to thaw out a tense situation. He recognises that *how* one says things is as important as *what* is said. He displays vitality and an enthusiasm for the job which rubs off on the rest of the group. He is humble and teachable, making it clear that he does not pretend to know all the answers. He studiously avoids overshadowing others, and is appreciative of the contributions made by everyone in the group.

Leadership tasks
The primary groups envisaged in this chapter, 'should as far as possible express the full nature and message of the church' (Osmaston 1979:11). This being so the leader is responsible for a wide range of tasks. The complexity of his role is often masked by the smallness of the group, and does not become evident until the new leader has worked his way into the job. The scope of the task and the range of responsibilities need to be spelt out and agreed upon before any appointment is made so that no one takes on more than he finds he can manage. The following paragraphs attempt to describe his range of responsibilities.

The leader's prime task is to enable the group to come together to achieve the objectives for which it has been established. He must, therefore, be able to define clearly the nature of the various tasks to be undertaken or the problems to be considered. He must establish rapport between members so that they can relate creatively to one another. 'Leadership involves sensitivity to the feelings and attitudes of others, ability to understand what is happening in a group at the unconscious as well as the conscious level, and skill in acting in ways that contribute to, rather than hinder, task performance' (Rice 1965:5). He works to draw out the insights and views of the group. People begin to share when they are encouraged to feel that they have something valuable to contribute.

The group leader does not immediately jump in to answer questions, but bounces them back for the group to respond. When someone becomes muddled and confused he saves them from embarrassment by a face-saving interjection, such as, 'Did I understand you to mean . . . ?' He looks out for the flaring up of private feuds, the surfacing of red herrings or the emergence of 'hidden agendas' which might subvert the purpose of the group. He calms the argumentative, restrains the over-talkative and spots the shy person who has withdrawn into a mental backwater. When the pace flags he fires the group with a fresh idea or a provocative question. He is not embarrassed by, but rather encourages, periodic silences for the incubation of new ideas. He discourages sloganising and repetitions. He is concerned to see that much talk about God results in a closer walk with God for all. He is therefore alert to challenge the group in considering ways of applying practically what has been discussed.

The leader is also responsible for ensuring that practical arrangements and details are cared for. He will be concerned to see that the meeting begins and ends on time. He will undertake to introduce newcomers and visit absentees. He will maintain good relationships with the wider congregation and liaise with other groups.

To be an effective group leader requires the acquiring of skills and dedication of time. It cannot be taken on as yet another chore for the already over-taxed church leader.

Job description

As we commented earlier, it is essential that the leader understands what the job entails and what is expected of him. This may be achieved by means of a written job description, which is talked over, modified where necessary and then agreed to. The job description might look something like the following:

JOB DESCRIPTION: HOME GROUP LEADER

The task of the leader is to direct the group to fulfil its stated purpose:

1 To be responsible for the group to the minister and church leadership.
2 To conduct the teaching programme within the guidelines agreed by the minister or pastoral eldership group.
3 To encourage the participation of all the group members in discussion, prayer times and other activities.
4 To endeavour to establish an atmosphere of trust, in which people feel free to air their problems and concerns and ask for the support of the group.
5 To visit all members in their homes at least once every three months.
6 To help each of the members to identify their gifts and skills, and to encourage their use in the group, the life of the church, and the community at large.
7 To report to the minister or church leadership any special needs arising in the group.
8 In the case of neighbourhood groups, to ensure that group members are monitoring the needs of the locality, making contact with new neighbours, visiting any individuals or dealing with specific needs, and to require adequate reporting back on results.
9 To initiate at least two invitation evenings each year, one of these to be for church members in the locality who are not group members and the other for group members to share their faith with non-Christians.

10 To train assistant leaders who can act for him in a temporary capacity and eventually take on responsibility for their own group.

Appointment

As home groups are not autonomous bodies but sub-units of a larger fellowship, the leaders should not be appointed by the group members but by the minister who has overall pastoral responsibility and will in effect delegate pastoral responsibilities to them. A wise minister under normal circumstances will also take the precaution of seeking ratification by the parochial church council, deacon's meeting or other appropriate body. In the case of an existing group requiring a change of leadership, it is usually advisable to discuss the matter with the group or consult with one or two members who would be considered representative of the group prior to making an appointment rather than to approach candidates privately and individually. Such behind-the-scenes tactics can have an unsettling influence on the group, and make them feel that they are not considered mature enough to arrive at their own decisions. If the group cannot provide a new leader from within, then the minister must bring in a new leader from elsewhere.

Wherever possible the minister should avoid being a group leader. The presence of an ordained man can be inhibiting to laymen. But, most importantly, he should be free from other commitments to call in on groups to evaluate how effective the leader is proving to be, and be prepared to step into the breach should an emergency remove a leader without an assistant being readily available. If the minister has spotted any mistakes in the leader's approach he can then counsel him on ways of improving his performance.

It is advisable for the period of the appointment to be specified both in the interests of the church, the group and the leader. The leader may prove to be unsuitable and the fact of the agreed time limit makes it easier to arrange a replacement, avoiding embarrassment or ill-feeling. Obviously on occasion the minister must act at once for the good of the group. As for the leader, his circumstances in terms of his family responsibilities or work commitments may change, making it difficult for him to continue. Leaders should not be left to soldier on when they find they can no longer give the time or the energy which the job requires. Leaders placed in this predicament serve as a warning to other prospective leaders that they might well find themselves in a similar position if they allowed themselves to be persuaded to become home group leaders! A time limit encourages the leader to re-assess his commitments to decide whether or not to agree to a renewal of the appointment for a further period.

The appointment is not simply the concern of the group but is to an office which is part of the total congregational structure. As such it should be recognised and supported by the whole church. This can be expressed in a commissioning service of the leaders held at the beginning of the church's new yearly cycle of activities, which normally gets under way after the long summer holidays.

Training and co-ordination
It is vitally important for the minister to keep in regular contact with the various group leaders in order to provide them with adequate personal support and to obtain feedback. This may either be arranged on a one-to-one basis or through a monthly or quarterly group leaders' meeting. Able leaders tend to have many commitments so the minister must be prepared to meet at their convenience and not simply at his own. If all else fails contact can be maintained by a regular telephone call. If the leadership are not regularly comparing notes the cell structures will be in danger of losing momentum and cohesion.

If regular monthly sharing and training sessions prove too frequent to sustain, it may be necessary to work to a three- or six-monthly programme. At the training sessions the teaching programme can be arranged and any alternative agreed to. In programming for groups a degree of flexibility is necessary. Some groups may be of a different social, cultural and age mix from the rest, which may mean they will have to follow a distinctive approach or have a programme of their own.

Training topics may include the following:

1 How to lead a discussion.
2 Encouraging group sharing and prayer.
3 Visiting church members.
4 The art of listening and counselling.
5 Identifying gifts.
6 Visitation evangelism.
7 Holding an evangelistic Bible Study.
8 Relating to community needs.
9 Arranging a local community outreach.
10 What to do when the group becomes too large.

Avoid leadership bottlenecks

As a church grows, so groups multiply and before long things grind to a standstill through a shortage of trained leadership. To avoid the leadership bottleneck ensure from an early stage that each group has an assistant able to work alongside the leader. He is then ready to stand in should the leader be absent for any reason, and is also available to spearhead new groups. Assistant leaders should be encouraged to participate in all the leadership training opportunities to equip them to run a group of their own. However, they should not be encouraged to assume that they are the automatic choice when the group needs a new leader.

Distinguish between leader and host

This is a helpful and often necessary distinction to make to
ease the burden on the leader. If the meeting is held in his
home and he is responsible for all the practical arrangements in addition to the meeting programme he is unlikely
to be able to give of his best. This is especially the case with
a married man or woman with children. By the time the
children have been put to bed, toys put away, room tidied,
furniture rearranged and the refreshments prepared, they
flop back exhausted as the members begin to arrive and the
programme gets under way! When the leader is not the
host, he can arrive fresh to conduct the evening's programme. It must be recognised that some leaders, while
having the essential pastoral and teaching qualifications,
may not possess the gift of hospitality.

A further advantage is that the location of the group can
be changed with minimum disruption to the group. If the
leader who is also the host suggests moving the meeting
elsewhere to ease the hospitality burden from his family,
this may seem to imply that he has lost interest in the
group, or that he is questioning its importance.

SUMMARY

This chapter has attempted to demonstrate the importance of small groups for the growth of the church both in
regard to quality of corporate life and by multiplying
points of contact with and outreach into the surrounding community. Assess their significance to date in the
life of your church. How can they become more meaningful for those who attend? By what means can other
members of the congregation become involved? How can
their leadership be improved? How can new groups be
formed to undertake specific tasks, while at the same
time ministering to one another? How can the resources
given by God to the Church be channelled into the

community to get done what God wants us to achieve? These are key questions which every growing church must squarely face if its growth momentum is to be maintained. Otherwise it will simply grow flab rather than muscle.

CHAPTER SEVEN

Structures and Strategy

Human growth entails, in addition to the multiplication of cells, the development of the skeletal structure to support them. For the body of Christ to grow, structure is equally important. Without an adequate and expansible framework the Church will be in danger of an organisational overload leading to institutional collapse. In order to prevent such an unfortunate eventuality many churches operate a self-limiting structure which determines the ceiling level of performance.

David Wasdell of the Urban Church Project presented a report to the General Synod of the Church of England which showed conclusively that the answer to the problem of achieving an increased level of penetration in a densely populated urban parish is not merely to increase the numbers of clergy. 'In parishes of over 2,000 the single-clergy model church levels off at an average congregation of 175 regardless of parish population' (Wasdell 1974:5). He quoted an earlier piece of research which had shown that a two-person team adds an average ninety Christmas communicants, and increasing the team by a further full-time worker added an extra eighty-one Christmas communicants. He writes, '. . . the only way to break out of the self-limiting church structure is to increase lay mobilisation in mission and to minimise lapse rate. In other words we need structures of high motivation, maturation, education, training and pastoral care, together with a sense of belonging' (Wasdell 1974:12).

In the previous chapter we examined the small group, emphasising its importance for providing a sense of belonging and pastoral care. In this chapter we will be concerned with further structures for education and inspiration. Chapter eight will focus attention on lay mobilisation.

The study of local church structures is a neglected area in the thinking of many clergy because their main preoccupation in ministry is with people rather than structures and organisation. Some suspect all organisation as having a depersonalising influence. However, when properly understood, applied and implemented, organisation can help a growing church to retain its emphasis on the importance of the individual. It achieves this by providing two-way channels of communication which can help everyone to know what is happening and which allows everyone to be heard and to participate. The Church in today's urban world with its mushrooming population needs structures which facilitate its own potential for mushroom growth.

DEFINING GROUPS

Peter Wagner in his analysis of growing urban churches in the United States, identifies as his fourth vital sign of a healthy growing church the interrelationship of a three-tier structure, which he expresses in the formula: celebration+congregation+cell=church. Each tier is represented by a different size of group, designed to fulfil a distinctive function. Sociologists distinguish between three types of group which differ in size and function.

The smallest of these is the '*primary group*' which consists of twelve members or less. This is the intimate face-to-face unit, which provides the possibility of developing in-depth, personal relationships. But as numbers grow much above twelve it becomes difficult and then impossible to maintain this level of intimacy.

The next stage is the '*secondary group*' with a membership ranging from thirteen to a maximum of 175. Within this range it is possible to know everyone by name, be on casual speaking terms and experience a group identity. The group stresses social activity rather than personal interaction. It is more task- than people-orientated.

The third tier begins at 175 plus with no upper limit. This is the '*tertiary group*' in which it is not possible for people to know one another. The tertiary group provides the opportunity for celebratory events on a grand scale.

Primary, secondary and tertiary groupings each have a significant role to play in the life of a growing church. In modern urban society the small group is not the whole answer. We therefore need to appreciate the distinction between the three levels of groups, understand their distinctive dynamics, and establish a dynamic relationship between them.

In the previous chapter we examined the nature of groups at the primary level and their leadership. We now proceed to describe the secondary and tertiary levels.

SECONDARY GROUPS

The secondary group is more task-orientated than person-centred. With up to 175 members, it is large enough to contain an interesting variety of people, yet small enough for each person to know everyone by name. For the small church the 'secondary group' will be the congregation. When people come to the church service there is a likelihood that the worshippers know one another, although recognition is usually minimal due to the seating arrangements of the building or the members' understanding of worship. One South Wales worshipper was heard to say to her vicar as she left after a service in which the congregation had been invited to greet one another, 'I come to church to worship God not to be friendly!' Even the small church of less than 150 members may subdivide into a number of secondary groups with twenty to sixty members, such as the youth organisations, women's meeting etc.

The secondary groupings are important for the church growth, as they cater for a variety of church-based activities for particular age groups or special interests. People are made to feel that they belong and can begin to get involved and make an individual contribution.

When a small church becomes too large to function as a healthy single unit, it becomes what Lyle Schaller describes as a 'supersaturated solution with more members than can be absorbed into one group. These congregations usually are able to assimilate replacement members to take the place of members who move away, drop out or die; but rarely are they able to grow' (Schaller 1978b:59).

The groupings become increasingly important as the Sunday services grow beyond the point where it is possible for all the worshippers to know one another, or for members to be able to spot the newcomer and take steps to get to know, welcome, and introduce him to others. Frequently this problem is signalled by church members commenting, 'This church is getting too big.' This should not be interpreted by the church leaders as a comment on *size* but on *structure*. What they are really saying is, 'Help, I'm lost here' or, 'I no longer count around here.' The organisational structures have begun to creak or break apart under the strain of additional mass. If the growing church fails to build intermediate structures then the growth dynamic will be destroyed. Strangers will go unnoticed among the crowd of regulars. While these gather in groups, the visitor stands near the wall to hide the fact that he has been left out, or simply slips quietly away.

In large churches people are much more likely to 'stick' when they have been successfully incorporated into face-to-face groups either at the primary or secondary level. The unspoken questions are: Do people know my name? If I am absent am I likely to be missed? Do people want to know me better? Would my contribution be invited and welcomed?

Many churches are a hive of activity throughout the

week, especially when public amenities are scarce in the area. They provide premises which are attractive and adaptable to a wide range of activities – uniformed organisations, dance, drama, social clubs, badminton, judo, painting, pottery etc. The trouble is that in most cases the church acts as little more than a landlord. This can cause complications with financial haggling and competing claims.

Mid-week activity groups

I believe that the church should be the focal point of a hive of diverse activities, because urban society brings together different kinds of people in large numbers. But wherever possible it is preferable for the church to identify and anticipate the likely interest and to initiate activity groups with able Christian leadership. In this way the church can avoid being driven into fulfilling a landlord role, hosting activities over which it has little or no control, and can integrate those activities as aspects of its total mission in the community.

The key problem area for implementing such a policy is to identify appropriate leaders who are technically competent to lead the activity and are spiritually mature to relate the specific activity to a wider Christian framework.

The significance of the secondary groupings is likely to increase in the foreseeable future, with the prospect of more people out of work, shorter working weeks and earlier retirements. The church will have a greater opportunity to help people cope with the increased amount of time they find on their hands.

In the present economic climate, government education cuts mean that many of the adult education and creative leisure opportunities will now have to be provided on a voluntary basis. The level of demand increases as the opportunities and options shrink, as people become disenchanted with television and increased petrol prices restrict their mobility.

I would like to see more churches encouraging family nights, providing an opportunity for the whole family — mum, dad, teenagers and youngsters to go *together* to the church for an evening of fellowship, relaxation and fun. A well-equipped and spacious church hall can provide facilities not normally available at home. So often the church has tended to divide, rather than draw together families. In an age when there are so many influences at work to break down the family unit, such an activity night will help to provide a much needed corrective. The programme could include table tennis, badminton, five-a-side football, games for young children, handicrafts (with the whole family making things for the Missionary Sales or Christmas Market), barbecues, 'spic and span' (when we join forces to decorate, clean or garden). Such occasions can be great fun, and particularly effective in bringing the menfolk together.

Gavin Reid, however, sounds a warning bell with regard to activity groups. He observes, '. . . some churches have run social activities hoping that they would "bring people in". But church dances only "bring people in" to church dances . . . when we set up clubs for social and recreational activities we must be quite clear that they will not win people for Christ, but they will end up by attracting people because of their activity and not because of their associations with the church' (Reid 1979:47). I agree that this is frequently the case. Equally, because of the church link many will think there is a hidden trap and just stay away. But when such groups serve to provide a relaxed atmosphere in which Christians and non Christians can mingle, when the leadership is clearly Christian, when the church members are fully involved with everyone fulfilling their role of witness and those equipped to do so exercising the gift of evangelism, then social activity groups can provide the occasion when individuals are befriended and introduced to Christ.

Multiplying congregations

Some churches do not believe in becoming too large. They, therefore, take steps to ensure that they do not grow beyond the 'secondary level'. This is ensured through the imposition of self-limiting structures such as the seating capacity of the church premises or a restricted leadership base. Such a maintenance attitude reflects a static concept of the church.

A more dynamic small church approach is for the congregation, when it grows beyond the 150–200 membership mark, to begin to think about dividing and establishing a new church elsewhere. These can be regarded as completely independent offspring, or as satellite congregations relating to a mother church which continues to provide celebration events, training facilities and personnel and financial assistance.

An alternative approach to establishing satellite congregations is to duplicate services in the one location in order to keep the worshipping congregations to a size in which it is still possible for people to relate to one another. If this seems the best option, it is inadvisable to attempt this by trying to divide the existing congregation into two. Such a strategy frequently destroys the dynamic rather than stimulating further growth. For, whereas previously the church was full, with the crowd serving to attract a crowd, now that the congregation has been split into two congregations meeting at different times, the church has suddenly become half-empty. As a consequence, people become disheartened. To avoid this danger, the second congregation may be developed from a small nucleus of 30–40 people who have the vision and drive to involve themselves in a fresh undertaking. Should this experiment fail to get off the ground the originating group can go back to the parent congregation without any damage having been caused.

Sometimes the motivation to create a second congregation is not lack of space but the need to provide a contrasting style of worship. Some members prefer a traditional form of service, in contrast to younger people, or those with no church-going background, who prefer a more informal and spontaneous style of worship. Tension frequently arises in churches with family service in which the children are present for most or all of the time. The noise and disruptions are off-putting to older people who no longer have the patience with children that they once possessed. They find they need quiet and dignity to enable them to worship.

When services are duplicated because of numbers, or the need to offer alternative types of worship service, careful thought must be given to the increased demand which this extra work places on the leadership. If the service is a straight repeat with only a measured output of nervous energy (as in a liturgical service with a brief, coolly-delivered message) then the one minister may be able to cope. Where there are contrasting styles of worship, it may be necessary to appoint assistants to pastor these congregations.

A multi-congregational church has the drawback of causing a degree of fragmentation. However, this is a preferable option to our impersonal crowd which is too big for people to get to know one another. Its advantage is that it enables the church to offer worship options to meet the needs of members and provide the atmosphere which they find most conducive to worship. It also calls forth a wider range of openings for leaders. The formal church choir, for instance, may not attract the gifted young folk, jazz or pop musician, while the family, youth or newcomers service will provide scope for creative talents to blossom and express themselves in a Christian context.

All-age Sunday School

So far we have considered the 'secondary group' in terms of a midweek activity group and as a Sunday congregation. The secondary group's most significant form in the North

American pattern is in the all-age Sunday School. Families come to church around ten o'clock and divide into a range of classes for the first forty-five minutes to one hour. In addition to the graded classes for children and the crèches and play groups for tinies, there is a range of groups, for young marrieds, singles and senior citizens, all engaged in programmes which relate to their differing interests and stage in life. At the end of an hour all the groups come together for an act of worship with a brief inspirational message.

In Britain we have relied on week-day activities to provide secondary groupings. These supply the needs of young people, the elderly and mothers who are not able to go out to work. But they are not so effective in attracting fathers, working mothers and singles. Furthermore, lack of a regular teaching curriculum means that we have a congregation of adults who are theologically ill-equipped, spiritually under-nourished and lacking the skills to apply Bible teaching to their everyday lives. Brief monologue sermons on isolated topics provide an inadequate diet of teaching, so most Christians who want to grow in their spiritual understanding have to rely on Christian literature; hence the Christian paperback publishing boom.

In recent years a number of churches in England have responded to the problems of pioneering the all-age Sunday School. In doing so they have had to face three major problems. The first is a time constraint which is not shared in North America. Here in Britain there is a tradition of 'the Sunday roast lunch', so that many Mums have half their mind on the oven during the Sunday morning worship. Among middle-class churchgoers in the USA the tradition is to go from church to a restaurant with many going on to a 'ball game' afterwards. Most only go to church once on Sunday, so are prepared for a full Sunday morning programme.

The second problem is a serious lack of teaching

materials to sustain an adult Christian education programme. These constraints probably mean that the all-age
Sunday School may be most applicable to the city-centre
church with resourceful members who can develop their
own curricula, and provide luncheon facilities.

The third problem relates to inadequate facilities in the
form of classrooms for a number of groups of up to sixty
members.

Groups for men

Although figures are not available for the proportion of men
among church attenders in the United Kingdom, for many
churches it is in the region of one quarter to one third. Why
should it be that women outnumber men? Is the explanation that women are more spiritual than men? It seems hard
to justify this biblically. What then is the reason for
the imbalance? I would offer the following five suggestions
which either singly or in various combinations could
explain the fact.

1 In many churches, of all theological persuasions, there is
a dependency style of ministry in which women are more
prepared to acquiesce than are men. To rectify the situation, ministry must be regarded as the activity of the whole
congregation with responsible leadership positions open to
men. If men are shaping policy and deciding on courses of
action at work, they are unlikely to be attracted to churches
where they are blocked from contributing at this level. This
area will be considered at greater length in chapter eight.

2 In the adult programme of most churches the organisations and teaching content are more geared to the needs of
women than of men. The pulpit approach tends to be
individualistic, introspective and domestic in application.
Menfolk come to church with a range of work and family
problems to which the church seldom addresses itself.

3 Men on both sides of industry face moral problems relating to their work which their wives, especially if they are at home or in part-time employment, do not face. They therefore have to weigh up the cost of Christian discipleship, which in some types of employment may be very high.

4 Because women are more often at home when the minister is free to do his visiting – namely during the afternoon – they are contacted more readily. This is especially the case with young wives who are unable to work while the children are on their hands due to inadequate pre-school, play group facilities. Wives therefore get together for coffee chats and invite one another to the church women's fellowships, pram services etc, and so begin to get involved while their husbands remain largely uncontacted. In some cultures the result of winning the women first is to make it all the more difficult for their husbands to follow. The women's circles are then left to pray for their unconverted husbands – as a direct result of this faulty strategy. Ways must therefore be found at an early stage to contact the husbands through other men.

5 When a woman attends church on Sunday she is far more likely than her husband to know other people in the congregation. She will have more contact with the neighbours and is more likely to belong to a 'primary' or 'secondary group' in the church – the Mothers' Union, Women's Fellowship, Coffee Chat, Bright Hour etc. She therefore feels a sense of belonging, which her husband does not share because most likely he does not see people with whom he mixes socially on or off church premises.

In middle-class areas men can frequently be reached through home-based groups. This is especially the case where men are articulate and are accustomed to attending social functions with their wives. It is however less easy in an artisan culture where men find it difficult to join in discussion when wives are present, especially when the subject is 'religion'. In general men are less likely to be attracted to the 'talk shop' kind of meeting as distinct from the 'planning occasion'. They are more attracted to the task-orientated group or to sport pursuits. There should be not one route but many ways into membership of the local church, through a wide variety of activities. People are most likely to get involved through the avenue in which they feel they can contribute most.

One minister in a Hertfordshire parish has a novel method of contacting men effectively. His church holds a monthly evening women's meeting. Having glanced in to see who is there, he and a group of Christians then spend the evening visiting the husbands most of whom are at home child minding! In a Western culture the most difficult, yet strategically most important member of the family to win is the husband. We must therefore resist the temptation to concentrate on mothers and children as an easier option, in the hope that fathers will be won at a later stage. By concentrating more effort on reaching men there is more likelihood that complete families will be won, leading to greater family unity and stability.

TERTIARY GROUPS

Tertiary groups number 175 or more members, with no upper limit on numbers; in fact, the more the merrier. Wagner describes this as the 'celebration' level. He writes, 'One of the things a large church can do well is to celebrate. . . . When a lot of people come together hungry to meet God, a *special* kind of worship experience can occur. That experience is what I want to call "celebration"' (Wagner 1976:97). This is a level of corporate religious experience with which most European Protestant Christians are unfamiliar. The great majority of Protestant churches are small, or if the buildings are large the congregations occupying them are depleted.

In the religious sphere, in contrast to sporting events, we are unaccustomed to crowds. Furthermore, our remnant theology has idealised smallness so that we are suspicious of 'popular' religious events.

When one speaks of the mammoth super-churches to be found in Latin America, Asia and North America, many Europeans respond negatively, declaring, 'we wouldn't want to belong to a church like that!' If we instinctively react adversely at the thought of crowds we should reflect that we are going to have to get used to crowds one day. Consider the Apostle John's vision of life in heaven: 'After this I looked, and there was an enormous crowd – no one could count all the people! They were from every race, tribe, nation and language, and they stood in front of the throne and of the Lamb, dressed in white robes and holding palm branches in their hands. . . .' (Rev. 7:9). From his description it is clear that we will have to get used to crowds one day!

The celebration event is not however postponed until then. It has great significance for church life today. It comes as a great surprise to many British Christians to learn that there are between seven and nine times as many people in church on Sunday as at professional soccer matches on Saturday afternoon. We do not recognise our numerical strength because we are scattered throughout 51,000 Protestant and Catholic churches in the United Kingdom, with little opportunity or inclination to gather together in strength.

Celebration expresses identity
'The individual believer must be able to feel himself a part of the larger corporate unity of the people of God' (Snyder 1975:106). Our fragmentation horizontally into different congregations and vertically into denominations has destroyed our sense of 'peoplehood'. Visitors from other congregations are treated almost as though they were adherents of another

religion and no concern of ours. Loyalty to *our* church or *our* denomination can so easily take precedence over our loyalty to Christ.

The people of God in the Old Testament preserved their identity not simply through their distinctive way of life, but through their sense of 'belonging', heightened through regular pilgrimages. In March/April as many as could make the journey went to Jerusalem for the feast of the Passover. Seven weeks later the crowds gathered once more for Pentecost, which marked the end of the grain harvest. September/October was heralded with a fanfare marking the Jewish New Year. Special celebrations were followed by the solemn Day of Atonement when the nation confessed their sin and asked for cleansing. A few days later the people observed the Festival of Shelters – a national camp-out, when they built shelters of branches to remind themselves of their wanderings in the desert and of God's provision for his people. This came at the end of the olive and grape harvests. Israel was a nation of pilgrims, not hermits. They loved to congregate to express their identity. Such gatherings helped to keep scattered clans together. This was needed in a hilly terrain which tended to divide communities.

Celebration provides inspiration

It can be a moving experience to be part of an enormous crowd. When the crowds converged on Jerusalem there was a sense of occasion and expectations were heightened. The significance of the celebration event today is recognised more within the Catholic than the Protestant tradition. In Southern Europe, Poland and throughout Latin America popular pilgrimages capture the imagination of masses of people, causing hundreds of thousands to gather at popular shrines.

Yet, celebration doesn't just happen. It requires a 'charisma' of leadership. Many an ecumenical occasion has gone

off like a damp squib through lack of ability to handle such
an event or understand the dynamics of the occasion. The
dignitaries drone on, and the choir render their anthems
with esoteric detachment. Such events are endured rather
than enjoyed.

For the celebration event to fulfil its inspirational role
there must be a sense of occasion, with individuals gifted to
hold the attention of the crowd, and musicians spiritually
motivated to lift the entire gathering in worship.

Speaking of the church where he worships regularly,
Lake Avenue Congregational Church, Peter Wagner
declares 'that 52 times a year 2,500 people go home to
Sunday dinner feeling that they have just had an important
meeting with Almighty God and that because of it they are
not the same' (Wagner 76:59). He also recognises that to
achieve this a great deal of work goes on behind the scenes,
for good worship doesn't just happen. On this scale it
normally depends on the consecrated professionalism of a
lot of people with a wide range of gifts.

Here in Europe where there are very few, if any, Protestant congregations to match this size, when 'celebration'
has been experienced it has been outside the local church
in the context of a city-wide gathering of Christians for a
renewal worship experience or an evangelistic crusade.

Celebration crystallises intention
One of the reasons why worship presentations such as
'Come Together' proved hard to follow, and why the charismatic renewal meetings are difficult to sustain, is that they
lack the structure to implement the expectations aroused.
The celebration event can only serve to supplement what is
happening at the grass roots level; it cannot substitute for
what is not happening. So often people return to their
locations to continue doing what they are accustomed to
doing. What happened at the celebration left a warm glow
but was as remote as a day trip to heaven!

Celebration restores confidence
Elijah felt that he was struggling on alone. He was unaware of the existence of 7,000 others who had not succumbed to pressure to worship Baal. If our experience of the church is limited to the one or two places where we have regularly worshipped, then we will tend to imagine that all the rest are like these – or worse! Here in the United Kingdom it is estimated that about five million people are in church on Sunday. When we make the effort to meet with the many other Christians in our area we begin to realise that we are not just a surviving handful, but a numerous army with enough manpower to make an impact on the entire nation.

Celebration establishes visibility
In Brazil and Chile the indigenous Pentecostal movements have developed an effective structure for church growth especially suited to urban life. People are coming in their millions to the big cities in search of work, schooling and housing. These new arrivals are contacted by the church and house groups in the shanty towns and new housing developments. They are welcomed by people like themselves into those small support groups. Then at the week-end they go to the mammoth mother church where they meet tens of thousands of fellow believers. Those who have been attracted from the country by the bright lights of the city are delighted to find that the company they have joined has its prestige place among those bright lights. The 25,000 seater São Paulo Church and the 15,000 seater Jotabeche Methodist Pentecostal Church give the denomination visibility. The city centre streets of the big Latin American cities are crowded during the week-end so that the Christians converging on their mother churches cannot go unnoticed.

Crowds also attract the attention of the media. Around the world hundreds of millions of people have seen the Pope address a sea of faces stretching to the horizon during one of his Papal visits. Large churches in North America use their financial resources to buy television time and their professional resources to sustain a series of programmes, which would be beyond the capacity of the small church. In some urban situations the only ways into the home are often via the television or the telephone. Home calling is rendered very difficult by the security systems installed in apartment blocks.

In the United Kingdom time cannot be bought on the commercial television channels. It can only be earned by the quality of the communication or the significance of the event. A programme of celebration events which had the whole-hearted backing and support of Christians in the regions where they were to be held would, I believe, attract media coverage, if not at national level then certainly through the local radio station and press. This would serve to replace the one-sided presentation of the outmoded, irrelevant and dwindling Church so often portrayed in current affairs and light entertainment programmes.

For the church of two hundred plus members, 'celebration' level of worship can be experienced at congregational level, provided that it is not dispersed in a seven-hundred-and-fifty-seater building. Most European and North American churches have a membership below the two hundred level. This being the case, the 'celebration' event has to be staged at a multi-congregational level, organised denominationally or ecumenically. One town in Kent which has run a programme of such meetings on a Saturday night once a month from time to time attracted a crowd of 600–900 people. On one occasion the police station rang the organisers to be kept informed of future meetings so that they could provide traffic control!

The celebration level becomes significant when a fresh surge of spiritual vitality is being experienced within the local church, when churches are open to each other to be mutually encouraged by each other's faith (Rom. 1:11, 12), and when they have a united evangelistic vision to share the Good News with their locality. But if these conditions have not developed then the celebration can prove more of a diversion than provide a dynamic.

INCORPORATING NEWCOMERS INTO MEMBERSHIP

It is not sufficient for growing churches simply to establish a three-tier system of primary, secondary and tertiary groups and then just leave individuals to find their way around. There needs to be a clearly defined structure which shows how the various groups relate to one another in the achievement of overall objectives. Each group must see its own specialist contribution within the context of a wider strategy and framework. The leaders must have a vision which reaches beyond their group activities, otherwise the groups will begin to compete and this will only serve to fragment the church's life rather than provide the building-blocks.

A number of larger churches have tackled the problem of incorporating new people by forming a *Welcome Group* to which those who are not yet committed are invited. This will include those who are considering the claims of Christ upon their lives and those who have transferred from other churches.

The Rev. Paul Berg of Christ Church, Clifton, a residential suburb of Bristol, runs eight such Christian Basics Groups a year which have resulted in a steady trickle of enquirers. These then go on to a beginners' group before being integrated into one of the neighbourhood groups. A similar scheme is operated at St Thomas's, Crookes, an inner city district of Sheffield. The Rev. Robert Warren reports that they run five six-week courses a year with an average attendance of between twelve and fifteen. The new members are then introduced to one of their twenty-four area-based home groups.

In what ways does the Welcome Group differ from the Membership Class? It provides an immediate 'half-way house' for the enquirer who is not yet at the stage of wanting to commit himself. There are those who were baptised in infancy and formally received into membership in adolescence without any personal commitment. Soon afterwards they quickly fell away to live in a spiritual wilderness during the disruptive years of 18–28, when they went from college to work, left home, changed houses, got married and began a family. Then when they settle down with family responsibilities they come back to church, and come to personal faith. How do such people *join* their local church when they have already been through denominational membership procedures years before? The Welcome Group provides an opportunity to re-lay foundations. As for those who are transferring from other churches, it provides an opportunity for them to familiarise themselves with the spiritual priorities of their new church and to learn about its objectives and organisations. New Christians in the group and those who come to faith or wish to make further enquiries can then proceed to the Membership Class. Those restored to membership or who transfer from elsewhere can be welcomed immediately into the congregation by publicly extending the right hand of fellowship.

Considering the high lapse rate in many churches, as much emphasis needs to be placed on their restoration as on contacting non-members. Lyle Schaller suggests four ways of strengthening the notion of membership (Schaller 1978b:219, 220).

1 Treat the transfer of members as a celebration event and not just a paper routine. The new person or family should be publicly welcomed.
2 Each member is asked to come forward and publicly reaffirm his membership vows annually.

3 Establish a probationary membership which is a pre-
   liminary step before achieving full membership.
4 Develop clearly stated expectations of the responsibility of membership in that congregation in operational
   terms.

The Rev. Jeffrey Yates of Bamford Chapel, a United
Reformed Church near Rochdale, Lancs. also lays great
stress on clear new members procedures. His church,
located in a growing middle-class area, sees a high level
of response as a result of their house-to-house visitation
programme, their range of recreational activities and lively
Sunday services. During the past four years 250 people have
come into the church, seventy of whom had no previous
church membership. They are prepared for membership in
classes led by the minister. As an additional point of contact
four new couples are invited to the manse once a month.

As we saw in the previous chapter there does seem to be
a correlation between church growth and the existence of
primary groups. However, with few exceptions it seems that
the new church members are not being recruited by these
groups. Rather, the groups provide the opportunity for the
Christian community to develop so that when they gather
on Sunday there is a new quality of friendliness, acceptance,
trust and 'family feeling'. This sense of community communicates itself to the newcomer who then wants to come
again on another Sunday and eventually gets further
involved, until he also finds himself within a primary or
secondary group.

Most groups have not proved effective so far in the area of
evangelism because they consist of groups of long-standing
church members with a programme designed to meet their
needs. These may not be appropriate for the enquirer or
beginner in the Christian life. The best group for the nurture of the new believer is a group composed largely of
people who are just starting out.

New churches which have grown through neighbourhood
groups eventually find that these groups have moved so far
away from 'base' that they have opened up a communication gap and as a result they no longer attract new people
so readily. There are two ways around this problem. One
is to hold the occasional evangelistic group meeting, with
any converts then being escorted to the 'Welcome Group'
for the duration of the course and then brought back into
the group where having been given the basic they will be
better able to cope. The other way is to be continually
forming new groups of new Christians led by people
who can relate to the perceptions and problems which they
face.

EVANGELISM AT ALL THREE LEVELS

We conclude this chapter with a brief look at the evangelistic significance of the primary, secondary and tertiary
groups, for each has a distinctive role to play in a total
evangelistic strategy.

Evangelism in primary groups

The small neighbourhood group can provide an ideal base
for contact visiting, that is, identifying the seekers, and also
for the following-up of contacts in a home visitation programme. For this to happen, church members in these
groups must have both concern for and contact with their
neighbours. Regrettably many churches have an over-full
programme based on a 'come-to-us' philosophy which
keeps their committed people so busy that they have no
time to develop friendships in their immediate community.
A large church has the advantage of providing a full and
varied programme, but church members must be disciplined enough to be selective, and in particular, to resist
pressure to support those activities which appear to have
long since outlived their usefulness.

Primary groups which have been preoccupied solely with

the spiritual nurture and social intercourse of the existing membership need to be gently but firmly challenged to face their evangelistic responsibilities. Within every group each member is called to fulfil the role of witness. The group must also seek to discover whether one or more of their members appears to have the gift of evangelism. If not, then it may be necessary to import someone who is gifted in this area to be present when they hold an evangelistic event.

Evangelism in a small group situation is most appropriate among people with whom we have had previous contact and experience a measure of compatibility. The people we decide to invite may be either neighbours or work colleagues, etc. When the small group consists of complete strangers it is extremely difficult to break the ice and to conduct a conversation at a deeply personal level.

Conversely, where people know one another, the small group situation provides a positive, informal atmosphere for frank speaking.

While the overall programme for the outreach meeting should be informal and flexible, it is advisable to have a well-thought-out conversation opener. Some begin with a brief statement, lasting for no more than ten minutes, of the central issues to be discussed, after which opinions are invited leading into a dialogue situation. This part of the programme may either be conducted by a spokesman for the group or be in the hands of an invited, outside speaker. Others prefer to base their discussion on a specific passage of Scripture. If this approach is adopted it is essential that everyone in the group has the same version of the Bible so that page numbers can be given, and people are not confused by chapters and verses and a variety of renderings. Instead of using whole Bibles some groups have individual Gospels or even brief Scripture selection leaflets for use in such evangelistic groups. The advantage of this approach is that invited non-Christians can then take the booklets or pamphlets home with them to continue to consider the passage studied at the meeting.

When basing the evangelistic programme on a text of Scripture it is important to let the passage speak for itself. Rather than drawing up a list of prepared questions, an alternative approach is simply to ask individuals in the group to say what the passage has said to them. Having invited one person to express an opinion or voice a response, find out from others in the group if the passage made the same impact on them. This avoids the problem of posing questions to which there is a 'right' or 'wrong' answer or which introduce issues which are of no immediate concern among the individuals present.

One rapidly growing house fellowship considered that one of the secrets of their success in attracting new people was their refusal to precipitate an 'us' and 'them' situation. They included newcomers as 'insiders', leaving them to discover for themselves that they had not yet arrived at the point of commitment or level of experience described by others in the group. By that time they had picked up enough knowledge to make a meaningful decision.

The handling of evangelism in small groups requires particular leadership skills and sensitivity on the part of Christians in the group. In order to avoid any appearance of undue pressure the non-Christians should outnumber the Christians present. Some people with experience in this field would also recommend that the meeting be held in the home of an interested person who was not yet a committed Christian or church member. It is important that the Christians present be as ready to listen attentively as to speak themselves. We must look for opportunities to affirm all that the other person is saying rather than look for points of confrontation. When people come to groups aware of their personal needs, they are not so much looking for answers to their problems as for people who can help them. The great advantage of the small group is that it provides the opportunity for two-way communication on the basis of shared experience.

Only occasionally do individuals come to the act of commitment to Christ during the actual meeting. It is therefore important to conclude the programme at the pre-arranged time, allowing opportunity for those who want to talk further to do so. This may be the time when someone will take the life-changing step of faith. Others may come to the point of decision during a subsequent contact when members of the group are in personal conversations with an invited person.

It is important not to overstep the mark in our eagerness to influence our neighbour and friends for Christ. We must always leave the conversation where we can take it up again on a subsequent occasion. Those with little or no contact with the Christian message and community may take months or years to be won. We must therefore think in terms of both a short and long-term strategy.

Evangelism in secondary groups
The small face-to-face primary group may not provide the best environment into which to invite the comparative stranger, or be suitable in areas where it is not the custom to open one's home to the neighbourhood. Furthermore, some people would recoil at the thought of being exposed in a small group. They may find conversation difficult or are fearful of their ignorance being exposed. This, incidentally, is one reason why those who are long-time office bearers in the church but have little understanding of the fundamentals of the faith and no personal commitment to Jesus Christ as Lord, keep at a safe distance!

For both the types of people mentioned above the secondary group may provide a more relaxed and gradual pathway to Christian commitment. People are invited to join with Christians to engage in activities which already interest them. As they work and play alongside each

other, openings will eventually arise during the course
of conversation for personal testimony in specific areas
of life and for an explanation of the content of the Good
News.

The secondary group is small enough for personal relationships to develop between members and for subgroups to
form spontaneously. Yet the secondary group is also large
enough for the new person not to feel himself the focus of
attention. He can therefore progress at his own pace. Many
people in coming to faith do not follow a steady path of
progress. Usually they fluctuate, taking three steps forward
and two back. Sometimes they may encounter a 'sticking-
point', and if too much pressure is applied to drag them
forward they may turn tail. Such long-term response patterns are more easily handled in the larger group with
which the individual can merge.

In order that a secondary group may realise its evangelistic potential the leader must exercise pastoral care over the
members who in turn must function effectively in their role
of witness. Furthermore, at least one person in the group
should have the gift of evangelism.

Evangelism in the tertiary groups
Some people who shrink from contact either with a primary
or secondary group are prepared to listen while lost in a big
crowd. They wish, for the time being at any rate, to be left
alone to come to their own conclusions. Then there are
those who are impressed by the colourful, big-scale event,
because they are gregarious by nature or larger-than-life
personalities. Such people are more likely to respond to the
'celebration event'. Such occasions provide the opportunity
for church members to invite their personal friends to something out of the ordinary, and for the church to circularise
the institutional fringe. Within the community at large
a well-publicised celebration event makes an impression,
rouses curiosity and becomes a topic of conversation. Such

an impression is considerably enhanced by good media coverage.

However, effective celebration evangelism depends upon widespread support from the local churches. It must be a scaled-up version of what they are regularly doing at local level. If the celebration event is no more than a substitute for, rather than a supplement to what should be happening in individual congregations, then it will prove to be an expensive diversion. Regrettably this has been the case in much of our experience in mass evangelism in Britain during the last thirty years. Nevertheless, when such events are an integral part of an ongoing strategy they can play a highly significant role.

Large churches which operate Sunday by Sunday at the celebration level need to give a great deal of careful thought as to how the visitor is to be identified and welcomed and how the enquirer is to be followed up. In this area many of the large churches in the United States are more efficient than their European counterparts. It is the custom in some for everyone present to fill in an attendance card, so that absentees can be spotted and newcomers identified. These completed cards are either placed in the offering plate or passed to the end of the row for the sidesmen to collect. New people are then contacted by phone during the next twenty-four hours and visited that week by a lay person in the church.

While I know of no church on this side of the Atlantic which has succeeded in persuading church attenders to fill up a card on a regular basis, a number use visitor's cards with varying degrees of success. Where this system is adopted, the minister welcomes the newcomer. He should hold up the card to identify it from the other literature which may be in the pew rack. If the system proves to be effective it is recommended that the cards be kept tidily in a special holder on the pew lodge or seat back to prevent becoming dog-eared or buried under the hymn-books, pew

Bibles and service sheets. The wording needs to be friendly
and minimal. One church has devised the following wording:

> We are a large family, and it's easy to get lost in the
> crowd. Please help us to get to know you by supplying
> your name, address and telephone number.
> Name ....
> Address ....
> Tel. No. ....
> We sincerely hope that you have enjoyed worshipping
> with us.

Having filled in the card the visitor must be given clear
instructions as to how to hand it in. If it is to be handed to
the stewards (or sidesmen), they should wear an identifying
badge, and be given training in what to do when they are
handed a card. They should welcome the visitor warmly
and introduce him to another member of the congregation with whom he is most likely to have something in
common. An increasing number of churches follow their
services with coffee, which provides a further ready-made
opportunity for a newcomer to be introduced to other
church members.

The visitor's card should be left in the vestry or parish
office for the minister to see and to be handed promptly to
the appropriate home-group leader. The person responsible
should establish contact that week, to chat about the
various activities which may be relevant to the needs of that
person. People don't like feeling that they are being
stampeded, so the visitor must be sensitive to the person's
initial level of enthusiasm and commitment.

In order that the church leadership may be aware of new
people joining the church and provide an opportunity
to meet them, St Andrew's, Chorleywood, in the North
London commuter belt, has initiated an evening occasion
when those who have linked up with the church during the

past year are invited to a reception to meet the clergy and the Parochial Church Council and to hear about the church, its activities and its plans for the future. This occasion is valued as much by the council members as by the newcomers.

Evangelism also has its rightful place within the main worship service. Occasions such as Christmas, Easter, Mothering Sunday, Harvest and Remembrance Day provide opportunities for a clear and winsome presentation of the claims of Christ to people who are unlikely to be in church at other times of the year. I recall visiting a West Midlands Anglican Church one Remembrance Day. The minister spoke to a packed congregation of man's desire for peace and of that peace which the world cannot comprehend but which Christ alone can offer. If people wanted to know more they were invited to take a leaflet which outlined how to know God's peace. Forty people asked for one on their way out. Many people come to church uttering a silent cry for help, yet leave without being given the opportunity to be heard.

Evangelism should be built into the church's programme at every level, using a variety of methods, so that by the use of all means we might at least succeed in saving some.

SUMMARY

This chapter has argued in some detail the need for appropriate and extendable structures to facilitate growth. Churches with a regular attendance of more than sixty must begin to develop primary small-group structures. Congregations of more than 150 must pay close attention to the need for secondary in addition to primary groupings. They may decide to plant new churches or to subdivide the existing congregation into several worship, educational and fellowship groups. If they fail to develop an adequate structure they will soon see an increasing proportion attending Sunday worship services without making relationships with others in the church, which will be to their own spiritual detriment and that of the church. The desire for and experience of renewal does not obviate the need for facilitating structures.

Examine your congregational roll to ascertain how many are in primary and secondary groupings. Are the groups to which they belong enabling them to identify their gifts and to contribute to one or more of the many ministries of your church? Who are excluded from any of the groups, and for what reasons? How many of your groups have proved to be effective avenues into the fellowship of your church in the past year? Let us seek a variety of ways to realise the growth potential of the many kinds of groups in the life of the church.

CHAPTER EIGHT

Equipping and mobilising

Church growth cannot be sustained unless the laity are mobilised to fulfil their distinctive ministries both in the Church and the world. The problem of how to motivate and sustain lay participation concerns many, if not the majority, of church leaders. Someone has indelicately commented that the trouble with the Church as a body is that it is all mouth and bottom! The majority of church members have little understanding of their place and function as members within the body of Christ. For them belonging to a church means no more than turning up, singing up and paying up. Developing an adequate theology of the laity is an urgent task which faces the Church. Nothing less than a lay people's liberation movement will be adequate to release the Church's manpower resources to meet the challenges and opportunities in the world today.

The missionary and ecumenical theologian Hendrik Kraemer observes that while the Reformation emphasised the doctrine of the priesthood of all believers, it failed to give the concept an ongoing practical expression. 'In spite of the fact that the layman's place of responsibility in the church and the principle of the universal priesthood of believers were strong ingredients in the Reformation Movement, in respect of Continental Europe it is largely true that, after the consolidation of the Reformation in various countries, the laity receded into the background and the ministry or clergy, although with different

motivations and in different forms, was again established as
the "office" and body which represent the Church'
(Kraemer 1958:25). We might add that this clericalism
was not restricted to Continental Europe but crept through
Britain as well. The priest moved from the altar to the
pulpit, but the people remained undisturbed in their
pews!

From the Catholic side Yves Congar also emphasises
the priestly and apostolic role of the whole people of God.
'Lay people, each one according to the conditions of his life
and his state in the Mystical Body, truly bring something
to God's Temple and help to build it up. It is in and
through the life of the faithful (and of the clergy as members
of the faithful) that Christ's saving powers are made
manifest within the dimensions of history and of the world,
so as to bring back to God all the richness of his creation,
of which Christ is the first-born and the king' (Congar
1959:109).

As a consequence of the contribution of the lay apostolic movement 'Catholic Action' and the influence of
Congar among other Catholic theologians, the role of the
laity found its way on to the agenda of the Second Vatican
Council. 'This was the first time in the history of the
Church that a council had concerned itself with lay
people as such' (Schillebeeckx 1973:106). In the resulting
document, *The Dogmatic Constitution on the Church*, lay
people are described as 'all Christian believers outside
the members of the priesthood of holy orders and of the
religious state recognised by the church; those Christian
believers namely who have been embodied into Christ by
baptism and set up as the people of God, who participate in
Christ's priestly, prophetic and royal office in their own way
and who consequently for their part carry out the mission of
the whole Christian people in the church and in the world'
(4,31). We see here a significant move away from a paternal-
istic attitude towards the laity, with a growing recognition

of their importance if the Church is to fulfil her mission in the world.

With such an emphasis placed upon the laity in both Protestant and Catholic theology how is it that the majority of lay people still keep to the side-lines?

WHY PEOPLE ARE RELUCTANT TO GET INVOLVED

There are a variety of reasons for the serious lack of lay participation in many churches. In attempting to deal with this problem, ministers and church councils must be prepared to face the causes within their particular situation. The views not only of the clergy but also of the lay leaders must be taken into account, and the situation must be perceived from the perspective of those who 'follow' (and maybe are excluded from participation) as well as from the appointed leadership. An accurate and balanced assessment can only be reached by examining the situation from all sides, in an open and frank spirit. In order to create a positive atmosphere in which there is the possibility of changes for the better, people must be as ready to affirm one another's strengths as to expose weaknesses. Frank speaking is a characteristic of true friendship. 'A friend means well, even when he hurts you. But when an enemy puts his arm around your shoulder – watch out!' (Prov. 27:6).

The following represent the principal causes of lack of lay involvement:

The majority of the congregation have not yet placed their lives under the lordship of Jesus Christ. This is the problem of 'nominality' which to some degree or other afflicts almost all churches. Nominal Christians are Christians in name only. They are second, third, or fourth generation Christians without a personal experience of God's saving grace. They are present in church largely for reasons of historical association or cultural conformity rather than out of personal commitment. They lack a basis of belief and a vital personal faith. In such a situation there will be no spiritually significant growth until the minister provides a sound basis of biblical teaching, coupled to a life-related, personal challenge to commitment.

Many churchgoers undervalue the corporate nature of the Christian faith. This is especially true for Western Christians for whom religion is essentially a personal and private matter. People must be encouraged to establish relationships with other members in the body before they can begin to function through the fulfilment of a role within the life of the Christian community. It is usually a futile exercise to try and encourage people to do a job in the church through a general announcement to the congregation when the majority of those listening to the exhortation are on little more than nodding acquaintanceship with each other. Relationship precedes function. As people feel accepted so they gain in confidence to contribute.

Many churches have no clearly defined aims and in consequence no cohesive programme. Some congregations would be hard pressed if asked to give an agreed statement on the reason for their existence. Their activities serve to conceal a lack of purpose rather than to achieve one. 'A congregation without specific goals may be compared to an apathetic football team engaged in a "game" on a field without goal lines. The players are content to kick and pass the ball but no one tries to score. If one were to cross the line where the goal ought to be no one would be sufficiently interested to record the points' (Curry 1968:63). The participants in a 'kick-around' become uninterested after a time, and such an activity is unlikely to attract others to see what is happening and to move from the touch-line on to the field of play.

Lay people may not be convinced of the relevance of the church's programme or of its chances of success. Many churches saunter along with pedestrian programmes which lack imagination and challenge. People of ability and vision feel frustrated and don't want to get involved. This is especially the case in churches where the leaders insist on repeating events which have not worked in the past either because they have shut their eyes to the results or haven't bothered to consider them. No one wants to be identified with a lost cause. Those with the insight to see what will not work and to appreciate why it will not, need to get alongside those with vision to picture what might work, and to redirect those with dedication from the futile to the more promising!

Sometimes the obstacle lies more in the absence of leadership skills than in the inadequacy of the programme ideas. If this is the case then the church must take urgent steps to extend its base of leadership.

Lay people may be discouraged by their ministers from taking leadership initiative. There are some clergy who regard themselves as omnicompetent and resent any lay initiative. They regard the congregation as little more than customers and consumers, whom they are called to satisfy. Members who do become involved are largely confined to practical matters relating to the running of the church as an institution and the care of its property. They have little place in formulating policies, or in establishing objectives with regard to the spiritual ministries of the church. Their expertise is regarded as being principally in such areas as property maintenance, raising funds and running organisational activities.

Lay people may be excluded by the established lay leadership from joining their number. This is especially so in small churches which can often be dominated by a small tight-knit group of powerful personalities. As the church develops it begins to attract people who are more able and who are viewed as posing a challenge to the existing leadership. Instead of welcoming those with leadership gifts the church committee or board of deacons closes ranks. The newcomers are thereby relegated to the sidelines and may eventually move elsewhere where their gifts will be recognised and used and their desire to contribute can be satisfied.

Lay people may be reluctant to get involved because they fear that their willingness will be abused. Many churches find themselves having to sustain a programme which is too large for their available manpower. The short-cut expedient to deal with the situation is to make yet more demands on the already over-committed. Such a practice is self-defeating in the long term. Not only does it exhaust those who shoulder the additional responsibilities; it also warns off those who might otherwise have offered their services, but who suspect that they in turn would end up in the same situation.

THE RESOURCES WHICH THE LORD SUPPLIES
If the church is to grow and move forward in effective mission, then it must solve the unemployment problem within its ranks. It must deal with the underlying causes whether they be in the area of clerical domination or lay abdication. It is not that jobs do not exist or that there is no work to be done. The church urgently needs to mobilise its manpower to tackle more effectively its global commission. Lloyd Perry exhorts the clergy, 'We must learn to look at the laity as people of potential rather than people with problems' (1977:106). People with problems help the minister to feel wanted. To regard them as people with potential might make him consider them as a threat. Despite all the teaching of the New Testament on ministry as the function of the total membership there is still

a persistent tendency to make a dichotomy between the sacred and the secular. The 'spiritual' ministry is the concern of the clergy, while the 'practical matters' are largely cared for by the laity.

As we have already seen, lay people with initiative and a desire to get involved often find their way blocked. 'Laymen are often disillusioned, dissatisfied and disorientated, because they cannot figure out how to become vitally involved in a church which appears to be merely struggling to survive rather than seeking to fulfil a God-given mission' (Lloyd Perry 1977:107). It is our concern in this chapter to seek ways to identify and bring together in a creative relationship the full range of resources that God has bestowed upon his church so that it can function imaginatively and effectively.

The Lord has not left it to his Church to generate her own resources. From the moment of his ascension into Heaven he did not expect his followers to go it alone. They had more than the stimulus of their fading memories to rely upon, and those whom they would recruit would be given more than second-hand evidence. The Lord keeps in vital day-to-day contact with the entire operation because he is present with them by his Holy Spirit. For this reason he had instilled in his disciples that it was to their advantage that he was going away (John 16:7). In the future he would be with them far more intimately and universally by his Spirit who would indwell every believer. In practical terms this stupendous truth means that the risen Lord is not merely masterminding a grand strategy at Supreme Headquarters level, but is also present with the smallest group and the most isolated individual.

The Holy Spirit is able to fill each believer and every Christian community with power so that they can become channels for the implementation of the divine will. Such first-hand experience will enable them to become prime witnesses to a doubting, questioning and accusing world.

They will bear witness to the fact of the Lord's crucifixion and resurrection as recorded by apostolic testimony, and from their own experience they will speak of the power of the gospel at work in their own lives (Acts 1:8). They will both point people to Christ and invite them to join their company. A spirit-filled community is able to communicate powerfully. But for the Church to fulfil adequately such a witnessing role it must be able to speak from first-hand experience. 'What we have seen and heard we announce to you also, so that you will join with us in the fellowship that we have with the Father and with his Son Jesus Christ' (1 John 1:3). The 'fellowship' of which John speaks is much more than human comradeship, it is the communion in the Holy Spirit, who indwells each member, and binds them together as adopted children in the family of God (Rom. 8:16; Gal. 4:6).

The Holy Spirit shapes our character
The evidence of the presence of the Holy Spirit in a person's life is to be seen not primarily in sensational exploits but in Christ-like character and conduct. His instantaneous work of regeneration is followed by his gradual, progressive work of sanctification. This character formation is described as 'the fruit of the Spirit' in Galatians 5:22. His life within us produces discernible qualities. Paul lists these as, 'love, joy, peace, patience, kindness, goodness, faithfulness, gentleness and self-control' (Gal. 5:22,23 NIV). Such qualities are in marked contrast to the 'works of the flesh' which Paul identifies in the verses immediately preceding.

Fruit tells us two things about a tree. First, it enables us to identify what kind of tree it is. Many people may fail to recognise an apple tree by the shape of the leaf, or the appearance of the blossom. But all doubt is removed when the fruit begins to form. The appearance of the apples enables the least expert to identify it unmistakably as an apple tree. That is also the way to tell a true prophet from a false one, according to our Lord's teaching. 'Watch out for false prophets. They come to you in sheep's clothing, but inwardly they are ferocious wolves. By their fruit you will recognise them. Do people pick grapes from thornbushes, or figs from thistles?' (Matt. 7:15, 16 NIV). The clear answer is 'No'.

Secondly, the appearance of the fruit tells us something about the health of the tree. A well-nourished tree produces an abundant crop of large, juicy fruit. A diseased tree produces unhealthy and inedible fruit. 'Likewise every good tree bears good fruit, but a bad tree bears bad fruit. A good tree cannot bear bad fruit, and a bad tree cannot bear good fruit. Every tree that does not bear good fruit is cut down and thrown into the fire. Thus, by their fruit you will recognise them.' (Matt. 7:17–20).

It is no wonder then that the letters of the New Testament lay such great stress on the character of the Christian and on the personal qualities which are essential for Christian leadership (1 Tim. 3; Titus 1). The fruit of the Holy Spirit provides the Christian's mark of identity and guarantee of authenticity.

The fruit is the evidence of the 'abundant life' which Christ came to give (John 10:10). Such life cannot simply be contained by the tree, it must burst out in fruit. This represents the give-away life of the Church. It is life which others can pick and sample. The fruit contains the seeds which can in turn germinate in the receptive soil of other people's lives. Without such fruit the Church's activism may produce congregational enlargement but it will not be authentic church *growth*. Above all else growth depends on the quality of life. A barren tree may succeed in gathering birds on the leaves of its activism, but it will never produce saplings, for that requires seed-bearing fruit.

While Peter does not use Paul's phrase, 'fruit of the Holy Spirit' he has a similar list of qualities which are the evidence of 'God's divine power'. Having listed them he goes on to say, 'These are the qualities you need, and if you have them in abundance, they will make you active and effective in your knowledge of our Lord Jesus Christ' (2 Pet. 1:3–8). The secret of effectiveness lies not in a frenzy of activity but in the fruit of character.

The Holy Spirit equips us for service

Ministry, as envisaged in the New Testament, is not the prerogative of one man, or an élite corps. Ministry is the function of the whole people of God. Our call to serve Christ entails a call to serve one another in the Church, and extends to meeting the needs of our neighbour in the world. 'Neighbour' is not a narrow concept, but includes all with whom we come into contact.

Every Christian shares in the mission of the Church. He does this in a general way through his personal witness, which he should be constantly bearing as he takes Christ to all the world. In addition he is equipped by the Holy Spirit to fulfil specialist roles, for God's mission entails a vast range of activities.

During the past decade there have been a number of excellent books dealing with the subject of gifts of the Spirit. All we will attempt to do here is to raise the most common questions which are still in the minds of many Christians, and give a brief answer to each. For a fuller discussion the reader is advised to consult one of the books listed in the bibliography.

GIFTS FOR SERVICE

What is a 'gift of the Spirit'?

The *Dictionary of New Testament Theology* edited by Colin Brown defines 'charisma', the principal word used by Paul to denote a 'gift of the Spirit' as, 'The manifold outworking of the one grace in individual Christians through the one Spirit' (Vol. 2 p.121 H.-H. Esser). Arnold Bittlinger provides

the following definition. 'The concept of charisma is understood in the New Testament as "the concrete realisation
of divine grace". It characterises a function – whether
"ordinary or extraordinary" – that serves to build up the
body of Christ' (Bittlinger 1974:16). For Peter Wagner,
whose special contribution to the subject has been specifically to relate the topic of spiritual gifts to church growth, 'a
spiritual gift is a special attribute given by the Holy Spirit
to every member of the Body of Christ according to God's
grace for use within the context of the Body' (Wagner
1979b:42). From these definitions we can see that the gifts
are related to the grace of God. As such they are neither
acquired skills nor are they rewards for devotion or service.
They are given by God according to his sovereign will.
Following one of the lists of gifts in Paul's letters he goes on
to say, 'All these are the work of one and the same Spirit,
and he gives them to each man, just as he determines'
(1 Cor. 12:11).

Who are given gifts of the Spirit?

The New Testament makes it quite clear that the gifts are
distributed throughout the entire body of believers. Every
Christian has at least one of the gifts and many Christians
have more than one. However, no individual Christian has
by any means *all* of the gifts of the Spirit. Unlike the
manifold fruit, the gifts are dispersed among the body.

1 Corinthians 12:7	'To *each* is given a manifestation of the Spirit for the common good' (RSV)
Ephesians 4:7	'But grace was given to *each* of us, according to the measure of Christ's gift' (RSV)
1 Peter 4:10	'As *each* has received a gift, employ it for one another, as good stewards of God's varied grace' (RSV)

This underlines the truth that no Christian is self-sufficient. We all need each other as other members of the Body of Christ. 'So, the eye cannot say to the hand, "I don't need you!" Nor can the head say to the feet, "Well, I don't need you!"' (1 Cor. 12:21). There is a mutual dependency at every level with everybody making his or her distinctive contribution to the whole. The gifts are given irrespective of sex, age, social standing, intellectual level, or academic attainment.

How many gifts of the Spirit are there?
Many of the books on the subject written from the classical Pentecostal position speak in terms of nine gifts, which neatly match the nine-fold fruit of the Spirit described in Galatians 5. Nine gifts are in fact listed in 1 Corinthians 12:8–12. But towards the conclusion of the same chapter still more gifts are mentioned (1 Cor. 12:28–30). In Romans 12 yet another list is to be found, and Ephesians 4 lists five leadership roles which are described as the gifts of the risen Christ to his Church. 1 Pet. 4:10–11 mentions two broad categories of preaching and service. Even then the list is not exhausted, because in other places in the New Testament reference is made to isolated gifts. When we turn to the Old Testament, mention is made of the Holy Spirit coming upon individuals to equip them to perform specific acts of service to fulfil the divine will. It is, therefore, evident that none of the five main lists of gifts is meant to be exhaustive. John Stott comments that, 'No single gift occurs in all five lists, and thirteen gifts occur only in one of the five lists. The arrangement seems almost haphazard, as if to draw attention to the fact that each is a limited selection from a much larger total' (Stott 1975a:88). For instance it seems that Paul made his selection in 1 Corinthians 12:8–12 because there was misunderstanding and malpractice in the church in Corinth over these particular ones.

When listing gifts of the Spirit the New Testament makes

no distinction between what we might call the extraordinary and the ordinary, or the supernatural and natural. It is not possible to draw up a complete list. Each of the lists in the New Testament is illustrative rather than exhaustive. Peter Wagner argues that there are apparent gifts in the New Testament which are not explicitly called by that term. He lists for instance: intercession, exorcism and missionary gifts. There may also be further gifts which are not even mentioned in the New Testament.

Should every congregation manifest the complete range of gifts?
Gifts are given on God's initiative in order that the Church may fulfil its mission in a specific locality. God will therefore select those which are relevant to the needs of the hour. He may gift one church in one area and another church in a different direction, because each is facing a different situation. The range of gifts in evidence should not be the result of the church's theological filter or cultural disposition, but represent those which are essential and strategic for the church to fulfil its mission. Furthermore, as Scripture nowhere provides a fully comprehensive list we do not know the complete range.

Are all the gifts of equal importance?
The New Testament makes it clear that not all the gifts are of equal importance. While none is to be despised, for all are from God, there are some which are described as 'higher gifts' which are to be earnestly desired (1 Cor. 12:31). The higher gifts are those which edify, i.e. do most to build up the Body of Christ. The advice Paul gives to the miracle-mongering believers in Corinth was, 'since you are eager for manifestations of the Spirit, strive to excel in building up the church' (1 Cor.14:12 RSV). The speaking of intelligible, relevant words from God has top priority in the building up of the Church. 'Make love your aim, and earnestly desire the spiritual gifts, especially that you may prophesy'

(1 Cor. 14:1 RSV). People need to hear truth from God if the Church is to grow. John Stott writes, '. . . the teaching gifts have the highest value, for nothing builds up Christians like God's truth. It is not surprising, therefore, to find a teaching gift or gifts at the top of each of the five New Testament lists. The apostles' insistence on the priority of teaching has considerable relevance to the contemporary Church. All over the world the churches are spiritually undernourished owing to the shortage of biblical expositors. In areas where there are mass movements they are crying out for teachers to instruct converts. Because of the dearth of teachers it is sad to see so many people preoccupied with, and even distracted by, gifts of lesser importance' (Stott 1975a:112).

What is the relationship between natural talents and gifts of the Spirit?
We have noted above that not all of the gifts of the Spirit appear as 'miraculous' phenomena. Some of them are very 'natural' and ordinary, such as teaching, helping, administration, serving, hospitality, performing acts of mercy and craftsmen's skills. These maybe exercised by a non-Christian as well as by the Christian. What then is the relationship between natural talents and gifts?

Peter Wagner draws a sharp distinction between the two. He heads a section dealing with the distinction, 'Don't Confuse Spiritual Gifts with Natural Talents' (Wagner 1979b:85). He writes, 'Spiritual gifts are reserved exclusively for Christians. No unbeliever has one, and every true believer in Jesus does. Spiritual gifts are not to be regarded as dedicated natural talents. There may be a discernible relationship between the two, however, because in some cases (not all, by any means) God takes a natural talent in an unbeliever and transforms it into a spiritual gift when that person enters the Body of Christ. But even in a case like this the spiritual gift is more than just a souped-up natural talent. Because it is given by God, a spiritual gift can never be cloned' (Wagner 1979b:86, 87).

I do not agree that gifting can only take place subsequent to a person's conversion. The Holy Spirit is active in our creation as well as in our regeneration. Wagner concedes in response to the question, 'Where do these natural talents come from?' – 'Ultimately, they are given by God, and as such they should be recognised in a sense as gifts' (Wagner 1979b:86). Prophets like Jeremiah and John the Baptist were set apart to be prophets from their mother's womb (Jer. 1:5; Luke 1:15, 76). 'This fundamental truth that God has planned the end from the beginning should warn us against too facile a discontinuity between nature and grace, between pre-conversion and post-conversion life' (Stott 1975a:91).

However, it cannot be automatically assumed that every natural talent will be converted into a gift of the Spirit. Some Christians who have exercised some great gift before their conversion do not feel moved to do so by the Holy Spirit after their conversion. This can occur for a variety of reasons. They may have so misused, distorted and debased the gift in the past that it is difficult to resurrect and apply it to the work of the Kingdom. As new and immature Christians they may be held back from exercising a spectacular gift, at least for a time, because it might destroy them spiritually, leading them to pride. God may say, 'Not yet', until they have learned how to utilise their gift for the glory of God.

Furthermore, we should not restrict our thinking to the gifts we had before our conversion as we make ourselves available to God for his service. We must be open to the 'surprises of the Holy Spirit'. He may wish to equip us in new ways for fresh spheres of ministry.

Are gifts a permanent possession?
They are gifts bestowed by God and not personal acquisitions. He gives when and how he will, and is free to

withdraw a gift again at any time. We therefore must guard against a presumptive attitude, taking for granted that the gift is there for us to use when and how we like. 'Charismata' are by definition gifts of *grace*. On the other hand God does not play games with us. There is a consistency in his operations. Gifts are not given and withdrawn arbitrarily. They may be withdrawn because they have been grievously misused, or allowed to become dormant because they are no longer relevant to our present opportunities. Peter Wagner argues that gifts are, normally speaking, a lifetime possession. He explains, 'This rather dogmatic opinion is derived from Romans 12:4, where Paul established the analogy of the physical body as the hermeneutical key for understanding spiritual gifts. If spiritual gifts are to the Body of Christ as hands, tongues and other members are to the physical body, there is no question in my mind that once we know what our gift is, we can depend on keeping it' (Wagner 1979b: 106). The fact that the three main lists of gifts in the New Testament occur in the immediate context of teaching about the body adds further weight to his line of argument.

Others take a different line, arguing that 'gifts' are distinguished from 'ministries' in that the former are temporary while the latter are permanent. Ph.-H. Menoud writes about Paul's list in 1 Cor. 12:29–30, 'He designates them by terms which are abstract and not personal, for they are beyond doubt spontaneous and sporadic manifestations of the Spirit, which do not possess the permanence of a ministry' (J-J. von Allmen Ed. 1958:265). The distinction may however lie more in the area of official recognition and leadership implications than in permanence. The ministries represent those activities which are essential for building up the body. The fact that Christians are exhorted to utilise their gifts responsibly as 'good stewards' (1 Pet. 4:10, 11) also implies a measure of permanence, and implies that we are accountable.

Were the gifts withdrawn at the end of the apostolic age?
Many Protestant Christians in the reformed tradition have argued that the supernatural gifts of the Spirit were characteristic of the apostolic times. When the period of 'redemptive history' was replaced by 'church history' these gifts ceased to operate. They were phased out with the passing of the last of the apostles.

This line of argument is based upon a desire to safeguard the normative nature of apostolic tradition and of the completeness of revelation as enshrined in the canon of Scripture. This is argued at length by Oscar Culmann in *The Early Church*. He regards the period from the birth of Jesus to the death of the last apostle as a time of direct revelation. This was recognised by the Church in the second century when it fixed the canon of Scripture. 'The Church was getting to the point where it was too distant from the time of the apostles to be able to guard the purity of the tradition so she drew a line under apostolic tradition. In doing this she demonstrated a clear line of demarcation between apostolic and the church period; between the time of foundation and of construction' (Culmann 56:89).

There are three other principal considerations which have further underlined this negative stance. Firstly, they look back through two thousand years of church history and note that many of the gifts have fallen into disuse for much of this period. Secondly, looking at the crude religious magic of the medieval Church, and some of the practices of 'folk catholicism' at the present time, 'It is not surprising that main-line Protestantism, . . . suspicious of anything mysterious or miraculous, . . . turned its face against a revival of the apostolic gifts' (Bridge and Phypers 1973:30). Thirdly, in observing the manifestation of some of the 'supernatural' gifts within the classical and neo-Pentecostal movements, they have been unconvinced about their authenticity.

In response to these genuine concerns, I would make the following brief comments. First, there is undoubtedly a uniqueness about the period of our Lord's ministry and the apostleship of the Twelve. Therefore, the terms 'apostle' and 'prophet' have undergone some modification when applied outside their ranks and after their period. Indeed, within the pages of the New Testament there is evidence of these terms taking on a wider, secondary meaning. We will look at this more closely in the following section.

Secondly, the Bible nowhere explicitly states that the gifts, or certain of them, have been withdrawn. On the contrary, 1 Cor. 13:8–10 infers that prophecies, tongues and knowledge will be needed until the 'perfect comes' i.e. until Christ returns. Ephesians 4:11 teaches that the gifts of apostles, prophets, evangelists and pastors and teachers are all required to prepare God's people for works of service, so that the body of Christ may be built up until we all reach unity in the faith. Surely, the need for this is as great today as it was then?

Thirdly, when the Epistles speak about the gifts, it is to instruct Christians in their proper use – 'never how to phase them out' (Bridge, Phypers 1973:28).

Fourthly, as we have previously noted, the Scriptures nowhere draw a distinction between 'ordinary' and 'supernatural' gifts. They are intermingled without comment. By what authority therefore have we the right to perform a scissors-and-paste exercise to edit out certain gifts which we consider have been withdrawn?

Part of the problem may be more cultural than theological. As Western Christians we have serious inhibitions in coming to terms with the supernatural, which are not shared by the majority of our brethren in Africa and Latin America. Signs and wonders are sovereign acts of God. He causes them to happen as and when he pleases to authenticate his word. Perhaps at times we too glibly say that these are more appropriate in the pioneer missionary situations overseas. The missionary frontier is as much on our own doorstep, and we are not performing so startlingly well without them. Perhaps their scarcity may have as much to do with our little faith (Matt. 13:58), as with their inappropriateness.

Michael Griffiths, principal of the London Bible College and one-time director of the Overseas Missionary Fellowship, who does not identify personally with the charismatic movement, has written concerning the gifts. 'Common objections or apprehensions about certain gifts can be met, not by denying that they are still given, but rather by insisting upon a careful biblical study of what these gifts mean in the New Testament and by exercising them only in the way which Scripture itself clearly teaches' (Griffiths 1978:9).

A COMPOSITE LIST OF GIFTS MENTIONED IN THE BIBLE

This list does not claim to be exhaustive and a number of the descriptions are tentative, as it is not always possible to know the exact nature of every gift to which the Scriptures make passing reference. In classifying the gifts I am following Michael Green's helpful categories (Green 1974:161–192).

Gifts of Utterance

1 *Prophecy* (Rom. 12:6; 1 Cor. 12:10; 1 Pet. 4:11). Prophecy is a message given directly from God through men who have learned to listen to him and are prepared to speak on his behalf. The message may come as a result of study or be spontaneous. It may be a proclamation regarding the present or a prediction relating to the future. It may be addressed to the Church for her upbuilding, encouragement and consolation, to an unbeliever to convict him of sin, or to society at large. Prophecy is a gift which is characteristic of the 'last days'. It is given to all regardless of age, sex and

social standing. It is the most commonly referred to of all the gifts.

2 *Teaching* (Rom. 12:7; Eph. 4:11; 1 Cor. 12:28). To explain and apply the word of God in such a way that people can understand and are encouraged to respond. It is not restricted simply to the imparting of information, but calls people to commitment which produces a behavioural change. It is therefore closely related to the gift of pastor, and overlaps with prophecy and encouragement. Teaching need not be equated with formal lecturing; it may be given in a variety of styles and using different media appropriate to the occasion, content, audience and desired response.

3 *Exhortation* (Rom. 12:8). The Greek word translated 'exhortation' literally means to draw alongside in order to strengthen. It signifies to challenge, comfort, console, rebuke and encourage, so that people move forward rather than shrink back, and pass the breaking-point without breaking. The encourager is the positive, patient, resilient motivator. His exhortations serve to dry out the gunpowder and light the fuse.

4 *Tongues* (1 Cor. 12:10). These are generally understood as 'languages' which have not been learned but are given by the Holy Spirit, for private or public use, to express our praise to God or to communicate his message through a divinely anointed utterance. In the latter case it must be accompanied by the gift of interpretation for it to become intelligible. Some Christians understand 'tongues' to mean a definite language form with vocabulary and syntax, while others regard it as an expression of feeling and emotion – 'rather like the love language of a happily married couple, which may not *mean* anything, when the words are analysed; but which *denotes* the intimacy and trust of the couple concerned' (Green 1975:162). Still others interpret the phrase 'various kinds of tongues' to mean simply an unusual aptitude to learn languages (Stott 1975a:112–15, Griffiths 1978:57–60).

5 *Interpretation of Tongues* (1 Cor. 12:10, 30). This is the ability to give the substance of a message delivered in a tongue. It is not strictly speaking a translation. Those with the gift of tongues are encouraged to pray for this complementary gift so that they will be able to understand what they are saying (1 Cor. 14:13). Without the gift of interpretation the tongues can have no place in the Church (1 Cor. 14:27, 28). Tongues followed by interpretation become equivalent to prophecy.

Gifts of Action

6 *Apostolic* (1 Cor. 12:28; Eph. 4:11). This gift, together with Prophet, Evangelist, Pastor and teacher we will be discussing at greater length in the following section devoted to leadership. Here we take this to mean responsibility for a number of churches, exercised so as to enable those churches to grow in spiritual maturity. It also expresses a pioneering spirit to establish a Christian witness where the gospel has not yet been heard, with a view to gathering converts and planting churches.

7 *Missionary* (Eph. 3:7–9). Peter Wagner draws attention to this as a distinct gift. He defines it as 'the special ability that God gives to some members of the Body of Christ to minister whatever other spiritual gifts they have in a second culture.' (Wagner 1979b:205.) Most people find it difficult to function adequately outside of their own culture. They are unable to make the necessary adjustments to adopt another language, enter the frame of reference of another culture, and adapt their style of working.

8 *Evangelist* (Eph. 4:11). The ability that some people have to know to whom, when and how to share the gospel so that others become disciples of Christ and responsible members of his church.

9 *Pastor-Teacher* (Eph. 4:11). To assume the spiritual care and nurture of a body of believers.

10 *Gifts of healing* (1 Cor. 12:9, 30). The ability to heal various kinds of sickness whether of the body, mind or soul. The healing may be instantaneous, gradual, complete or partial, with or without the aid of medication or surgery.

11 *Miracles* (1 Cor. 12:10, 28). These refer to any mighty act of God performed through one of his servants. While including healings, the term 'miracles' embraces other signs and wonders which 'are received by observers to have altered the ordinary course of nature' (Wagner 1979b:237).

12 *Faith* (1 Cor. 12:9; 13:2). This does not refer to saving faith but a gift of 'mountain-moving' faith to overcome difficulties and achieve the seemingly impossible. It should not be confused with brash presumption which is confidence in one's own abilities, or the mistaken assumption that God places a safety-net under every tight-rope. Rather, it is taking God at his word and acting upon it. It is thanking God for what I believe he is going to do before he does it (Yohn 1974:47).

13 *Leadership* (Rom. 12:8; 1 Thess. 5:12). The ability to set goals in accordance with God's purpose for the future and to communicate these goals to others in such a way that they voluntarily and harmoniously work together to accomplish those goals for the glory of God' (Wagner 1979b:162). The Greek word literally means 'the one who presides'. To fulfil this role effectively he must be able to see the parts in relation to the whole; to reconcile conflicting interests, and to inspire trust and confidence. The Old Testament example of Daniel's God-given ability to act as a supervisor in the Persian court demonstrates that gifts of leadership are not restricted to the ecclesiastical realm. He was gifted for political leadership (Dan. 6:3). Closely associated with the gift of leadership is the following gift:

14 *Administrators* (1 Cor. 12:28). In the New Testament this word is also used of a ship's captain or steersman. It describes the ability to keep the vessel on course and safe

from navigational hazards so that it arrives at its destination in good shape. Administration is the drawing up of realistic plans and the establishing of effective procedures, so that goals can be achieved and all involved enjoy job satisfaction as they can see the significance of their contribution to the success of the whole enterprise. It may also have a link with the administration of finance.

15 *Help* (1 Cor. 12:28). The word literally means 'to take firm hold of someone, in order to help' (Robertson and Plummer 1911:281). Others apply the gift to the general area of administration. In view of the paperwork burdening every minister simple secretarial and organisational skills are invaluable. In the context of New Testament church life it probably refers to the offer of practical assistance to the poor, the orphaned and the widowed. It is closely associated, if not synonymous with the next gift mentioned in our list.

16 *Service* (Rom. 12:7; 1 Pet. 4:11). It is from this word that we get the term 'deacon'. It is a task-oriented gift which prompts a person to see what needs to be done and then set about doing it.

17 *Mercy* (Rom. 12:8). Like the previous two this gift is practical and unostentatious. It represents kindly acts of all kinds performed out of compassion for those in need.

18 *Giving* (Rom. 12:9). While it is the duty of every Christian to give sacrificially, regularly and cheerfully to the Lord's work, some Christians have a particular burden to give generously themselves and to stimulate others to give.

19 *Voluntary Poverty* (1 Cor. 13:3). Peter Wagner describes this gift as the special ability 'to renounce material comfort and luxury and adopt a personal life-style equivalent to those living at the poverty level in a given society in order to serve God more effectively' (Wagner 1979b:96). It is demonstrated by those who take the vows of monastic order and by many missionaries serving overseas. Many

Christians are being led by God into a simpler life-style in response to the selfish over-affluence of the surrounding society.

20 *Hospitality* (1 Pet. 4:9). The readiness to keep an open home to which the visitor is invited and in which he immediately feels welcome and at ease. Where this gift is present a relaxed atmosphere prevails. There is no unnecessary fuss and bother, and the practical details are attended to in a quiet and efficient manner, so that the visitor never feels an intruder.

21 *Martyrdom* (1 Cor. 13:3). The ability and willingness to endure suffering to the point of death in a joyful and victorious attitude which brings glory to God.

22 *Suffering* (Phil. 1:29; Col. 1:24). 'For it has been granted to you that for the sake of Christ you should not only believe in him but also suffer for his sake' (RSV). I am grateful to an Anglican clergyman, a Jewish Christian who lost both of his parents in Auschwitz for pointing out this gift to me. The verb translated 'granted' might equally well be translated 'gifted'.

23 *Celibacy* (1 Cor. 7:7; Mat. 19:12). Those who remain unmarried in order to be freer to devote their time and energies to the Lord's service (Bridge, Phypers 1973:84).

24 *Craftsmanship* (Ex. 31:3–6). The Spirit of God inspired Bezalel to give him skill in design and working with wood, precious metals, building stone, in cutting precious stones for jewellery and in weaving curtains and garments.

Gifts of Knowledge

25 *Word of Knowledge* (1 Cor. 12:8; 13:2). The God-given ability to understand truth, or knowledge of events or motives, which has not been acquired by normal means. Peter Wagner also understands the gift as the ability 'to discover, accumulate, analyse and clarify information and ideas that are pertinent to the growth and well-being of the body' (Wagner 1979b:218). In either case it includes the

ability to apply information so that it has a significant bearing on a situation.

26 *Word of Wisdom* (1 Cor. 12:8). A special insight to apply knowledge to resolve a difficulty. It helps a person to remain objective and provides him with a sensitivity to what people are saying and to handle them appropriately. It is the ability to see things as they really are and to work towards an appropriate solution. This gift is necessary both in personal counselling and labour negotiations.

27 *Discernment* (1 Cor. 12:10). The Revised Standard Version translate the phrase denoting this gift as 'the ability to distinguish between spirits'. It describes the ability to discern whether a person's words or actions, which are claimed to be of God, are in reality divinely inspired or whether they are the manifestations of merely human activity or are satanic in origin. It enables the false prophet to be distinguished from the genuine one. As every genuine work of God is challenged and counterfeited by Satan this gift is of abiding importance.

Attempting to draw together a composite list highlights a number of facts with regard to the gifts of the Spirit. It demonstrates that there are a large number, covering a wide variety of activities. As mentioned at the outset it is not always possible to describe them with any degree of precision.

GIFTED FOR LEADERSHIP

In the New Testament leaders are not thought of in terms of dignitaries but as functionaries. The emphasis there is on service rather than status. Furthermore, various leadership specialisations are envisaged. No single individual, no matter how versatile he may be, is competent in every sphere. For a church to move ahead in numerical growth and diversification of ministries there needs to be effective leadership in each area. Five such spheres of ministry were in operation among the churches of Asia Minor as recorded in the letter to the Ephesians, which many New Testament scholars regard as addressed not just to one church but possibly to a number in the region. Michael Harper in *Let My People Grow* sees these five ministries as five interlinking spheres, rather like the Olympic symbol.

He describes them succinctly as:

Let my people go – the apostolic function of the Church
Let my people hear – the prophetic function of the Church
Let my people care – the pastoral function of the Church
Let my people know – the teaching function of the Church
Let my people grow – the evangelistic function of the Church

(Harper 1977:44, 45).

For the churches in Asia Minor to sustain their life and spread their influence throughout the province they needed effective leadership in each of these specialisations. As most of the individual congregations were probably quite small, with no adequate premises in which to come together regularly, they possibly were little more than an extended family gathering or large house meeting. The specialist leadership roles had to be provided on an inter-congregational level. The various groups were 'visited' as often as possible by itinerant leaders exercising their particular ministry.

The role of the '*apostle*' was to ensure that the teaching was in line with the sayings of Christ and the body of doctrine which the apostles had established as foundational. Their visits also served to remind the local congregations that the Church was a dynamic, expanding body. In addition to the twelve unique *apostles of Christ* (among their essential qualifications was that they had to be eye-witnesses of his resurrection) were the *apostles of the Church*. They were the trail-blazers and travelling representatives, working on the spiritual and geographical frontiers to bring individuals to faith and establish new congregations. The New Testament names Barnabas (Acts 14:14), Andronicus and Junias (Rom. 16:7), Timothy and Silas (1 Thess. 2:6) and Epaphroditus (Phil. 2:25) as among those fulfilling this kind of function. The apostles were not cautious, bureaucratic leaders, but bold, pioneering adventurers, ensuring not simply the orthodoxy of the Church, but also safeguarding its continuing mobility and flexibility. Such a steadying and inspiring ministry was particularly relevant to the small, struggling groups of relatively new Christians, many of them fighting for life in a hostile environment.

In addition to the 'ambassador' and 'pastor-pastorum' the church needs a new generation of leaders with a truly apostolic gift of the trail-blazing kind. We need leaders who are freed from administrative and maintenance tasks. Once a leader becomes overburdened with management problems he quickly loses his vision and perspective. The urgent crowds out the significant. We need leaders with time to reflect, diary flexibility and visionary qualities who can be with the troops not just for the ceremonial parades and in the casualty stations but share in the strategic advance. They should be released to roam freely on the growing edge. Their task is as much concerned with preparing for tomorrow as preserving yesterday

Of equal importance was the '*prophetic*' function. Among some groups, especially those predominantly Gentile in membership, the Old Testament Scriptures may not have been readily available. This problem must have become acute as the followers of Christ became more and more distanced from the synagogues where the scrolls were deposited. At this early stage in the Church's life many of the New Testament books had not yet been written. The production problems were immense in a day when every manuscript had to be copied by hand and personally conveyed. When specific issues arose in the Church concerning doctrine and practice, which were not covered by the portions of Scripture in their possession or in the apostolic teaching which they had received verbally, they had to rely on the prophet who spoke a Word from God as the Spirit moved him for the guidance of the Church.

Michael Harper helpfully distinguishes between the role of the prophet and that of the teacher. 'A prophet is not a Scripture exegete. He knows the scriptures, but he does not teach from his knowledge of the Bible, which is the role of the teacher; he hears that which is particularly appropriate for the hour, and he faithfully passes on the message to the appropriate quarter, wherever and whoever that may be' (Harper 1977:52). The prophet in no sense adds to God's self-revelation in Christ, but he does bring a practical word of encouragement, warning, exhortation and guidance, which must then be tested by the Church, in the light of Scripture and according to their Spirit-led discernment.

The task of the *evangelist* is located within each individual church. Apart from the mention in Ephesians 4 and the example of Philip as an evangelist in Samaria (Acts 21:8), and the exhortation to Timothy to do the work of an evangelist (2 Tim. 4:5), there is no stress in the New Testament on the office of 'evangelist'. The overwhelming evidence is of the church itself actually engaging in the evangelistic task. We may therefore conclude that the task of the visiting evangelist was to help the local churches to become more effective in their outreach. He evangelised among them as one specially gifted, not to remove the responsibility from their shoulders, but to inspire them by his example. As distinct from the 'apostle' who is the pioneer church planter, the evangelist works from a local church base and in conjunction with local Christians. He will help each local church to identify those within their midst who are the potential evangelists. This will often only be discovered and developed as the congregation responds to the outside stimulus of those with a recognised evangelistic gift.

The small, scattered Christian fellowships of New Testament times also required the help of visiting *pastors and teachers*. Small groups are prone to foster intense relationships which exclude others, and to generate personality conflicts which are not easily resolved from within. Furthermore, among those joining the Church will be those with pressing personal problems. They will also be stepping into a very different environment as they came in from the surrounding pagan world, bringing a lot of their beliefs, attitudes and habits with them. The fact of their becoming Christian may have resulted in their being disowned by their families, thrown out of home or losing their jobs. Many of these problems would be dealt with by the local leadership, but there were no doubt some thorny issues which would require the attention of a visiting pastor responsible for shepherding a number of groups. Paul's letters reflect his wide-ranging pastoral concerns, and as he travelled he was acutely conscious of the pastoral burden which he carried for all of the churches.

Similarly, not every group would have someone within it capable of fulfilling an adequate teaching role. So there were visiting teachers providing instruction of a more systematic kind, on which the local leadership could base their own exhortations for the coming months.

The Ephesians 4 pattern of inter-congregational ministry makes more sense to me as a result of serving overseas for a brief four years, sharing in a church planting team in Chile, South America. Many missionaries report that such experience provides insights which are seldom reflected in academic commentaries on the text.

The five leadership spheres described in Ephesians 4

represent supra-congregational ministries exercised by individuals travelling among the groups of Christians scattered throughout Asia Minor. Their roles were appropriate to the structure and needs of the church at that time. Each group would have its local leadership, which was developing to the point where it could assume many of the functions previously exercised by leadership from outside the fellowship. As local congregations become established, developing community life and growing numerically, so their ministries become diversified. In this way the ministries increasingly find expression in the life of the local church.

With the institutionally developed church life of today we must look at the leadership spheres described in Ephesians 4, asking ourselves how they apply to our times and our local situation. They will vary from congregation to congregation according to the ministry emphases of each church and the constituencies which they believe God has called them to serve.

It is the responsibility of the ordained minister, with his church council, to ensure that effective leadership is being exercised in each sphere and that there is cohesion within the leadership team. It is not, however, his responsibility to give a personal lead in each sphere. His ordination did not endow him with all the gifts necessary to fulfil every role. Churches which expect their minister to be effective in every area of ministry will soon become disillusioned. As a consequence of such unrealistic expectations many churches engage in the game of 'scapegoating', in which they compare the weaknesses of their present minister with the strengths of his predecessor. To avoid this futile pastime churches should help their minister identify his gifts and encourage him to develop his ministry in those areas. Some churches have taken the step of drawing up a job description in cooperation with their minister, which recognises his particular contribution. Such an exercise also exposes those areas where he is unable to give an effective lead. These must be met by others within the church who have corresponding leadership gifts.

A LEADERSHIP TEAM TO FACILITATE MEMBERSHIP MINISTRY

As a church grows, so its ministries diversify. Just as in Ephesians 4 we have distinct inter-congregational leadership roles fulfilled by different individuals, ('. . . he [i.e the Risen Christ] appointed some to be apostles, others to be prophets, others to be evangelists, others to be pastors and teachers' [v. 12], so distinctive roles begin to emerge in the local church.

The need for a leadership team which demonstrates a range of gifts
Those who are in a leadership position do not merely exercise their gift on behalf of the congregation and with their official recognition; they are also responsible for stimulating those similarly gifted (but not necessarily with accompanying leadership ability) in the congregation. In their ministries they will inspire others by their example and invite them to work alongside them. So the church becomes a 'gift evoking' community.

I am convinced that often gifts are suppressed because of the lack of leadership models, which is the result of ministry being channelled through too narrow a funnel. Thus church members see their leaders inadequately trying to fulfil impossible demands which either they have placed upon themselves or which they have been loaded upon them by a congregation who have assumed an 'observer only' role. They witness the uninspiring and sometimes embarrassing spectacle of a leader trying to fulfil roles for which he has no gift. They are constantly comparing the weaknesses of the present man with the strengths of the predecessor. The minister for his part is subjecting the person in the pew to repeated exhortations to do this and that, without anyone to hand to show how it could be done. When people can move from the theory to seeing the gift in action, then they are motivated.

At the other extreme, the leader must guard against thinking that because he can do something everyone else should be able to perform in the same area of competence. This will only serve to cause frustration, with people trying and failing and eventually being forced to the conclusion that they have nothing to contribute. Paul makes this clear to the gift-laden church in Corinth. 'If the foot should say, "Because I am not a hand, I do not belong to the body," it would not for that reason cease to be part of the body.' Feet must not be mistaken for hands. They must be identified, deployed and trained for what they were meant to do!

The need for a personal pastoral relationship

This picture of a shepherd with his flock of sheep as a model of the relationship between a religious minister and his people, is unique to the Hebrew-Christian tradition among the religions of the world. (Ps. 23; Jn. 10:12; 1 Pet. 2:25; Heb. 13:20; Jn. 21:15ff). An eastern shepherd spent most of his life with the flock. He knew every one of his sheep by name, and noticed when just one went missing. He was prepared to give his life for the sheep. The shepherd has a daily relationship with the sheep. In the church today the relation of the minister to his flock is more like that of the vet or the sheep-shearer than the shepherd. He can only deal individually with the sheep at infrequent intervals or in response to an emergency or domestic crisis.

The pastor has to know his flock individually if he is to identify their actual and potential gifts. He must know what his members do for a job, what their leisure interests are and if they are involved in community service. These may give some clue to their gifts. For churches with over 150 members this will inevitably mean the pastor delegating some of his pastoral responsibilities to a team of lay pastors. As the pastors get to know those for whom they are responsible a card index can be built up, which shows the gifts each person possesses and is perhaps already exercising in the world. Often times those gifts have not been made available to the church because he either does not see its relevance or has not been given opportunity.

The need for a group context

It is often within the small group that gifts are first identified and begin to function. I have already dealt with this aspect in our chapter on groups so there is no need to elaborate further here. I make just one observation, namely, the larger the church the more important become the primary and secondary groups for the release of the congregation's gifts. The Sunday worship is on such a scale that gifts have to be highly developed to operate effectively at that level. Many people are therefore discouraged, thinking that they would never utilise their gifts in the presence of so many people. The small group situation on the other hand helps gifts to blossom in the warm, friendly atmosphere of mutual friends. If mistakes are made at this level, they are considered as 'within the family' and can be overlooked or laughed away without embarrassment. As people gain confidence in the primary group they can then begin to function in the secondary group and eventually be introduced, where appropriate, to the tertiary level.

The need for an inspiring, well-publicised programme

Many people are reluctant to offer themselves for service, not because they lack dedication but because they lack information and inspiration. The fault often lies with the leadership, who have not communicated the fact that the church has a programme which is designed to achieve God-given objectives. Jobs are undersold, and those invited to take on responsibilities are not encouraged to 'dream their dreams' to envisage what that work might one day become. In the final chapter I will spell this out in much greater detail. Suffice it to say here, many churches have not identified gifts because they have no programme to which the gifts which God has given could be usefully put. Or if they have such a plan it is concealed behind a 'Top Secret – Restricted Circulation' file cover!

SUMMARY

The issue of gifts is crucial for church growth. We have attempted to show that gifts are distributed among the people of God so that no one is exempt. We have also noted the wide variety of these gifts. The task of the ordained ministry is not simply to minister to the congregation but to create and direct a ministering congregation through the detection, development and deployment of God-given resources. The church members are not there to enable the ordained minister to do his job; he is there to enable the congregation to fulfil theirs. This being so, we must examine our situation to discover how these principles are being worked out in practice.

What proportion of the congregation have identified their gifts? What steps do we envisage taking to help everyone identify their gifts? Once recognised, are our structures elastic and diverse enough to encourage people to develop and employ their gifts in fellowship with others?

Increased diversification will necessitate an enlarged leadership team with new specialist skills and the need for coordination so that the diversification does not result in fragmentation and frustration. I believe that there are enormous supplies of untapped resources within the Church. The present high level of unemployment in the nation palls into insignificance in comparison with that which prevails in the Church. Unidentified gifts represent unlived life. Let us find ways of helping each other identify our gifts and affirming one another in their development. The mission which Christ has committed to his Church represents the greatest enterprise with which we can be identified. Its implementation requires the total mobilisation of all our God-given resources in unending waves of committed creativity.

CHAPTER NINE

Leadership and Relationships

The church growth literature emanating from North America emphasises the vital role played by leadership in facilitating growth. Peter Wagner, for instance, in *Your Church Can Grow – Seven Vital Signs Of A Healthy Church*, rates strong pastoral leadership as the first of these signs. He writes, 'Vital Sign Number One of a healthy, growing church is a pastor who is a possibility thinker and whose dynamic leadership has been used to catalyse the entire church into action for growth' (Wagner 1976:57). His sheer ability, love and dedication have earned him a place of authority in his church. This is not an authority of status invested by the ecclesiastical hierarchy, but generated from below; built up through living relationships with people. 'Strong pastors of strong churches have earned the fierce loyalty of their parishioners' (Wagner 1976:57, 58).

The Southern Baptist denomination tested out Peter Wagner's seven vital signs in 277 of their fastest growing churches in the United States, and interviewed the pastors of the top fifteen in growth terms. They found that although the leaders of their fastest growing churches were self-effacing, yet they were the undisputed leaders. 'Overwhelmingly, lay persons describe their pastor as "shepherd of the flock" and 78 per cent of those interviewed considered him to be "a strong leader".' Pastor O'chester of Allandale responded, 'I have always been an authoritarian leader, but I'm not the man I used to be. My church didn't always follow me because I wasn't follow-able. Today, my church would charge hell with a thimble full of water if I said this was where God wants us. They would follow me because I would be out front!' (*Home Missions* Magazine Dec. '77).

This kind of language is hard to take from a European perspective. We react strongly against the dynamic image and success language which casts the church minister in the role of the business tycoon. The Rev. Gordon Jones, Education Secretary of the Church Pastoral Aid Society, reflects the sentiments of many British clergy when he exclaims, 'Phew!' in response to Peter Wagner's 'first vital sign', and then comments, 'If that is true most of us had better start packing our bags now. See you at the station' (*Church of England Newspaper*, May 18, 1979). In the second part of his article he expands on the theme, concluding, 'If such charisma and dynamism is essential for church growth then it has to be said that a large number of churches will never grow. Most of us are not in the star-studded first division of the clergy league' (*CEN* May 25, 1979).

It is difficult to hear one another through the 'static' created by differences of culture and ecclesiastic structure. The North American culture is success and growth-orientated. Achievement is acclaimed and rewarded. Everyone loves a winner. Furthermore, there is a much higher percentage of new churches than is the case in Europe, due to US population growth and urban migration, coupled with an entrepreneurial approach to religion.

THE NEED FOR LEADERSHIP

While many of us would want to challenge the super-star approach with all the personality cult-following which it engenders, and the traumas which occasion the star's departure, we cannot duck the important issue of leadership. If we react adversely to the North American stress on ability and achievement we must also come to terms with European constraints on leadership, where so much depends on class, privilege and the 'old boy' network. In their book *Turning the Tide* Paul Beasley-Murray and Alan Wilkinson quote numerous statistics gathered from 350 Baptist churches throughout England. One section explores this first 'vital sign' by gathering data about the minister, his dominant characteristics, his theology, his relationships with lay members, and his usage of varied activities and techniques.

Their findings broadly support Wagner's premise that the pastor should be a possibility thinker and a dynamic leader for growth. It is, however, just as important that he should have a willingness and the ability to delegate or share his responsibilities with the members in his fellowship. There is a fruitful interdependence which neither party can achieve on its own.

When one considers the totality and variety of the pastoral care, the teaching, the evangelism and the administration needed within a fellowship, it is improbable that any one man – no matter how creative a thinker or dynamic a leader – can cope with the total spectrum. The leadership base must be extended to include others who are appropriately gifted and show leadership potential.

We may be nervous of success-orientated language with regard to leadership for both theological and pragmatic reasons. At the theological level we may feel that the leader will be judged on his faithfulness and effectiveness in fulfilling his calling, irrespective of results. Thus the faithful prophet may be rejected for his bold and frank speaking, while the false prophet who tailors his message to appeal to his audience may pull in the crowds. Success is not necessarily to be measured in terms of a full church and a mountainous budget.

On the other hand we are surely not simply to soldier on without any concern for results. The New Testament clearly teaches and demonstrates that God wants lost people found. He wants them to be introduced to his only son Jesus Christ, who alone can give them eternal life. At the level of pragmatism, we shy away from success-orientated language because it is too threatening in the European context of sustained decline since the First World War. But this is a situation which calls for leadership. Throughout the Old and New Testaments, and across the centuries of subsequent church history, the great periods in the story of the people of God have been characterised by outstanding leadership.

Clearly a few individuals display a distinctive charisma and most well-known leaders certainly have had it, but many others have achieved great things for God and inspired thousands by their example, even though they did not possess such personal charisma. Leadership is not created by image as much as by performance. This is a point which Paul makes in 1 Cor. 3; where he hits out against the factions produced by personality cults among the various Christian groups in Corinth. Some said they followed Paul, others Apollos, a third group were attracted to Peter, while a fourth, apparently out of a false sense of spiritual superiority, said they followed Christ. (1 Cor. 1:12.) With regard to Apollos and himself, Paul draws attention away from their personalities to the essential functions which they each performed. 'The one who sows and the one who waters really do not matter. It is God who matters because he makes the plant to grow.'

But supposing after all the planting and regular watering nothing comes up. Do we simply shrug our shoulders and shift the responsibility on to God? Clearly not. Although it does not matter *who* does what, it is of crucial importance *how* it is done. The way we do things affects the outcome. There are more effective ways and less effective. Faithfulness implies more than stickability, it embraces being teachable, gaining skills and remaining expectant.

STYLES OF LEADERSHIP
Styles of leadership vary. They depend upon a number of factors: the personality of the leader, the nature of the task

to be accomplished, and the conditions prevailing at the time. There are also cultural influences which predispose societies to accept certain styles of leadership.

Autocratic leaders

Some leaders are *autocratic* by nature. They steamroller things along. Some do this in a benevolent manner as paternal autocrats. Others are more bureaucratic in style. They go by the book of rules. Still others are more visionary and inspirational.

Democratic leaders

Other leaders are *democratic or participatory* in approach. This is the style favoured in the majority of Protestant churches. It seeks to give organisational expression to the theological truth that the Church is the Body of Christ, and that we should normally expect the Lord to make his will known through the membership or their elected representatives. This is where the snags begin to arise. For it to work the group must be agreed on their fundamental beliefs and have arrived at a consensus on the objectives that they are consti-tuted to fulfil as a local church. They must be sensitive to God's leading, in tune with one another, and with a breadth of vision to evaluate alternative routes to achieve an agreed goal. Where this is lacking then the church wanders along without either vision or motivation on a 'lowest common denominator' approach to opportunities and obstacles.

Furthermore, many so-called democratic systems are not so truly representative as they would appear on the surface. Sometimes the leadership group has a stranglehold on the situation. New people with a great deal to contribute are held at bay because they present too much of a threat to the less able people who have been occupying the seats of power for many years. The attitude prevails that those new people must serve a long apprenticeship before they begin to think of stepping into leadership positions.

The democratic processes can be used to neutralise leadership initiative. The leader resigns himself to a laissez-faire approach, allowing everything to run its natural course, knowing that he would be blocked at every turn if he were to propose anything which either threatened his people's security or questioned their priorities.

From the side of the congregation the attitude is that of 'genteel anarchy' which expresses itself in a defiant attitude of 'Whatever you decide, we will continue to do precisely as we have always done, and if you persist in pressing the matter either we leave or you leave.' Faced with this kind of entrenched attitude it is all too easy to succumb to institutional pressures and abdicate from leadership on the basis of 'anything for a quiet life'.

Theocratic leadership
The people of God in both the Old and New Testaments have been governed according to the *theocratic* principle. Perhaps within the modern western Church this has too readily been equated with the democratic approach. The organisational structures through which 'theocracy' – the rule of God – is expressed may vary according to the prevailing conditions and the nature of the task in hand.

Whatever the leadership style adopted the leader cannot escape the fact that he is an agent of change. Lyle Schaller describes the different roles: 'By action or by inaction every person does influence the future. Therefore, in one manner or another everyone is an agent of change. Some people are passive agents of change (let things happen), others are negative agents of change (they stop things happening), and an increasing number are becoming affirmative agents of change (they enable things to happen)' (Schaller 1973:12, 13).

In times of rapid change the church must seek to play a dual role. On the one hand she represents a conservative emphasis, seeking to remain loyal to a body of truth delivered once for all to the saints, and with a long and rich tradition built up through the many changing circumstances of her life. On the other hand she is called to fulfil a rejuvenating role, furthering the impact on the whole of life of the gospel which makes all things new. The Church as a Messianic community lives between the two comings of Christ. She experiences the tension of the 'now' and the 'not yet' of the Kingdom of God. The Church points back to the past, reaches out to the future, and expresses all she can of both in the *now* of day-to-day living.

AVENUES OF CHANGE

When considering the avenues of change there are four possible routes that the leader can follow. The path chosen must relate to his assessment of the situation and the degree of change envisaged. The first is that of *evolution*. This is the one most favoured by the conservative elements. It stresses continuity with the past, and thinks in terms of shaping what we have inherited to meet the demands of today and tomorrow. Such an approach is appropriate provided the pace of change in the society you seek to serve is fairly slow and the situation has not deteriorated beyond recall.

The second possibility is that of *reformation*. This also has a 'rear mirror' emphasis, but this time it is more critical. It is an attitude which sifts the past to distinguish between the good and the bad, and the more helpful and less helpful elements in our inherited structures. Some features are retained and reordered while others are discarded as a hindrance to effective performance.

The most radical route to take is the *revolutionary* road. It is also the most potentially traumatic as it entails a complete rejection of the past and overthrow of the established order. Some situations may be so appallingly and fundamentally wrong or corrupted that they have to be eradicated. However, the cost and outcome should be weighed very carefully. Power to turn the tables can so easily destroy the very idealism which motivated the action. 'Revolution' can come to mean no more than a turning of the wheel, with the last state simply a more extreme form of that which it replaced.

The fourth avenue is that of *innovation*. I believe this to be the most appropriate route for a leader to take in most church situations today. The innovative leader does not destroy all that he has inherited as an essential prerequisite for a successful investment in the future. He is appreciative of the insights and achievements of previous generations, and possesses discernment to identify those elements which are of lasting value. He is also aware that the 'latest' does not necessarily equate with the 'best'. So he tempers his enthusiasm with humility as he plans for the future. He is hesitant to sacrifice the existing set-up until he is reasonably assured of the success of its replacement. Furthermore he will have to bear in mind those among his church members who either through old age cannot cope with yet more change, or who have been hurt or disillusioned by traumatic experiences in the shape of unwanted changes which were inflicted upon them.

It will serve no useful purpose to threaten the existing set-up as a first step to introducing new approaches. Such action will only serve to raise barriers and block further progress in other areas. The innovative leader adopts a different strategy. He affirms all that he can in the existing situation. What his people are used to may be meeting their needs. It is an unloving act to inflict further changes with which they can neither cope, nor do they see its relevance to themselves. When confidence has been established through the existing members realising that their leader is on their side, he can then begin to talk, for instance, about the potential church members who may be from a very different background from those who have been church members for most of their lives. Such new people are unlikely to be reached unless the church is prepared to adopt alternative approaches, possibly through a different style of church

service and through other avenues than those provided
by the existing organisations. Thus, while enthusiastically
maintaining what is there already, the new grows up alongside and hopefully each benefits from the other.

There is always an element of risk in attempting to forge
new paths and some of the enterprises may fail or need to
be revised at frequent intervals. By using the innovative
approach, experimentation can proceed with minimum
damage to the existing patterns, so that change will not
automatically be equated with decay in the mind of the 'old
stagers'. Furthermore, the traditionalists can be involved
in the planning of new concepts and should certainly be
encouraged to take a prayerful interest in what is going on.
In the long term, those new ventures which succeed may well
eventually attract those who were cautious and suspicious
at the beginning. Any cross-pollination which occurs will be
to the benefit of all and therefore should be planned for and
encouraged.

LEADERSHIP MODELS

As we have previously noted, different situations require
distinctive leadership styles and mode of change employed.
A medical team at the scene of an accident has to take rapid
and co-ordinated action. To cope with the emergency, when
speed and efficiency are vital if lives are to be saved, an
autocratic model of leadership is essential. Orders have to
be given concisely and clearly. There is no time to argue
the pros and cons, they have to be smartly obeyed, at the
double! In the case of long-term planning or deciding on
how to deal with a situation which, although serious, does
not have to be acted upon immediately, a more democratic
approach can be adopted.

Within the church context there are a number of leadership models which the minister or priest may be called upon
to adopt. Different individuals will feel easier in one role
than in the other, and some personality types are more

adaptable than others. Very few individuals, however, are versatile enough in gifts and skills to adopt all the roles. Each must therefore recognise his limitations and seek to supplement these by well-chosen advisers who can compensate for his deficiencies. Let us now consider some of the more common models:

Competent teacher

This is the model most dominant within the majority of Protestant churches. The teacher's task is supremely to expound the Bible. When education was a privilege enjoyed by a select few, the clergyman was respected as the man of letters. However, the acquisition of learning is not the same as having the ability to teach. Many a polished three-point sermon fails to make a three-point landing!

The Church's established patterns of training for the ministry are partly to blame, as they train men to become amateur theologians rather than able teachers. Happily this state of affairs is beginning to change, but there is still a long way to go.

Far too many theological college lecturers hide behind a barricade of books which provide protection and conceal the world outside from them. They sit 'heads down' pursuing their specialist interest. The ministerial students are invited to share this erudition. As a result they learn a new vocabulary, become proficient at answering abstruse questions set by examination boards and thereby think they have learnt something. To dispel any sneaking doubts they are given a certificate to prove it.

What I have written does not constitute a swipe at theology. I am not intending to be anti-intellectual. But I am pleading strongly for a theology which is earthed in real life or – to use the jargon – a contextualised theology. As a regular feature of training we must be asking, 'How does that relate to situations I have already experienced or might conceivably have to face?' And 'How can I say that in a way

which enables me to be understood and which is authentic
to me?' I regret to say that while at theological college I had
neither the discernment nor mental discipline to do this for
myself, and so emerged with sheaves of notes for much of
which I could find little subsequent use.

To be fair to theological colleges, most of them have
precious little time-table flexibility to build in the
dimension which I suggest. The pressure of the syllabus
requirements, set either by university or denominational
educational boards, squeezes out alternative approaches
to the designated topics, and the students are assessed
largely on written examination performance. The situation
has however become more flexible in England within recent
years with the introduction of the Council for National
Academic Awards which allows accredited educational
establishments to devise their own courses. Some are taking
advantage of this opportunity to introduce courses which
are more closely related to the job for which ministerial
students are supposedly being prepared.

Being skilled in teaching requires, in addition to a thorough grasp of the subject, a profound understanding of the
audience and the questions in their minds. School teachers
are aware that pupils are seldom prepared to 'pay' attention. Attention has to be 'earned' by exciting their curiosity.
Teaching is not to be measured in terms of output but
intake. Nobody has been taught anything until someone has
learned something. An essential ingredient in Christian
education should be the opportunity to respond, for we are
required to be doers of the Word and not hearers only.
Latin American theologians make the helpful distinction
between orthodoxy and orthopraxis. Orthodoxy is what we
claim to believe. Orthopraxis is what we demonstrate that
we believe. And at the end of the day, they point out, we
shall be judged on the basis of our orthopraxis rather than
our orthodoxy.

Once, in South America, I was invited to lecture at a

Christian night school being set up by a group of Chileans, most of whom were from Pentecostal churches around the port of Valparaíso. As they discussed their plans, one of the church leaders began to express his doubts. He wanted to know what the students were going to *do* with all their newly acquired knowledge. For 'to whom much is given, much is required', he quoted. And if they were not going to do anything as a result of attending the institute, it would be better if they had never come in the first place. Their learning only serves to place them under greater judgement. This is an interesting third-world perspective on theological education!

Many books have been written on the craft of making sermons and the art of their delivery, but insufficient attention has been paid to their reception. What is to be done with them once the benediction has been pronounced? What change was the sermon designed to bring about, and what appropriate steps were taken to give opportunity for response? Rarely is there any provision for feed-back or time to discuss attitude changes, or specific courses of action. Because there is no opportunity for response, people are at a loss to know what to do with the sermon once it has been delivered. Being able to teach means far more than the ability to deliver a clear exposition of biblical passages; it embraces the art of raising questions so that people are stimulated to think for themselves. It also involves apprenticeship learning. The teacher cannot confine himself to the theoretical aspects of his subject, but must teach through being involved with his pupils in learning situations.

In the Church's selection of the top echelons of leaders I believe there is an over-emphasis on the scholar model, which has adversely affected the growth potential of the denominations. The wise scholar is a person who can see both sides of an argument. He can shuttle skilfully between the pros and the cons. Yet he may have great difficulty in making up his mind and in determining on one course of action rather than another. While not wanting to dispute that the Church needs erudite scholars, I suggest that it also urgently requires many more men on the ground who have vision, confidence and courage to lead; who have that sixth sense to size up a situation, to set a course and inspire people to go with them. Our performance must be brought into line with our declared purposes. Only then will our public statements sound other than platitudes.

Encouraging father

This leadership style has its roots in the patriarchal tradition. The paternal autocrat is the central figure in the extended family's complex network of relationships. He is the anchor man providing stability and cohesion. Today, this model is still to be found with a number of Christian churches with a wide range of traditions. The leader who is a firm-handed father figure is evident in Catholicism and in the Orthodox and Pentecostal churches. Within Catholicism the model arises not simply out of that Church's theology of the ordained ministry as mediating priest and dispenser of the sacraments. It is also explained by the fact that, being celibate, he has fewer conflicting loyalties and traditionally stays longer in one church than does his Protestant counterpart.

In the Orthodox and Pentecostal traditions the sociological explanation is somewhat different. There the leader has probably grown up in the community he serves and regards his pastoring of that congregation as his life's calling. This encourages and enables him to establish a depth of relationship which is not possible for someone who has come from elsewhere and expects that he will be moving on again within the space of five to seven years. The leader, therefore, never fully identifies with his people, preferring to distance himself. Such aloofness was actively encouraged in theological college training. Ministerial students were advised not to make their friends within the parish! When problems begin to arise among his church members he is more prone to complain about them than weep over them.

I remember kneeling in prayer on the dirt floor of a shack church alongside a Chilean Pentecostal pastor. He was a man of his people, indistinguishable from them either in his dress or his speech. He had dedicated his life to their service. Like most of his kind he was an older man with gnarled hands and a weather-beaten face. As he prayed earnestly for his congregation he named each in turn, and poured out his heart for them as though they were members of his flesh-and-blood family. They were like his own children for whom he felt personally responsible. He recounted before God the joys or sorrows which each brought to his heart. After a time tears were streaming down his cheeks. Was this depth of relationship between pastor and people one of the secrets of the incredible growth of the Pentecostal churches in Latin America?

Christian Lalive D'Epinay thinks so. He writes, 'The pastors are the authentic expression of the congregation, and the thing which distinguishes them from the mass of members is not their social origin or their way of living or their intellectual attainments, but simply certain qualities they have as leaders of men' (Lalive 1969:77). A further factor is that seventy-nine per cent, according to Lalive's research, are first-generation converts from the world, so they are acutely aware of what life is really like for their congregation. They themselves have shared its harsh realities, and as the majority of pastors still continue to earn their living in secular employment, they are in daily touch.

Supportive brother

'Brother' was the term by which the apostle Paul most frequently addressed his fellow Christians. It expressed the bond of spiritual kinship linking believers together. The Trades Union movement also uses the term to express to fellow trade unionists the sense of belonging together in the defence and advancement of their mutual interests. When, however, the mutual commitment is lacking, the title assumes a hollow ring, and may become an embarrassment. When used between theological students on the college campus it is an indication that 'the brother' has forgotten your name!

The title 'brother' was reinstated for me during my four years of missionary service in Latin America. There you are welcomed as *'hermano'* (brother) with a warm embrace. You are introduced to the congregation as to your family of adoption. Being an *'hermano'* may lead to an invitation home, a meal and a bed for the night. I have no doubt that the same would be true of the churches in Africa and other parts of the world. Here in Europe there is a disturbing lack of 'kinship' in many churches. A handshake is little more than a polite formality.

In leadership terms the 'understanding brother' is one who identifies with people and their problems. The 'brother' takes on the local culture. There is no sense of managerial aloofness or clinical detachment. Paul as an apostle sometimes had to lay down the law. But having done so, he then drew alongside as a brother to share his own internal struggles, fears and plans. He had that rare ability to slip from one role into another. He did not use his apostleship to secure aloofness from the personal involvements of brotherhood.

Within middle-class and artisan cultures there is a different attitude to employment which has a bearing on the acceptance of the minister. The middle class are concerned about job opportunities and promotion. The artisan is concerned about job security, status between grades and pay differentials. If a minister leaves his inner-city church he is regarded as leaving 'in order to better himself'. It is a boss who moves, but a brother who stays. The imported short-term minister can easily regard the Christian family as foster children. He takes in problem children for a brief span before handing them on with a sigh of relief to someone else! A brother, like the father-figure, cannot adopt that attitude.

To become a 'brother' means not only a readiness to get near to people, but being prepared for them to get close to us. In spiritual warfare, as in military combat, one of the enemy's tactics is to isolate soldiers from the main column and pick them off one at a time. There are many exposed, lonely men in the ministry who have become isolated because they will not be ministered to by others. Ministry is a two-way transaction. The bond of brotherhood helps us to enter the rough and tumble of life together, enjoying both mutual support and accountability.

Productive manager

In the pre-industrial times of the Bible, the closest we get to 'manager' is the 'steward' (*oikonomos* or *epitropos*). These two terms are used interchangeably to denote the 'house manager'. The steward would be responsible for running household affairs and for managing the estate. From the parable of the three stewards (Matt. 25: 14–26) we can see that he is expected to operate faithfully and effectively. Those who demonstrate that they can handle the resources entrusted to them will be rewarded with greater resources and wider responsibilities.

The Bible recognises that individuals have different levels of ability. This is expressed in the parable of the three servants by each one being given different amounts. In Luke's Gospel this is recognised in a different way. There ten servants are given equal amounts – a gold coin each (Luke 19:11–27). In response to the challenge, 'See what you can earn with this while I am gone!', one returned with ten times the original amount while another increased his five-fold. People who start off equal do not end up that way. Some will achieve more than others. But most of us can improve on our performance.

Many churches face serious management problems,
though these are often spiritualised to recast them in a form
with which the clergyman feels professionally competent to
deal. Many of the difficulties arise because management
skills are not taught in most theological colleges. We clergy-
men emerge from training with a theological and historical
understanding of the Church, but without sufficient understanding of it as a social institution. As such it is subject to
all the pressures of any other secular organisation. If management skills are required for running industry, they are
even more needed in the Church, for there the management
task is more complex. In the Church there is no narrowly
defined and clearly labelled product, and the labour force
consists of volunteers. The management of volunteer workers is far more delicate, with different rules applying, than is
the case when people depend on the work for their liveli-
hood. Some men entering the ministry bring management
skills which they have learned in their previous employment in business or military service. Where such skills have
been sensitively adapted to the peculiarities of church life,
congregations feel the benefit. Clergy without this background are 'forced to fly by the seat of their pants'. If they
have a sense of direction and succeed in getting a hang
of the controls they remain airborne, otherwise they have
to bail out or crash land when things get out of control.
Fortunately management skills can be learned, and
there are many qualified lay people in the Church who
would be delighted to render their services if invited to
do so.

Obedient servant

A Christian understanding of leadership excludes any idea
of power grasping or engaging in an ego-trip. He seeks to
serve God not *be* God. Paul, the apostle of Christ, was also
his bond-slave and conscious of his fraternal relationship
with every member of the family of God. When a leadership

struggle broke out among our Lord's disciples, Jesus pointed out the contrast between the world's understanding of leadership and that which was appropriate to his Kingdom. 'The kings of the pagans have power over the people, and the rulers are called, "Friends of the people". But this is not the way it is with you; rather, the greatest one among you must be like the youngest, and the leader must be like the servant. Who is greater, the one who sits down to eat or the one who serves him? The one who sits down, of course. But I am among you as one who serves.' (Luke 22:25–27.) In his understanding of both leadership role and style our Lord broke through all the conventions of his time. He did this not just by means of his teaching, but through his personal example.

This servant-leader model was dramatically demonstrated in the Upper Room when Jesus was at supper with his disciples and performed the foot-washing service. Custom required that this service would normally be performed by a household servant. John's account of the incident highlights its significance. 'Jesus knew that the Father had given him complete power; he knew that he had come from God, and was going to God. So he rose from the table, took off his outer garments and tied a towel around his waist' (John 13:3–5). This lowliest of acts is set in the immediate context of the loftiest of claims. It was intended as a example for his disciples to follow (v. 15). We are called to minister to one another. This entails being alert to what needs to be done, no matter how lowly the task, and then taking the initiative in doing it. Our commitment to one another is total, to the extent of being prepared to lay down our lives for one another, as Christ laid down his life for us.

Although Christian ministry involves wearing an apron, this does not mean becoming a door-mat. We are called to hold the towel of humility, not the door-mat of subservience which everyone can walk over. Service is not doing everything that everyone else should be doing; rather it is acting

in such a way that others are prompted to take up their
responsibilities willingly.

In summary, there are a number of leadership models,
and which model is appropriate at any given time will
depend on a combination of factors. Furthermore, these
models are not mutually exclusive, and the one which pre-
dominates will depend both on the personality of the leader
and the nature of the situation.

SKILL LEVELS

If any organisation, ecclesiastical or commercial, is to sustain growth, it must be prepared to restructure when the
need to do so becomes evident. Moving from one phase to
the next often requires a change in management style, and
the acquiring of fresh skills. I am grateful to the Rev. John
Wimber, an adjunct professor at Fuller Seminary, for the
following model which I have adapted slightly to fit the
British situation. He relates church size to the corresponding skill level in industry.

CHURCH SIZE	INDUSTRIAL SKILL LEVEL
1	Unskilled worker
2–65	Foreman
66–150	Supervisor
151–450	Middle management
451–1,000	Top management
1,000+	Chairman of the Board

Unskilled worker
When the congregation stands at zero, *unskilled worker* level
will suffice! The unskilled worker is merely concerned about
his own activities without any need to be responsible for
anyone else, or for the quality of the product or service he is
working on. There is widespread frustration among lay

people at the lack of management skill displayed by their clergy. As a clerical colleague admitted, 'As far as running anything is concerned, some of us couldn't run a tap!' If we lack skills to this extent then we must do some rapid reading on the subject or seek advice from those who have management expertise. We may not have far to look, for on many of our church committees are to be found people who are organising every working day, yet have not seen the usefulness of their skills for the life of the church, often because the minister has never encouraged their use.

A number of churches known to the author are facing this problem with a refreshing openness, and mutual expressions of relief as between the minister and his church council or deacons' court. While vision is an essential quality in leaders, management skills are not indispensable. He must understand management principles in order to assess his own management ability level. When a visionary leader, who shows his competence in other areas yet lacks management skills, is in the driving seat, it is essential that he has someone at his elbow who can translate vision and ideas into strategy, otherwise they will not remain on course. The distinction between management and leadership is an important one to maintain. The leader perceives *what* needs to be done. The manager demonstrates *how* it can be achieved.

Foreman

In a small church with a membership of up to say 65, the management style of the leader will probably be at the level of *foreman* or charge hand. He is one of a work-gang who is able to stand in for any of the members. He is available to be personally involved in every task which comes to hand. So the minister of the small church is expected to be a Jack-of-all-trades. He turns his hand to everything: mowing the grass, stoking the boiler, typing the letter, duplicating the magazine, leading the choir, etc., etc. He can probably sustain this pressure and diversity of work-load until the adult congregation tops 65, and then he will be in danger of driving himself into the ground. The church probably will not grow much beyond that point until he either leaves to establish another struggling church, or changes his ways.

Supervisor

In churches with a membership of between 66 and 150 the most frequently encountered leadership level is that of *supervisor*. In industry the supervisor is responsible for a line of people engaged in a number of routine operations or a small department whose job is to provide a service (e.g. invoicing). He shows everybody in his charge what to do, and constantly watches them to make sure that they continue to do it in the approved manner and to an acceptable standard. He is on hand to deal with any emergency and resolve any difficulties which may arise. Church ministers who operate in this way have their phones constantly ringing, or find people for ever at the door and have queues of church members at every service and function. These are people who have been given jobs to do, but have not been given the authority to make decisions relating to their tasks. Consequently, everything has to be referred back to the minister, who then begins to find that it is quicker to do things himself, as he is now spending the major part of his time chasing up other people. The situation becomes impossible as membership nears the 150 mark. Few individuals can cope with more than that number of people at more than surface level. Working relationships begin to break down. Also, as a church grows it diversifies its activities to the point where the leader is unable to make meaningful detailed decisions in every area. The Jack-of-all-trades has revealed himself to be incapable in the circumstances of becoming a master of any.

Middle management

The leader has to change his management style to *middle management* level to get far into the 151–450 member bracket. Middle management involves delegation *with accountability*. When people are invited to undertake some responsibility in the church they are given appropriate decision-making powers. The musical director, Sunday School superintendent, magazine editor, youth leader, parish administrator, require written job descriptions which spell out the requirements of the job and specify areas where the job holder has decision-making powers to avoid the need to refer back constantly to the minister or one of the church's management committees. (See page 186 for a sample job description for a home group leader.) In a large church the Sunday School superintendent, for instance, must be responsible for the teaching curriculum, training of teachers, discipline and home visitation of the children. He will work through his education committee and teaching team. Policy matters will be agreed with the minister and church committee, and the minister is on hand to offer a listening ear. Yet he must avoid getting over-involved in the detailed execution and allowing all the decision-making to float up the church's organisational structure. People have to be trusted. When others do a job in our place, it is to be expected that they probably won't do it our way. There is a wise missionary saying which reminds us, 'If you want a job done properly do it yourself. But if you want it to last, get someone else to do it!'

Management in a growing church of more than 150 members becomes increasingly complex, because the work force is made up of volunteers. The minister is the one person paid to run the church, and he is the one most likely to be available to attend to the hundred-and-one practical things which have to be dealt with during normal business hours. At this point the church will need to give serious consideration to the enlarging of its full-time staff, to diversify its ministries and provide the necessary administrative support.

Top management
The church with more than 450 members will have a growing full-time staff, each of whom operates at middle-management level. The minister in charge therefore needs *top-level management skills* to weld his professional team together. He is responsible for overall strategy and ensuring its implementation in the various departments. But he must leave room for initiative to be exercised by his team members. They will want to be treated as professionals who know their jobs, have ideas of their own and can carry responsibility. They must therefore be left to formulate their goals and draw up plans to implement agreed objectives.

Chairman of the board
When a church tops the 1,000 membership mark it enters the super-league. Some exponents of church growth theory have serious doubts as to whether churches should ever be encouraged to reach such proportions. They argue that it is preferable to sub-divide to maintain a growth momentum. The larger the church the higher the percentage of passengers it may find itself carrying. Superchurches, they argue, merely drain life from other congregations situated in their extensive catchment areas. Others take a different view, maintaining that urban conurbations with a densely populated, highly mobile society of people with wide-ranging interests and affiliations, require churches which are large enough to achieve visibility in the urban scene, and are able to sustain a wide range of activities corresponding to the community's diverse needs.

Our purpose here is not to enter into the pros and cons of this debate, but simply to indicate the leadership level at which the presiding minister of such a church will need to operate. He functions as *chairman of the board*. He dreams his dreams, formulates his plans, and excites others with the vision of his perceptions of where the church could be five years hence. He is looking for a hand-picked team of able people who can see their individual specialisations in relation to the whole. He ensures that there is free time in his diary to take soundings of the state of affairs at the grassroots level, otherwise he will quickly get out of touch, and he fulfils a wider ministry as ambassador of his congregation, sharing their vision with the church at large. There are very few examples of this kind of church in Europe, but they are to be found in the Americas and elsewhere. Some have proved to be an inspiration in many places around the world. Such a ministry is however not without its self-evident dangers.

LEADERSHIP QUALITIES
While leadership styles vary there are a number of characteristics which are apparent in the lives of outstanding leaders.

Strategic thinking
Many people get so entangled in the problems that they cannot 'see the wood for the trees'. The leader should be able to step back, to get outside the problem and see things in perspective. He must be able to set the situation out clearly and expose the heart of the matter. A great leader in fact makes few significant decisions, but he isolates the key issues. Having made up his mind about these, many other decisions fall into place. Until that central issue has been identified and decided upon, every other decision has to be considered in isolation, which makes for muddle and contradiction. Henry Ford's key decision was that the motor car should be cheap enough to be available to the average family. The rest of what Henry Ford did follows on from

that – a basic model, one colour only, assembly line production etc. Lord Alanbrooke in his position as Chief
of the General Staff in World War Two developed his
grand strategy of rolling back the Allied map, starting in
North Africa and continuing through Italy and southern
Europe. During the early part of the war he had to contain
Churchill's enthusiasm   he headline-grabbing, one-off
daring raids.

Task and problem definitions are a key role of the leader.
Having identified what needs to be done and having
explored and evaluated the possible ways of approaching
the task he then must identify the resources he will need.
'Effective leadership diagnoses where the greatest readiness and capacity exists to carry out the commitments and
priorities of the organisation. A good leader utilises the best
equipped person to act on those priorities' (Perry 1977:73).

Courage to act on convictions
A church must define clearly and concisely what it believes
to be its main objectives. It is the task of the leader to ensure
that this is done. He is also required to chart the possible
routes to their achievement. Leadership means the loneliness of being out front – but not too far ahead. A leader
ceases to lead when he is so far ahead that he is either out of
sight, or sets too fast a pace which none of his followers will
be able to sustain. Leadership entails being in touch with
the tail-enders as well as the front-runners.

There is a tendency for some ministers to abdicate from
a leadership position. It is safer and more secure to be a
neutral chairman ready to accept and implement committee decisions without questioning them too closely. There is
a feeble form of democracy which prevents any action until
there is unanimity. The result is that many long-overdue
decisions are kept in limbo, and the church can only
move forward on non-controversial and usually relatively
insignificant matters. In reality this state of affairs is not

democracy but rule by the minority who hold the rest of the congregation to ransom.

Due either to the influence of training, or the demands of parochial ministry, a number of clergy place the emphasis on counselling rather than leadership. They become so entangled in the problems of individuals that the church as a whole loses a sense of direction and lacks cohesion. A captain of a ship cannot confine himself to the sick bay. He must get back on the bridge. Furthermore his 'non-directive counselling' approach is carried over into his leadership functions with debilitating consequences. While it may be possible to act as a non-directive counsellor, it is a contradiction in terms to be a non-directive leader. A leader must lead.

Inspires confidence

A distinction must be made between the convictions people have regarding the suitability of plans and their confidence in the leadership seeking to implement them. Plans can be turned down without being given serious consideration through lack of trust rather than lack of commitment.

A leader must secure his leadership base by having an adequate support group. Such a group is not composed of pliable 'yes men' but of those who have leadership standing, a degree of discernment and a range of specialist skills.

Both the new minister and the old, established minister, who is seeking to lift both himself and his congregation out of a rut, must work hard to build trust and establish confidence. The inexperienced and impetuous are tempted to move too quickly into the areas of greatest controversy to establish their battle ground and force through sweeping changes. Such changes run the risk of proving to be for the worse rather than the better. Beware of change for change's sake.

A wiser strategy is to begin by affirming whatever is

praiseworthy in the inherited situation; then wherever possible, only introducing change where there is evidence of broad support and which looks reasonably sure of success. This establishes confidence in the judgement of the leader and creates working relationships and team cohesion. When bonds of mutual esteem and confidence have been forged they can then be tested in the more contentious areas. The leadership must reach a stage where they can disagree seriously on issues while still parting as friends. This leads us directly into the next point.

The course once set must be maintained. Nothing erodes confidence in a leader more than switching from one objective to another so that the whole progress of the church becomes erratic. Great leaders are not easily discouraged. They recognise that there will always be obstacles to progress. It is the task of leadership to blast through, climb over, or find a way round. The leader does not panic. He maintains his poise under pressure. Having accepted responsibility he does not then try to pass the buck or hide behind committee decisions. A leader must be able to live with tension. This demands a sense of personal security, the ability to make difficult and sometimes unpopular decisions, and the capacity to switch off and relax.

Influences others
One of the simplest ways to spot a leader is to notice those who people are following! The leader has a winsomeness which enables him to influence the thinking of other people and to motivate them to action. His presence instils confidence, heightens possibilities, and encourages people to get involved. Trust is gradually built up through the quality of personal relationships. Tactically, a minister is wise to spend the greater part of his first year in an established church situation in getting to know who the decision-makers are and in establishing rapport with them.

When the time comes to introduce innovative ideas, we

are saved from disappointment if we recognise that most good ideas are rejected first time and even second time around. The fact that they fail to achieve the necessary majority should not be regarded as the end of the road. It is better to withdraw the suggestion while the debate is still amicable, than precipitate a crisis which may debar the reintroduction of the idea for months or even years. If the discussion is allowed to become heated, on each subsequent occasion that the issue is raised, committee members will re-enter the fray in the same combative spirit. If, however, the idea is introduced first time as no more than a tentative suggestion, the responses, both negative and positive, can be evaluated with a view to its later reintroduction in a form which is most likely to secure the widest acceptance.

Fosters good relationships and builds up a cohesive team
This follows on from the previous point. The leader inspires confidence through his consistency and a measure of predictability. If those around him do not know where he is likely to jump next, they become understandably nervous and cautious. A leader who has patiently established a consistent and workable pattern of operation can then afford to adopt a more flexible approach from time to time. A totally predictable man becomes dull. The occasional unexpected, adventurous decision keeps people on their toes without setting them on the retreat.

One of the drawbacks of a 'strong natural leader' is that he often tries to project on to other people his high standards and total dedication, which they do not always share. He therefore becomes very critical of his colleagues and subordinates, and in turn they become cautious in their response to him. Thereby are sown the seeds which will jeopardise the future prospects.

The Christian leader is called to be a shepherd, not a jockey! He rounds people up and leads them forward rather than riding on their backs and driving them on to achieve his objectives. Good relationships are fostered through affirmation. We must have a ministry of encouragement to one another, helping each other develop those gifts with which God has endowed every one of us. Only then will we have access through each other's defences to offer constructive criticism.

SUMMARY

A good leader must be prepared to extend the base of leadership by encouraging others to share their particular expertise for the good of the whole. We must be ready to welcome other people to work alongside us, who have abilities in specific areas greater than our own, without feeling personally threatened by their presence. Remember, the chain is as strong as its weakest link. So a team will break apart unless weak links are reinforced.

There will be little in the way of sustained church growth without inspiring and facilitating leadership. Have you identified the leadership requirements of your church in terms of your spheres of ministry? Do each of your leaders have workable job-descriptions? Do they work together as a cohesive team? Are you alert to spot new and potential leaders, or is the leadership a closed circle? Does your leadership encourage initiative among the members, or does it regard any move among them as a potential threat? Do your leaders need further training to upgrade their skills to cope with a larger and more diverse operation? Are your leaders prepared for an evaluation of their performance? Do we pray regularly for our leaders, that their vision might be kept clear, that they will be able to sustain their creative drive, that through their decisions the whole congregation might be challenged, excited, involved and fulfilled?

CHAPTER TEN

Expectations and Planning

Some Christians are suspicious of planning and reluctant to get involved with policy statements, strategic thinking and defining objectives. Their hesitancy stems from the belief that the mission in which we are engaged is God's mission and not merely the Church's. While it is our responsibility to carry out his will, they argue, the planning and strategy remains in God's hands, and the results of our activities on his behalf are in accordance with his will, rather than commensurate with our efforts. They therefore consider that we must be prepared to operate on impulse as the Holy Spirit leads, preferring to remain in the dark regarding God's planning, and to rest content, leaving the result in his hands. They quote a number of Scriptures in support of this stance.

As Zerubbabel was pondering how Jerusalem could be restored and the Temple there rebuilt, the angel told the prophet Zechariah to inform Zerubbabel: 'You will succeed, not by military might or by your own strength, but by my spirit. Obstacles as great as mountains will disappear before you. You will rebuild the Temple, and as you put the last stone in place, the people will shout, "Beautiful, beautiful!"' (Zech. 4:6, 7).

When Christ was in conversation with Nicodemus, the Jewish leader, he underlined the fact that regeneration was a work of God the Holy Spirit. He achieves the seemingly impossible – 'How can a grown man be born again?' And his activities are totally unpredictable – 'The wind blows wherever it wishes; you hear the sound it makes, but you do not know where it comes from or where it is going. It is like that with everyone who is born of the Spirit' (John 3:8). As someone has delightfully commented, 'No weather forecasts are issued!'

Paul, in the course of his letter to the sadly divided church in Corinth, reminds his readers that it did not matter who did the sowing of the seed or the watering. God was the one who really mattered, because it was he who made the plant grow (1 Cor. 3:7). He had invented the germination process, had designed the seed, and was in control of the climate. This puts the part played by man in achieving a harvest in proper perspective.

To the self-assured, James issues this warning: 'Now listen to me, you that say, "Today or tomorrow we will travel to a certain city, where we will stay a year and go into business and make a lot of money." You don't even know what your life tomorrow will be! You are like a puff of smoke, which appears for a moment and then disappears. What you should say is this: "If the Lord is willing we will live and do this or that." But now you are proud, and you boast; all such boasting is wrong' (James 4:13–16).

Such passages of Scripture do not deny the possibility or legitimacy of planning, rather they warn against wrong attitudes in planning. They caution against substituting man-made schemes for a reliance on God's power. They remind us that nothing is impossible with God. They alert us to be prepared for the unexpected to happen, for God is not scheduled by our programmes. They emphasise that no matter how diligent and energetic man may be, it is still God who plays the major part. And they point out that there is a question mark hanging over every tomorrow. All plans are provisional.

PLANNING THAT IS PLEASING TO GOD

We plan in the knowledge that we serve a God who plans. He is a God of purpose and order. He does not simply respond to events, but plans in anticipation or, more accurately, in foreknowledge of developments. He had far-ranging plans for Abram (Gen. 12:3), but although Abram had certain knowledge about some things, it was none the less partial. It is only in the New Testament that the full ramifications are revealed. '. . . the promise was based on faith . . . – not just to those who obey the law, but also to those who believe as Abraham did. For Abraham is the spiritual father of us all; as the scripture says, "I have made you father of many nations"' (Rom. 4:16–17, see also Gal. 4:22–27). God's entire plan of salvation was formulated before the foundation of the world. Little by little it was revealed to his people in the course of history. God did not keep his people entirely in the dark concerning his purposes. 'I have not spoken in secret or kept my purpose hidden' (Is. 45:19). Through Isaiah and Jeremiah he informs Israel that he is in control of the future; they are therefore warned of the consequences of their disobedience (Is. 48:3–8) and reminded of the good things that he has in store for them (Jer. 29:10).

God's plans for man's salvation are fully implemented in Jesus Christ. The opening chapter of Ephesians is a classic statement of God's cosmic purpose expressed in the mission of his Son. 'Because of his love God had already decided that through Jesus Christ he would make us his sons – this was his pleasure and purpose . . . In all his wisdom and insight God did what he had purposed, and made known to us the secret plan he had already decided to complete by means of Christ. This plan, which God will complete when the time is right, is to bring all creation together, everything in heaven and on earth, with Christ as head . . . All things are done according to God's plan and decision; and God chose us to be his own people in union with Christ because of his own purpose, based on what he had decided from the very beginning' (Eph. 1:5, 8–10, 11).

We engage in planning in recognition that we are responsible co-workers with God.

Paul describes himself and his colleagues as working together with God (2 Cor. 6:1). God has created us as intelligent beings and works through our thought processes. He expects us to use our judgement and discernment in deciding issues rather than looking for sign-posts at every turning.

The delicate balance between divine guidance and dependence on him on the one hand, and human responsibility and resourcefulness on the other, is expressed in Psalm 32:8, 9. 'The Lord says, "I will teach you the way you should go; I will instruct you and advise you. Don't be stupid like a horse or a mule, which must be controlled with a bit and bridle to make it submit." ' God does not treat us like animals, demanding mindless obedience. Rather, he relates to us as rational and responsible human beings with whom he communicates via our thought processes. He guides us through consultation, not conditioning.

Two personalities in the Old Testament, Joseph and Nehemiah, illustrate the need to draw up and implement plans. Joseph was given the gift of interpretation to unlock the meaning of Pharaoh's dream. Having alerted the Egyptian ruler that seven years of famine would follow the seven of plenty, he then steps beyond his brief by outlining a job description and offering a plan of action to deal with the emergency (Gen. 41:33–36). He made such a favourable impression on Pharaoh that he himself got the job of organising the famine measures for the entire nation.

We see similar initiative and strategic thinking in the case of Nehemiah. On hearing the reports brought by his brothers of the ruined state of Jerusalem, he seeks an audience with Emperor Artaxerxes to ask permission to leave Babylonia to take charge of the rebuilding of his ancestral home. His bold request is granted and the subsequent account demonstrates the planning and leadership gifts of Nehemiah. He makes a thorough inspection to ascertain the size of the task and what must be given priority consideration. He allocates responsibilities so that each group knows the area in which it is to operate. He identifies the opposition and protects his work force from attack by arranging them in a shift system with half of them performing guard duty at any one time. By skilful planning, motivation and coordination he is able to complete the project, which had eluded his predecessors, in fifty-two days (Neh. 6:15). If the art of management is the ability to get things done through other people, then Nehemiah belongs to the top bracket of senior management!

As co-workers with God, Christians are held accountable for their actions.
This is emphasised in the parable of the three servants (Matt. 25:14–30). When their master was about to leave on his journey he 'put them in charge of his property'. They were expected to shoulder responsibilities and show initiative in the management of substantial resources.

When the master eventually returns 'after a long time', he calls the three servants 'to settle accounts' with them. The servant entrusted with five thousand silver coins and the one with two thousand each report a hundred per cent capital gain. To which the master responds, 'Well done, you good and faithful servant!' By their skilful trading they had shown their profitability. Having proved themselves at that level they are rewarded with increased responsibilities.

When the master calls to account the servant with the one thousand silver coins, the outcome is very different. This man reacts instantly with anger and bitterness. He fairly accuses his master of not providing the necessary resources. 'Sir, I know you are a hard man; you reap harvests where you did not sow, and you gather crops where you did not scatter seed.' He had appeared as a man without any resources at his disposal not because he had been deprived by his master, but because he had deprived himself by burying his capital. He had no one but himself to blame. The money was more of a burden than an asset. He demonstrated his inadequacy in his attitude of fear and by his failure to shoulder responsibilities. He played for safety by burying the resources so that he could hand them back intact. Because he had achieved nothing his master describes him as a 'useless servant' and deprives him of the resources which he had failed to utilise. He was castigated not for theft – his honesty was never in question – but for inactivity. He had failed to exercise initiative.

When God appoints us as co-workers he expects us to use the resources which he supplies, using our intelligence and endeavouring to be effective. We cannot 'pass the buck', for each will be held responsible, for to whom much is given from him much is expected.

We engage in planning in the understanding that in the final analysis we are utterly dependent on God's providence.
For planning to be pleasing to God it must be directed to the achievement of the objectives that he has stipulated, using methods which are worthy and effective to those ends. He guides us not by providing a celestial print-out, but by gifts of knowledge, discernment and faith which enable us to grapple with the issues. We begin by praying for guidance, and then plan, believing that he has answered our prayers. From time to time we may pause for further help in understanding and, when decisions cannot be postponed, be prepared to come down one side or the other confessing our confusion and asking for his overruling. In many instances a wrong decision is preferable to no decision at all.

We acknowledge our dependence on God not simply at the planning stage, but at every level of implementation. Spiritual results cannot be obtained apart from spiritual means. While planting and cultivating are man's responsibility, the provision of the harvest is God's. There are always imponderables involved. Results cannot be determined, they can only be estimated and anticipated, on the basis of assumptions which should be clearly stated.

Our planning is also inevitably provisional. We see through a glass darkly. Even on the clearest of days our vision is blurred and restricted. Although Paul planned to go to Spain the Acts record ends without his having achieved his objective. God is never limited or conditioned by our planning. He may surpass our expectations and surprise us by acting totally outside and independent of our planning framework. Planning which is pleasing to God is therefore flexible and open-ended.

ESTABLISHING GENERAL OBJECTIVES

In many organisations activity tends to crowd out purpose. We become so engrossed in doing things that we do not pause to ask why we are so engaged. Do we have a clear objective in view? Is the objective strategic? Is our method of achieving it the best way, given that conditions may have changed drastically? Like any other institution the Church should sit down from time to time in order to redefine its mission. The committed membership needs to ask itself: Why has God put us here? What kind of people does he want us to become? What should be distinctive about our motivation, goals and life-style? What does God want to get done through us? What are our inbuilt strengths and limitations? What other churches and groups are also serving the area? What are their distinctive contributions and how can we complement one another?

Many of our church planning meetings are disunited, inconclusive and prolonged through lack of any agreed statement of purpose and priorities. Consequently, all decisions are taken in isolation, with the result that a decision taken in one area is later found to be at variance with a decision taken in another. Opinions are moulded by tradition, the minister's views, influential cliques, financial limitations, frustration with interminable discussion, or a desire to find the easiest way out rather than to achieve mutually agreed objectives. If there is no eye to the future and no sense of destiny then in dealing with the items on a crowded agenda we will succumb to the temptation 'to fill in the background with so many details that the foreground goes underground'! A house which is divided against itself cannot even stand never mind about grow.

The driver of a parked car was disturbed by a man tapping on the near-side window. As he wound down the window the pedestrian asked, 'Excuse me, but is this the second turning on the right?' It was an impossible question to answer because the pedestrian had stated neither his starting-point nor his intended destination. Any road will do until we have decided where we are wanting to go.

Some churches in North America refer to their statement of objectives as their 'philosophy of ministry'. This is a concise, crisp and clear statement which attempts to set out the kind of church we believe God wants us to become as we currently perceive his mind. It should be kept short and succinct. The following considerations will all have a bearing on the formulation of a philosophy of ministry.

1 *Biblical priorities* as we understand them, covering the areas of worship, life-style, evangelism and service.
2 *Situational demands*. How we relate meaning to our area of ministry or constituency and the special emphases required.
3 *Denominational emphases* expressed. How these are expressed, modified or reinterpreted to make them appropriate to the area.

4 *Membership characteristics and resources.* Identifying what we have to contribute recognising who and what we are and defining the potential church member from among our personal contacts and the community.

5 *Leadership insights.* Inevitably these will both focus and restrict our vision. As we respond to God's will, so our perspective changes, causing us to re-examine our general objectives. They may then need to be clarified, enlarged or modified.

In drawing up your 'philosophy of ministry' do not be afraid of stating the obvious. What is clear cut and non-negotiable to one person may on discussion prove to be obscure or open to debate in the views of others.

WORKING FOR CONSENSUS

How should a church arrive at its philosophy of ministry statement? Is it introduced from above by the appointed leader? Are the objectives formulated by the church's management committee or crystallised through a process of congregational debate? There is no simple answer to this question. Much will depend on the leadership style of the minister, the effectiveness of the executive and the spiritual maturity and commitment of the bulk of the congregation. As the statement of general objectives will ultimately need to be owned by the congregation if it is to be implemented, they need to share in the formulation.

The congregation however will expect guidance from its leader in this exercise. Although they may rightly resent being treated as a rubber stamp, they will expect starting-points to provide a basis for further discussion.

Where congregational cohesion and commitment is lacking then the minister and church council will have to make the running, in drawing up general objectives.

The minister may need to go away privately to write his Parish Profile. When he has done this to his own satisfaction

he will need to ask himself if this is a vision with which he
can personally identify. Could he see himself working effectively and feeling fulfilled operating in that imaginary
framework? If he could, then his next step is to bring back
the summary to his leadership group for them to comb
through, suggesting possible amendments until it reaches a
form which is acceptable to all.

When the statement is presented for the vote either with
the church committee or at a congregational meeting the
following cautions outlined by the North American church
consultant Lyle Schaller should be borne in mind.

'*Do not ask people to vote prematurely.*' They need to become
thoroughly acquainted with all relevant facts, and the
various facets of each issue explored. Make sure that people
understand what they are voting for, otherwise they will
vote 'NO' to be on the safe side or to conceal their ignorance.

'*Present only one issue at a time.*' Take things step by step.
Seek agreement in one specific area before moving on to the
next, otherwise, people will be tempted to veto the whole
package for the sake of one controversial element. Suspicion
raised in one area is likely to spread into the others. Secure
the undisputed territory. Progress and improvement in this
area will generate confidence to tackle areas where there is
less unanimity of viewpoint.

'*Whenever possible avoid the use of "YES" or "NO" type of
questions in a ballot.*' These will tend to draw a dividing line
between positive and negative thinkers, rather than indicate
true levels of support. Furthermore, they drive the opponents
into a purely negative stance when they might want to
follow a more positive, alternative line. The 'YES/NO' vote
can polarise the situation and paralyse the group, prevent-
ing them from further action. People don't want to hear the
issue raised again, for each time merely stokes their feelings
of anger and frustration. Often there is more than one route
to achieve a goal, so keep the options open as long as
possible, and confront people with two affirmative choices.

'*It is unwise to let an issue come to a formal vote until most of the leadership are reasonably sure of the outcome of the balloting.*' When leaders lose contact with the followers they cease to be leaders and become loners. To allow an issue to be put to the vote when you have a strong inclination that it will be defeated, is to put yourself out on a limb and saw yourself off. Discernment and timing are of the essence of successful leadership. Schaller draws attention to the frequently overlooked fact that the formal vote is not the most decisive point in the implementation process. It is merely the legitimising of a decision that has already been arrived at informally (Schaller 1978a:149). If the most active part that people are going to play towards the implementation of an idea is to raise their hands or place a cross on a piece of paper, then little has been achieved. While the 'YES' vote may turn the traffic light to green it may not serve to take the brake off the waiting vehicle or engage the clutch.

'*Education is alienation from the rest of the congregation.*' 'Whenever a few people in a congregation share an educational experience that enlarges their vision, alters their definition of the purpose and mission of the Church, or changes their scale of values, this experience tends to alienate those few persons from the rest of the congregation.' It is all too easy to open up a communication gap between the front runners and the rest of the field. This occurs in churches which have over-secretive committees and poor internal communications, or may arise when thinking moves ahead quickly during a parish residential conference, causing resentments among those who were unable or unwilling to attend. The pace must be set at a rate which enables the main body to keep together (Schaller 1978a:147–149).

When an individual or small group become enthusiastic about an idea, the temptation is for them to seek out other likely supporters at the earliest possible moment to enlist them for the cause. Such a move, however, can be counter-productive in the long term. As soon as the opposition sense that the enthusiasts are on the move they will begin to exert a counter-pressure to maintain the congregation's equilibrium (or inertia, according to your point of view!). This in turn leads the innovators to exert still more pressure, which then has to be countered by the other side. If the pressure continues to mount, without either side giving ground, then the tension will become so great that the congregation will be in great danger of being torn apart into warring factions.

According to Kurt Lewin's 'force field theory' a better strategy is to go at an early stage to those who are likely to be most opposed or entertain the strongest reservations. Talking the issues through with them before plans have been detailed, or momentum allowed to gather, will give the leadership an indication of how far they are likely to carry people with them and where are the sticking points. In these initial consultations they may also discover that God has something to say through the 'opposition'!

Another important factor in attitude change is involvement. When people are encouraged to contribute their ideas and their opinions are actively sought and sympathetically listened to, a climate of trust and openness to innovation is created. As they get involved and become positive contributors to the change process so they become more flexible and adventurous.

In the previous section we emphasised the need to establish 'an overall objective'. While this is something which will need to be agreed eventually, in a seriously divided congregation it might be wiser to arrive at this statement in stages, rather than try to introduce the whole thing in one exercise. At the same time great care must be taken that by doing this the overall objective is not diluted or left to evaporate. The important point is that the leadership should at least know where they are going as they pick up the individual pieces and try to fit them together in a meaningful way.

ACHIEVING SPECIFIC GOALS

While an objective is a general statement of purpose, a goal is a specific result to be accomplished by a certain date. Many churches think they have goals, but in reality they are only vague intentions. A goal must be specific enough to eventually be able to measure whether or not you have attained it! To say that we want to increase the level of participation in the music of our church services is an objective. It is a statement of intent. To know to what extent we are successful in achieving it depends on goal setting. We might therefore decide:

1 To appoint a director of music.
2 To increase the choir memberhip from 12 to 25 in the next two years.
3 To teach the congregation one new hymn a month.
4 To begin the evening service once a month with a fifteen-minute congregational hymn practice.
5 To have a four-member singing group with guitars etc. to introduce modern music once a month.

Having clarified the distinction between an objective and a goal we proceed to examine goal setting from a Christian perspective in greater detail.

A goal is a statement of faith

It represents what we believe God wants done, and what he will provide the resources to enable us to achieve. Goals are not grasped out of the air. They must be set prayerfully and responsibly. On the one hand they help to release us from timidity. On the other, they must not lead us into arrogant presumption.

As a statement of *faith* it is not simply a projection based

on calculations from past performance. It is the product
of the gift of faith, which we have noted is given to some
Christians. However, a word of caution is necessary at this
point. Our congregational goals should not be uncritically
adopted. They must represent a corporate level of faith,
with which the leadership can identify and by which the
congregation are inspired. 'To have faith is to be sure of the
things we hope for, to be certain of the things we cannot see'
(Heb. 11:1). If assurance and confidence are lacking then
the goal may be a statement of folly rather than of faith!
Our faith is in order to achieve something which is over the
horizon, not on the far side of the moon.

Our goals pin-point our priorities
The range of goals should express the extent of our concerns. They should be in line with our objectives. Their
achievement will bring about detectable changes for the
better. Goals should be set to reflect a balance of concerns
in each area of the church's life. They might be conveniently
listed under the following headings:

    (a) Worship – styles, events, range of congregational
        participation.
    (b) Relational – knowing groups and individuals and
        relating to their felt needs.
    (c) Organisational – overall policy formulation, per-
        formance monitoring.
    (d) Educational – themes, methods, feed-back (i.e.
        opportunities to respond to the teaching).
    (e) Evangelistic – numbers trained, events held,
        response measured.
    (f) Missions Support – home and overseas.
    (g) Social concerns – in the community served by the
        church; further afield.
    (h) Resources – use of buildings; involvement of
        people; financial commitment.

A goal is a target for achievement

It is stated so as to define the point of aim, and to enable the degree of achievement to be assessed. McGavran and Arn caution that 'a goal is not a tyrant but a target' (McGavran and Arn 1977:108). It is something to aim at, not to be bound by. Some people are reluctant to set goals due to the fear of failure. However, failure can be itself a valuable part of the learning process. Failure, regarded positively, represents the elimination of possibilities. It contributes to the funnelling of effort towards eventual accomplishment. When we set a goal and aim for it, we are then in a position to measure how close we came to scoring a bull's eye. On the basis of our performance we can then take steps to improve our aim and increase our fire-power. We may even decide to move the target: nearer to us, if we even failed to register one hit, or further away, if we score a bull's eye every time. A goal should be seen as a movable target and not as a fixture. The quantities or timing may need to be adjusted in the light of experience.

Goal-setting challenges us to earth our fantasies. During the First World War, Will Rogers, the celebrated American raconteur, volunteered an idea for ridding the Atlantic Ocean of German U-boats. His novel answer to the problem was to bring the ocean to boiling-point, so that all the U-boats were forced to surface before their crews were pressure-cooked. Then waiting patrol boats could force them to surrender. When asked how he would go about heating the ocean, he replied, 'Oh! I'm just the ideas man. You work out the details!' Goal-setting provides the necessary discipline to ascertain to what extent ideas are achievable.

In addition to being measurable it must have a time-frame indicating what needs to be done by when. For some people time is an eschatological concept! They live in a never-never land. In the case of many projects the biggest waste of time is in getting started.

A goal provides a test of commitment

Goals spell out the practical implications of embarking on a course of action. As we describe our goals in precise terms we place a price tag on each item in terms of time, effort and financial outlay. We can then decide whether or not we are prepared to proceed.

From experience in the business world, it is clear that people are most prepared to accept goals which they themselves have had a hand in formulating. Imposed goals are regarded as a threat rather than a challenge. Goals must be accepted by the individuals or group responsible for their implementation. Larger congregational goals may therefore need to be broken down into sub-goals with which individuals and groups (i.e. organisations and home groups) can more easily identify. Alternatively, the agreed congregational objective can be taken into appropriate groups for them to draw up their own goals representing their particular organisation's contribution towards meeting the stated objective.

A goal should be established on the basis of research

Our goals will be in danger of being nothing more than castles in the air, unless in shaping them we have gathered as much relevant information as possible. Faith is not belief in spite of evidence, but living in scorn of consequences. Thus a church setting worship attendance goals will look carefully at trends during the past ten years. They will also take note of community developments. Is there any evidence of increased receptivity? What are the population trends likely to be? How many existing properties are scheduled for demolition? Are any new estates likely to be developed? Are new industries bringing families into the area, or is it a static and ageing community? What proportion of residents from our catchment area are we likely to attract, bearing in mind the kind of people we are and the activities in which we engage?

All these factors must be taken into consideration when formulating goals. But having done our homework, we do not simply let the facts determine the goals, else we may react as did ten of the twelve spies who reconnoitred the Promised Land and decided that the giants and walled cities presented too great an obstacle. We must take care to balance the positive alongside the negative factors. Many people find it helpful to draw up a 'for and against' list to help in decision-making.

FORMULATING WORKABLE PLANS

Plans are designed to convert intention into achievement. 'Planning is trying to discover how to accomplish goals *before* you commit yourself. Planning is moving from the *now* to the *then*, from the "way things are" to the "way we want things to be". Planning is trying to imagine the future as we would like it to be, and explaining how it could be. For the Christian, planning is trying to understand God's will and respond to that understanding by our actions' (Dayton 1974:125). Decisions commit us to a course of action. As someone has commented, 'Having fired a bullet it is very difficult then to catch up in order to move the target!'

We do well to remember that there is almost always more than one route to achieve a goal. Sometimes leaders conclude mistakenly that a goal has been rejected because a particular plan was turned down. First agree on the goal and then you are free to examine all the alternative routes which are open to you. If we are not clear about the goal, the plan will inevitably be confused. Albert Einstein once commented that 'few things characterise our day so much as perfection of means and confusion of goals.'

Therefore write up the goal for everyone to see, and keep looking at it during the planning session. Then invite ideas by means of a brain-storming session. List the suggestions on an overhead projector or blackboard without interrupting the flow of ideas by stopping to discuss them. If the planning group is too inhibited to participate freely, then divide them into buzz groups of four to six people for them to share suggestions among themselves before voicing them to the rest of the meeting. Once the list is complete, examine each idea in the light of the agreed goal. Delete those which will lead in other directions; they are the red herrings. Grade the remainder in order of likely probability. Take the 'A's' which represent the most promising and consider the pros and cons of each. If necessary follow with the 'B's' and 'C's'. In the light of your more careful considerations do you wish to revise the grading of any situation? Sometimes the least obvious suggestion proves on closer inspection to be the most ingenious. You may then want to take a break to allow the ideas to 'incubate' before you make your choice.

A plan by definition must be workable. It consists of a series of logical steps to convert aims into achievement. Each step must be within reach from the one before. Some plans are so ambitious that they result in pigmies struggling on a giants' causeway. The steps need to be attainable as well as logical.

DRAWING UP AN ORGANISATIONAL FRAMEWORK

An organisational framework shows the various steps in the achievement of a goal and indicates the relationship between them. Such diagrams are called 'PERT' in management circles – *P*rogramme *E*valuation and *R*eview *T*echnique. This provides a detailed breakdown and scheduling of all the steps involved. While at first glance this may to some look unnecessarily complex, it only takes a few minutes to draw up. As you undertake the planning exercise you will then become aware of the things you might otherwise have overlooked and you will see who will need to relate to whom and at what stage in the operation they should each begin to act. It also provides an invaluable record to help someone else to take over responsibility for its achievement on a subsequent occasion.

Such planning also entails the acceptance of mutual responsibility. We must move on from *what* needs to be done, to consider *who* is to do it and by *when*. This aspect of planning may be clearly represented on a 'Responsibilities Chart'. Once this has been agreed by all those involved it is distributed to everyone with a calendar of pre-arranged check-points to ensure that progress is being made. The establishing of clear areas of responsibility at the outset can help to save heartaches, embarrassment and frustration later on. The greater the complexity of the operation and the more people involved, the greater the chances of mis-understanding and organisational breakdown.

ALLOCATING ADEQUATE RESOURCES

The following cry from the heart appears on a partition in a certain open-plan London office:

> We, the willing,
> led by the unknowing
> are doing the impossible
> for the ungrateful.
> We have done so much
> with so little
> for so long,
> We are now qualified
> to do anything
> with nothing.

People are more important than plans. In Christian enterprises people should not be ruthlessly driven to breaking-point. Plans are formulated to inspire, not manipulate. Individuals and groups must therefore be convinced of the worthwhileness of the job they are being invited to undertake, and that they will be given adequate support and encouragement to enable them to perform to the best of their ability. In a previous chapter we have already discussed the principles involved in enlisting and handling volunteers. It is an irresponsible stewardship of human resources to give a person a job without the essential decision-making authority or basic resources to fulfil the task. This is an all-too-common occurrence in Christian work.

Every goal carries a price tag and each constituent item must be carefully costed. How many people will it need? What gifts, insights and skills are essential? What level of commitment will it demand in terms of hours per week (including preparation as well as performance)? How long should the appointment be expected to run for? What space will be required? What amenities? What expenditure for capital equipment and on-going expenses? These issues need to be faced *before* personnel are enthused and committed, otherwise they will become quickly frustrated and ultimately disillusioned. That is one of the reasons we have more vacancies than applicants in so much church work.

The church's budget
One of the major problem areas is a failure to bring budgeting into line with planning. In many churches the statement of accounts reflects precedents which have been established during the course of many years. The budget is drawn up on the basis of past performance rather than to achieve anticipated goals. Its bias is to ensure the maintenance of the status quo rather than responding to new challenges. Established items take precedent over new suggestions, which may only be added if there is surplus capital, or if ear-marked new money can be raised.

If a church is to adapt to new situations or gear itself for growth it must often revise drastically its budgeting procedures. The power of precedent needs to be broken. The budgeting exercise should be undertaken as part of the church's total programme planning. The budget must be structured to become more of an irrigation channel and less of a dam wall! Its purpose is not conservation but facilitation. Lyle Schaller, with penetrating insight, describes a church's budget as:

1 A theological document, identifying the gods that are worshipped, and ranking them in a hierarchy.

2 A statement of purpose – the priorities are reflected by the allocation of resources.

3 A political manifesto. Resources are scarce, and the budget is a result of bargaining. It reflects how the conflicts have been resolved.

4 A declaration of expectations. It shows what the organisation expects to achieve, and the sources from which it expects to receive them.

5 A precedent. Once adopted, a budget becomes a precedent for future decisions. It is more difficult to subtract existing items than add new ones (Schaller 1978a:38–46).

Review the current budget to ascertain to what extent it fails to reflect the church's policy and plans. If it is at serious variance, then isolate the points where there is an obvious divergence.

STIMULATING ENTHUSIASTIC PARTICIPATION
In the chapters dealing with every-member ministry and enabling leadership we considered at length a number of important issues relating to the identification, activation, deployment and developing of gifts. Under this heading we will confine ourselves to the following points:

1 The church's programme must be sufficiently relevant, imaginative and attractive to motivate people to want to be

party to its implementation. Simply stated, people must
a) understand it, b) believe in it and c) relate to it.
2 They must have confidence in and access to the leadership.
3 The overall programme should be broken down into
manageable parts so that it does not appear too daunting.
4 Do not rely on broadcast announcements to enlist support. Get people involved at the planning stage. When they
have had a share in their formulation they are more likely to
get involved in their implementation. Hand pick the key
people, and enlist the bulk of the support through the small
and intermediate groups.
5 Allow opportunity for the groups involved in each project
to exercise their initiative and creativity within general
guidelines.
6 Set a time limit so that volunteers know from the outset
that they have not committed themselves indefinitely. Often
people are reluctant to get involved for fear of not being able
to extricate themselves without a great deal of 'hassle' and
embarrassment.
7 Affirm and encourage people in their jobs. The bouquets
should outnumber the brickbats.
8 If any part obviously is not working don't leave it to limp
along indefinitely. Locate the source of the trouble and deal
with it.
9 Don't dwell on the difficulties – emphasise opportunities
and achievements. Foster a positive attitude and a buoyant
spirit.

ENSURING GOOD INTERNAL
COMMUNICATIONS

In many churches the congregations suffer from 'mushroom
management'. They are kept completely in the dark except
for brief moments when the door is opened for manure to be
thrown over them! This is not a style of management conducive to church growth! People must be kept informed and

not left in the dark until their help is required or blame apportioned. Few churches pay sufficient attention to their internal communications. There may be a great deal of planning activity at committee level but few of their concerns percolate through to the people in the pew. Churches tend to operate on the mystery tour principle. The coach-driver is the only one aware of the route. It is assumed that as far as the passengers are concerned, the attraction in making the journey is not knowing where they are going or blind faith in the driver's ability. Adopting such a style of operation means that the congregation will never be other than passengers, or more likely, that before long many will cease to turn up at all.

The church has a number of channels for regularly communicating with its membership.

A popularised budget summary

This should be a communication vehicle, not a confusion of mystery items. It is the church's action plan for a stated period in financial terms. It should clearly state in a readily assimilable form what the church intends to do. All figures should be rounded up to include only two significant digits, because this is apparently all people can take in at a glance. It should be structured according to overall objectives, with charts and pictorial diagrams used wherever possible.

The noticeboard

Some churches display their budget, for instance, in an attractive diagrammatic form on a notice board, and indicate month by month the progress being made as funds become available. People will give when they know what they are giving for with some hope that something will be done about it.

The magazine or news-sheet

This should also reflect the progress made in the achievement of objectives. The knowledge that you are succeeding in getting things done will encourage and generate more faith. The news-sheet can have more of a personal focus than the noticeboard, highlighting the various departments and their activities.

The notices

These should be more than a diary of events and should never be allowed to degenerate into a tale of woe. If the minister's instinct tells him that people are unlikely to support a particular event, no matter what he says, then he should not indulge in unproductive exhortations. They merely destroy credibility. Such items should be given the briefest mention, or relegated to the news-sheet.

The larger the congregation the more formalised the communication system needs to become. It is usually safe to assume that the message has not got through, or if it has, then it has probably become garbled in the process (Schaller 1978:134–140). Therefore, to avoid communication bottle-necks and 'static interference' use all the channels available to you. People need to hear the same things said in different ways, on a number of occasions, through different media, to be sure of getting the message. And even when every route has been exploited it can be assumed that some people will not have heard!

Two-way communication is preferable to one-way. The fact that people have assented does not mean that they will necessarily do anything about it. Therefore, whenever possible, build in opportunities for response by allowing for reactions and asking for specific commitments of time and talents.

A church with more than 150 members needs established procedures to encourage and handle suggestions and hear grievances. If not, people will vote in the only other ways open to them – with their pocket or with their feet. The quality of the commitment depends to a large extent on the quality of the communication.

COPING WITH CHANGE

The one thing certain about tomorrow is that it won't be like yesterday. Change is an indispensable ingredient of life, but in many areas the pace of change has increased unnervingly. Lloyd Perry maintains, 'Change in the local church is no longer an option, it is a necessity. Modern man feels a gap between the world of the church and the outside world. The world is changing rapidly and the present-day church with its rigidity of form, cannot cope with that changing world. We must be ready to face a changing world with a changing church' (Perry 1977:119).

The Church, like many other institutions, has to find ways of adapting to remain in contact with its potential membership, while at the same time avoiding alienating its long-term members. Most senior citizens, not to mention some younger churchgoers, cannot cope emotionally with too great a change inflicted upon them without due warning and preparation. If the changes proposed do not achieve their desired ends, they may alienate the existing membership without attracting the new constituency for which they were devised. It is all too easy to break eggs without succeeding in making omelettes.

In the chapter on leadership and relationships we argued the case for innovative leadership, which introduces the new without threatening the inherited patterns. By so doing the leaders are free to be creative without gaining the reputation of being subversive. As we have seen, people often resist change because they lack confidence in the one desiring it.

The innovative change agent needs to be open to suggestions. If he presents an inflexible image, insisting that his way is the only way, he will tend to generate the same attitude in those around him. Discussion has been described as 'seeking a meeting of minds without the knocking together of heads'. A flexible leader who is constantly inviting participation and encouraging suggestions generates a positive, creative attitude around him. People want leaders who know where they are going (or at least appear to), but who at the same time are open to explore alternative routes.

Change generates uncertainty. Therefore, focus attention on increasing the level of trust by highlighting the points of assurance rather than the dramatic nature of the change. The pace of change may suddenly increase as people become excited by the attractiveness of the goal, or as it comes within their grasp, or a sudden crisis galvanises them into action.

The change agent must be realistic enough to recognise that for many people any proposal for change constitutes bad news. He must therefore prepare himself for an initial adverse response. Many good ideas are thrown out first time. He may have to keep the idea simmering gently, choosing his moment wisely to reintroduce it. He must be prepared to rejoice if someone else subsequently produces it, claiming it as his own. The ideas of a successful leader carry no copyright. They are left for anyone to adopt. The goal is that the idea be implemented, not that the ideas-man be acclaimed. Many ideas are relegated to glass cases through the proud possessiveness of their inventors.

RESOLVING TO ACT

A depressing postscript can be added to many church projects, 'When all is said and done, too much is said and too little is done.' We need to guard against our conversations becoming a substitute rather than a preparation for action. In order to avoid action, churches either live in a nostalgic past or a fantasy future. We have to learn to live in the present, for now is the acceptable time, now is the day of salvation. What is our attitude to the present? Today is not an empty concept. I believe that we must become excited about today, for there are increasing indications that it is a day of opportunity for church growth.

Frequently we are more skilled in formulating plans than

in implementing them. Most churches have a poor track record in the area of numerical growth, especially in attracting those who have had little or no previous contact with the Christian Church. As a consequence we lack both experience and confidence. We have to remind ourselves that plans are made to be implemented. No matter how enthusiastic the planning, if they are then carried out in a hesitant and half-hearted manner the most promising of plans will fall to the ground. Their execution must be equal to the inspiration.

EVALUATING AND REFORMULATING

One of the greatest impediments to planning is the fear of failure. Win Arn responds to one of McGavran's comments regarding the psychological problem of goal-setting. 'True! If you have no goals you need not fear failure. Fear frustrates faith. I'm convinced that freedom to fail is a most important freedom and one that pastor and people must recognise as inherent in any significant effort' (McGavran and Arn 1977:160).

Goal setting is not carried out on the basis of 'direct revelation'. It represents an estimation of results. We therefore need to review our goals critically in the light of further reflection and more extensive experience, to see whether they are still the right goals. Not all plans work well. Many need to be modified in the light of experience, otherwise the goal may either contribute to despondency or complacency.

A further factor which underlines the need for periodic evaluation and reformulation of goals is the appearance of unscheduled developments. It is common experience among churches which have implemented goal-setting, then to find that God has introduced a few surprises! This may be to keep us on our toes or drive us to our knees. It also seems that when God sees that we are emerging from inertia and demonstrating that we are prepared to move in a given direction, he can then move us into other areas.

Our planning model is therefore not linear and climactic but cyclic. We must ever remain open and responsive to the revolutionary newness of the gospel. God's purposes will continue to unfold until he takes the stage in person once again.

CONCLUSION

Having concentrated so much on the practical aspects of church growth we must now return to the place where we started, namely the reason for church growth and the kind of growth we are concerned to nurture. God has declared his unswerving purpose for the world, namely that Christ should reign supreme over the whole creation. We humbly, and thankfully, acknowledge that it is he who brings into being his kingdom. In our day this is partly realised in provisional form through his Church. We are acutely aware of our weakness and imperfections. We confess our negativism and apathy. But thank God in many places today where once such attitudes prevailed there are an increasing number of churches which are becoming bored with their complacency! The Spirit is stirring dry bones into life. He is calling us to live adventurously and dangerously. We are emerging from our cul-de-sac to walk the Jesus Way. May this volume serve as a slight contribution to that end. To God be the glory, for what he has done, for what he is even now doing through his people, and for what he is yet to do – the splendour and magnitude of which will stagger us all.

Bibliography

ABERCROMBIE, D. 'Paralanguage', *British Journal of Disorders of Communication*, Vol. 3, pp. 55–59. Reprinted in *Communication in Face to Face Interaction*, ed. John Laver and Sandy Hutcheson. London: Penguin Books, 1972.

ALLMAN, J-J. von. *Vocabulary of the Bible*. London: Lutterworth, 1958.

ARGYLE and KENDON. *Communication in Face to Face Interaction*. London: Penguin Books, 1972.

BARCLAY, William. *Commentary on Colossians* (Revised Edition). Edinburgh: Saint Andrew Press, 1975.

BARRETT, C. K. *The Gospel According to St. John*. London: SPCK, 1960.

BAVINCK, J. H. *An Introduction to the Science of Missions*. Philadelphia: The Presbyterian and Reformed Publishing Company, 1961.

BEASLEY-MURRAY, Paul. *Turning the Tide*. London: The Bible Society, 1981.

BITTLINGER, Arnold. *Gifts and Graces*. London: Hodder and Stoughton, 1967.

——, *Gifts and Ministries*. London: Hodder and Stoughton, 1974.

BONINO, Jose Miguez. *Revolutionary Theology Comes of Age*. London: SPCK, 1975.

BRIDGE, Donald and PHYPERS, David. *Spiritual Gifts and the Church*. Leicester: Inter-Varsity Press, 1973.

BRIGHT, John. *The Kingdom of God*. New York: Abingdon, 1953.

BUCKLE, E. G. *Paroikia The House Alongside*. Diocese of Auckland, New Zealand, 1978.

CLEMMONS, William and HESTER, Harvey. *Growth Through Groups*. Nashville, Tenn.: Broadman.

CONGAR, Yves M. J. *Lay People in the Church*. London: Geoffrey Chapman, 1959.

COLEMAN, Lyman. *Serendipity*. Waco, Texas: Creative Resources, 1972.

COLEMAN, ROBERT E. *The Master Plan of Evangelism*. Westwood, N.J.: Revell, 1963.

CONN, Harvey M. ed. *Theological Perspectives on Church Growth*. Nutley, N.J.: Presbyterian and Reformed, 1976.

COOK, Harold R. 'Who Really Sent the Missionaries?' *Evangelical Missions Quarterly*, October 1975, pp. 233–239.

COSTAS, Orlando. *The Church and Its Mission*. Wheaton, Ill.: Tyndale House, 1974.

CULLMAN, Oscar. *The Early Church*. London: SCM, 1956.

CURRIE, R., GILBERT, A. and HORSLEY, L.. *Churches and Church-goers: Patterns of Church Growth in the British Isles Since 1700*. London: Oxford University Press, 1977.

CURRY, Mavis W. *Advancing the Smaller Church*. Grand Rapids, Mich.: Baker, 1968 (first printed 1957).

DAVIDSON, Leslie. *Sender and Sent*. Guildford and London: Lutterworth, 1969.

DAYTON, Edward R. *Tools For Time Management*. Grand Rapids, Mich.: Zondervan, 1974.

DOUGLAS, Tom. *Basic Groupwork*. London: Tavistock Publications, 1978.

DUBOSE, Francis M. *How Churches Grow In The Urban World*. Nashville, Ten.: Broadman, 1978.

ENGEL, James F. and WILBERT NORTON, H. *What's Gone Wrong With The Harvest?* Grand Rapids, Mich.: Zondervan, 1975.

——, *How Can I Get Them to Listen?* Grand Rapids, Mich.: Zondervan, 1977.

GAY, John D. *The Geography of Religion in England*. London: Duckworth, 1971.

GETZ, Gene A. *Sharpening the Focus of the Church*. Chicago: Moody Press, 1974.

GIBBS, Eddie. *Urban Church Growth: Clues from South America and Britain*. Nottingham: Grove Books, 1977.

——, *Grow Through Groups*. Nottingham: Grove Books, 1979a.

——, *Body Building Exercises for the Local Church*. London: Falcon, 1979b.

GOLDINGAY, John. *History, Culture, Mission and the People of God in The Old Testament*. Evangelical Fellowship for Missionary Studies Bulletin No. 5, 1975.

GREEN, Michael. *Evangelism in the Early Church*. London: Hodder and Stoughton, 1970.

——, *Evangelism – I Believe in The Holy Spirit*. London: Hodder and Stoughton, 1974.

——, *Now and Then*. Leicester: Inter-Varsity Press, 1979.

GRIFFITHS, Michael. *Cinderella's Betrothal Gifts*. London: Overseas Missionary Fellowship, 1978.

——, *Shaking the Sleeping Beauty*. Leicester: Inter-Varsity Press, 1980.

HARPER, Michael. *Let My People Grow*. London: Hodder and Stoughton, 1977.

HARRIS, Jeffrey and HARVIS, Peter. *Counting to Some Purpose*. London: Methodist Home Missions Dept., 1979.

HESSELGRAVE, David J. *Communicating Christ Cross-Culturally*. Grand Rapids, Mich.: Zondervan, 1978.

HIEBERT, Paul G. *Cultural Anthropology*. Philadelphia: J. B. Lippincott Co., 1976.

HOUSTON, Tom. *Communicating The Good News In a Television Age*. London: The Bible Society, 1978.

HUNTER, George G. *The Contagious Congregation*. New York: Abingdon, 1979.

JEREMIAS, Joachim. *New Testament Theology*, Vol. 1, *The Proclamation of Jesus*. London: SCM, 1971.

KELLEY, Dean M. *Why Conservative Churches Are Growing*. New York: Harper and Row, 1972.

KIDNER, Derek. *Genesis*. Leicester: Inter-Varsity Press, 1967.

KLAPPERT, B. Article in *Dictionary of New Testament Theology*, Vol. II, pp. 372–389, *King and Kingdom*. Exeter: Paternoster Press, 1976.

KRAEMER, Hendrik. *A Theology of the Laity*. Guildford and London: Lutterworth, 1958.

KRAFT, Charles H. *Christianity in Culture*. Maryknoll, Orbis Books, 1979.

LADD, George Eldon. *The Gospel of the Kingdom*. Grand Rapids, Mich.: Eerdmans, 1959.

——, *A Theology of the New Testament*. Guildford and London: Lutterworth, 1974.

LALIVE, Christian D'Epinay. *Haven of the Masses*. Guildford and London: Lutterworth, 1969.

LILLEY, J. P. U. Article in *The New Bible Dictionary*, 'Justification'. London: Inter-Varsity Press, 1962.

LUM, Ada and SIEEMENS, Ruth. *Creative Bible Studies*. Bombay: Jyoti, 1973.

McGAVRAN, Donald A. *Bridges of God*. London: World Dominion, 1955.

——, *How Churches Grow*. New York: Friendship Press, 1959.

——, *Church Growth and Christian Mission*. Pasadena, Calif.: William Carey Library, 1965.

——, *Understanding Church Growth*. Grand Rapids, Mich.: Eerdmans, 1970.

McGAVRAN, Donald A., and ARN, Winfield C. *Ten Steps for Church Growth*. New York: Harper and Row, 1977.

McGAVRAN, Donald A. and HUNTER, George G. III. *Church Growth: Strategies That Work*. New York: Abingdon, 1980.

McQUILKIN, J. Robertson. *Measuring the Church Growth Movement* (originally entitled *How Biblical is the Church Growth Movement?*) Chicago: Moody Press, 1973, 74.

MENOUD, PH-H. Article in *Vocabulary of the Bible*, pp. 259–266, 'Ministry', ed. J-J. von Allman. Guildford and London: Lutterworth, 1958.

MEYER, Ben F. *The Aims of Jesus*. London: SCM, 1979.

MILLER, Keith. *The Taste of New Wine*. London: Word Books, 1965.

MURRAY, Iain. *The Puritan Hope*. Edinburgh: Banner of Truth, 1971.

NEILL, Bishop Stephen. *Call to Mission*. Berkeley, Calif.: Frontier, 1970.

NEWBIGIN, Lesslie. *The Open Secret*. London: SPCK, 1978.

NIDA, Eugene A. *God's Word in Man's Language*. New York: Harper and Row, 1952.

———, *Customs, Culture and Christianity*. London: Tyndale Press, 1954.

NIEBUHR, H. Richard. *Christ and Culture*. New York: Harper and Row, 1951.

NOLAN, Albert. *Jesus Before Christianity*. London: Darton, Longman and Todd, 1976.

O'CONNOR, Elizabeth. *Journey Inward, Journey Outward*. New York: Harper and Row, 1968.

OLSON, C. Gordon. 'What About People-Movement Conversion?' *Evangelical Missions Quarterly*, July 1979, pp. 133–142.

ORTIZ, Juan Carlos. *Disciple*. London: Marshall, Morgan and Scott, Ltd. Lakeland Books, 1976.

OSMASTON, Amiel. *Sharing the Life: Using Small Groups in the Church*. Nottingham: Grove Books.

PACKER, James I. *Knowing God*. London: Hodder and Stoughton, 1973.

PADILLA, C. Rene ed. *El Reino de Dios y America Latina*. Buenos Aires: Casa Bautista de Publicaciones, 1975.

PANNENBERG, Wolfhart. *Theology and The Kingdom of God*. Philadelphia: Westminster, 1975.

PERRY, Lloyd. *Getting the Church on Target*. Chicago: Moody Press, 1977.

PETERS, George W. *A Biblical Theology of Missions*. Chicago: Moody Press, 1972.

PIPPERT, Rebecca Manley. *Out of the Saltshaker*. Leicester: Inter-Varsity Press, 1980.

REID, Gavin. *Good News to Share*. London: Falcon, 1979.

RICHARDSON, Don. *The Peace Child*. Glendale, Calif.: Regal Books.

RICE, A. K. *Learning for Leadership*. London: Tavistock Publications, 1965.

Root, John. *Encountering West Indian Pentecostalism*. Nottingham: Grove, 1979.

Roberts, Ted. *Partners and Ministers*. London: Falcon, 1972.

Robertson and Plummer. *International Critical Commentary – 1 Corinthians*. Edinburgh: T. and T. Clark, 1911.

Rowley, H. H. *The Biblical Doctrine of Election*. Guildford: Lutterworth, 1950.

Schaller, Lyle E. *The Pastor and the People*. Nashville, Tenn.: Abingdon, 1973.

——, *Parish Planning*. Nashville, Tenn.: Abingdon, 1978a.

——, *Assimilating New Members*. Nashville, Tenn.: Abingdon, 1978b.

Schillebeeckx, Edward. *The Mission of the Church*. London: Sheed and Ward, 1973.

Schuller, Robert H. *Your Church Has Real Possibilities*. Glensdale, Calif.: Regal, 1974.

Shenk, Wilbert R. ed. *The Challenge of Church Growth*. Elkhart, Indiana: Institute of Mennonite Studies, Herald Press, 1973.

Sheppard, David. *Built as a City*. London: Hodder and Stoughton, 1974.

Simon, Ulrich E. *A Theology of Salvation*. London: SCM Press, 1953.

Smail, Tom. *Reflected Glory*. London: Hodder and Stoughton, 1975.

Snyder, Howard A. *The Problem of Wineskins*. Downes Grove, Ill.: Inter-Varsity Press, 1975.

——, *The Community of the King*. Downes Grove, Ill.: Inter-Varsity Press, 1977.

Stauffer, Ethelbert. *New Testament Theology*. London: SCM Press, 1975.

Stott, J. R. W. *Baptism and Fullness*. Leicester: Inter-Varsity Press, 1975a.

——, *Christian Mission in the Modern World*. London: Falcon, 1975b.

Tippett, Alan R. *Church Growth and the Word of God*. Grand Rapids, Mich.: Eerdmans, 1970.

TOZER, A. W. *The Root of the Righteous*. Harrisburg, Pa.: Christian Publications, Inc., 1955.

TRUDINGER, Ron. *Cells for Life*. Basingstoke: Olive Tree Publications, 1979.

TRUEBLOOD, Elton. *The Company of the Committed*. New York: Harper and Row, 1961.

VON RAD, Gerhard. *Genesis*. London: SCM Press, 1961.

WAGNER, C. Peter. *Frontiers in Missionary Strategy*. Chicago: Moody Press, 1971.

——, *Look Out The Pentecostals Are Coming*. London and Eastbourne: Coverdale, 1973.

——, *Your Church Can Grow*. Glendale, Calif.: Regal Books, 1976.

——, 'How Ethical Is The Homogeneous Principle?' *Occasional Bulletin*, Vol. 2, No. 1. Fuller Seminary, 1978.

——, *Your Church Can Be Healthy*. Nashville: Abingdon, 1979a.

——, *Your Spiritual Gifts Can Help Your Church Grow*. Glendale, Calif.: Regal Books, 1979b.

——, *Our Kind of People*. Atlanta: John Knox Press, 1979c.

WARREN, Max. *I Believe In The Great Commission*. London: Hodder and Stoughton, 1979.

WASDELL, David. *Let My People Grow*. A workpaper presented to the General Synod of the Church of England, November 1974.

——, *Divide and Conquer*. AGM of the Archbishop's Council on Evangelism, November 1975.

——, *Long Range Planning and the Church*. Urban Church Project, 1979.

WAYMORE, Bob and WAGNER, C. Peter. *The Global Church Growth Bulletin*. Santa Clara, Calif., 1980.

WINTER, Ralph D. *The Decade Past and the Decade To Come: Seeing The Task Graphically*. Evangelical Missions Quarterly, Jan. 1974.

——, *The Two Structures of God's Redemptive Mission*. Missiology, January 1974.

YOHN, Rick. *Discover Your Spiritual Gift and Use It*. Wheaton, Ill., Tyndale, 1974.

Reports and Periodicals

BRITISH COUNCIL OF CHURCHES. *Stand Up and Be Counted*. Report of the Committee on Mission, 1972.

EVANGELICAL MISSIONS QUARTERLY. January 1974.

H.M.S.O. *Annual Abstract of Statistics*. 1979 Edition.

INFORMATION SERVICE, Lausanne Committee for World Evangelization, June 1979, May 1980.

INTERNATIONAL REVIEW OF MISSIONS, October 1965. July 1968.

NATIONWIDE INITIATIVE IN EVANGELISM. *Perspective for the Eighties* – a 1979 Census of Churches in England.

PASADENA CONSULTATION – *Homogeneous Unit*. Lausanne Committee for World Evangelization.

SIGNS OF HOPE. London; the Baptist Union, 1979.

THE WILLOWBANK REPORT. *Gospel and Culture*. Sponsored by the Lausanne Theology and Education Group, 6–13 June, 1978.

1. A lot of stringing proof-texts together
   accepting historicity of FG